Disclaimers

This book is in no way affiliated, associated, authorized, endorsed by F5 Networks, Inc. or any of its subsidiaries or its affiliates. The official F5 Networks web site is available at www.f5.com.

F5, Traffix, Signaling Delivery Controller, and SDC are trademarks or service marks of F5 Networks, Inc., in the U.S. and other countries. A full list of F5 Networks' marks can be found at https://f5.com/about-us/policies/trademarks. Trademarks used with permission of F5 Networks, Inc.

This book refers to various F5 marks. The use in this book of F5 trademarks and images is strictly for editorial purposes, and no commercial claim to their use, or suggestion of sponsorship or endorsement, is made by the authors or publisher.

Permission Notice

The F5 Certified logo used on the front cover of this book is a registered trademark of and is copyright F5 Networks, Inc. F5 Networks, Inc has granted this book's authors permission to use the logo in this manner.

Copyright © 2014 by Philip Jönsson & Steven Iveson

All rights reserved. This book or any portion thereof may not be reproduced or used in any manner whatsoever without the express written permission of the authors except for the use of brief quotations in a book review or scholarly journal.

First Printing: 2014

ISBN: 978-1-312-94023-9

Revision: 2015.v5

TABLE OF CONTENT

Preface	13
About The Authors	13
Dedications	13
Acknowledgements	14
Feedback	14
1. Introduction	**16**
The Book Series	16
Who is This Book For?	16
How This Book is Organized	16
F5 Networks the Company	18
F5 Terminology	21
What Is BIG-IP?	21
BIG-IP Hardware	22
BIG-IP Software – TMOS	23
2. The Application Delivery Fundamentals Exam	**26**
The F5 Professional Certification Program	26
Why Become Certified?	27
Choosing a Certification	28
Getting Started/First Steps	28
Taking Exams	28
Additional Resources	29
AskF5	29
DevCentral	29
F5 University	29
Exam Blueprints	30

BIG-IP LTM Virtual Edition (VE) Trial	30
BIG-IP VE Lab Edition	30
BIG-IP VE on Amazon Web Services (AWS)	30

3. The OSI Reference Model — 31

Layer 1 – Physical Layer	34
Layer 2 – The Data Link Layer	34
Layer 3 – The Network Layer	35
Layer 4 – The Transport Layer	35
Layer 5 – The Session Layer	37
Layer 6 – The Presentation Layer	37
Layer 7 – The Application Layer	38
Chapter Summary	39
Chapter Review	39
Chapter Review: Answers	40

4. The Data Link Layer in Detail — 41

Ethernet Access Method CSMA/CD	41
Carrier Sense Multiple Access	42
Collision Detection	42
Collision Domains	44
MAC Addressing	44
MAC Address Table	45
Broadcast Domains	45
Issues with Dividing Broadcast Domains	46
The Difference between Collision Domains and Broadcast Domains	46
Address Resolution Protocol (ARP)	47
The ARP Process	48

VLANs & VLAN Tagging	49
VLAN Trunking	51
The Benefits of Using VLANs	52
Layer 3 Switching	52
VLANs in Real-Life Scenarios	52
Link Aggregation Control Protocol (LACP)	53
Chapter Summary	54
Chapter Review	55
Chapter Review: Answers	56

5. The Network Layer in Detail — 58

Understanding IP Addressing	58
Structure of an IP Address	59
Converting Between Binary & Decimal	60
Converting from Binary to Decimal	60
Converting from Decimal to Binary	60
Addresses Classes	62
Private Addresses	63
Calculating Networks and Hosts	64
Subnet Masking	65
Variable Length Subnet Masking (VLSM)	66
Classless Inter-Domain Routing (CIDR)	71
Broadcast Addresses	71
Fragmentation	72
Time to Live (TTL)	73
TCP/IPv6	74
Different IPv6 Addresses	75
Unicast Addresses	75

Multicast Addresses	75
Anycast Addresses	75
The Structure of an IPv6 Address	75
The Loopback Address	76
Chapter Summary	76
Chapter Exercises	78
Decimal and Binary Conversions	78
Subnetting	78
Chapter Exercises – Answers	79
Decimal and Binary Conversions	79
Subnetting	80
Chapter Review	81
Chapter Review: Answers	82
6. The Transport Layer in Detail	**83**
Transmission Control Protocol – TCP	83
TCP Options	84
The Three Way Handshake (3WHS)	84
User Datagram Protocol – UDP	87
TCP Device Communications	88
Retransmission	89
Selective ACK – SACK	91
MTU & MSS	90
MTU	95
MSS	95
Exceeding the MTU	96
Flow Control & Window Size	96
Silly Window	100

Ports & Services	100
TCP Reset Packets	102
Delayed Binding	103
Chapter Summary	106
Chapter Review	107
Chapter Review: Answers	108

7. Switching & Routing — 109

Switching	109
Routing	109
A Router's Role	110
Different Types of Routers	110
The Routing Table	111
Dynamic Routing Protocols	113
IP & MAC Address Changes - Routing In Action	115
Network Address Translation (NAT)	122
Static NAT	123
Destination NAT	124
Source NAT	125
What happens with return traffic?	126
Chapter Summary	128
Chapter Review	129
Chapter Review: Answers	130

8. The Application Layer in Detail — 131

Hypertext Transfer Protocol (HTTP)	131
URLs – Uniform Resource Locator	133
Versions	134
Status Codes	135

Methods	136
HTTP Header Features	136
HTTP Persistent Connections	139
Cookies	141
Further Reading	141
HTTPS (Secure HTTP)	142
Domain Name System (DNS)	142
Top-Level Domains	144
Second-Level Domains	145
Zones and Resource Records (RRs)	145
Reverse Lookups	147
How Does a Computer Resolve a DNS Name (To An IP Address)?	148
Session Initiation Protocol (SIP)	149
File Transfer Protocol (FTP)	149
The Difference between Active FTP and Passive FTP	150
Active FTP	150
Passive FTP	151
Simple Mail Transfer Protocol (SMTP)	152
Chapter Summary	156
Chapter Review	156
Chapter Review: Answers	158
9. F5 Solutions & Technology	**161**
Access Policy Manager (APM)	161
Advanced Firewall Manager (AFM)	162
Application Acceleration Manager (AAM) Core Module	162
Application Acceleration Manager (AAM) Full Module	163
Application Security Manager (ASM)	164

Local Traffic Manager (LTM)	164
Global Traffic Manager (GTM)	165
Enterprise Manager (EM)	165
BIG-IQ Product	166
Cloud	166
Security	167
ADC	167
Device	167
Carrier Grade NAT (CGNAT) Module	167
iApps Analytics (aka Application Visibility & Reporting - AVR)	168
IP Intelligence Service	168
Link Controller Product (& Module)	168
MobileSafe Product & Service	169
Edge Gateway	169
Policy Enforcement Manager (PEM)	169
Secure Web Gateway (SWG) Cloud-based Service & Module	170
Silverline Cloud-based Service	170
WebSafe Service & Module	170
ARX	171
End of Life Products	172
iRules	172
iApps	173
iControl	173
iHealth	174
iQuery	174
Full Application Proxy	175
Packet Based Proxy/FastL4	176

High Availability (HA)	177
Active/Standby	177
Active/Active	179
Device Service Clustering (DSC)	180
ConfigSync	180
Traffic Groups	180
Floating Self IPs	181
MAC Masquerade	181
Force to Standby	181
Chapter Summary	181
Chapter Review	183
Chapter Review: Answers	184

10. Load Balancing Essentials — 187

What Is A Load Balancer?	187
Load Balancing Methods	191
Round Robin	192
Least Connections	193
Persistence	194
Source Address (aka Simple)	194
Cookie persistence	195
OneConnect	196
The Client & Server	197
What Is a Server?	198
What Is a Client?	198
F5 Device Acts As Both Server and Client	198
Chapter Summary	199
Chapter Review	199

Chapter Review: Answers	200

11. Security — 201

Positive & Negative Security Models	201
Real-World Scenarios	202
Conclusion	203
Authentication and Authorization	204
Authentication Processes	204
Centralized Authentication	204
RADIUS	205
TACACS+	206
Authentication, Authorization & Accounting (AAA)	206
Virtual Private Networks (VPNs)	207
IPsec – IP Security	207
When Should You Use IPsec?	208
SSL VPN	208
Chapter Summary	210
Chapter Review	210
Chapter Review: Answers	212

12. Public Key Infrastructure (PKI) — 214

What is Public Key Infrastructure?	214
The Basics of Encryption	214
Symmetric Encryption	214
Symmetric Algorithms	215
Asymmetric Encryption	216
Asymmetric Algorithms	218
Asymmetric Signing	219
The Hash Process	220

Hash Algorithms	220
Digital Signing	220
Combining Asymmetric Signing & Hash Algorithms	221
Certificates, Certificate Chains and Certificate Authorities	222
Certificate Revocation Lists (CRLs)	224
The Different Revocations	224
Chapter Summary	225
Chapter Review	225
Chapter Review: Answers	226

13. Application Delivery Platforms — 227

BIG-IP Hardware	227
VIPRION	228
BIG-IP Virtual Edition (VE)	230
Virtual Edition vs. Hardware	231
TCP Optimisation	233
HTTP Pipelining	234
HTTP Caching	236
HTTP Compression	238
Further Reading	238
Chapter Summary	239
Chapter Review	239
Chapter Review: Answers	240

Appendix A - How Does SAML Work? — 241

Appendix B – A History of Load Balancing — 244

Preface

About The Authors

Philip

Philip Jönsson was born in Malmö City, Sweden 1988 where he still lives with his wife. He gained interest in technology at an early age. When he was eight years old the family got a home PC which was the first step in his career.

Since Philip had a big interest in technology, choosing an education was easy. His IT-studies started at NTI (The Nordic Technical Institute) where he studied the basics of computer technology and eventually focused on network technology. Later on he studied IT-security at Academedia Masters.

Philip's first job in the IT business was at a home electronics company in Sweden. He worked at the IT-department and was responsible for managing and troubleshooting the sales equipment in the different stores and managing the IT-infrastructure within the organization. This is where Philip first encountered a BIG-IP controller.

Philip eventually started working in a NOC (Network Operations Center) department at an IT security company that works with some of the largest companies in Sweden and as of this book's printing he's still there. For about 2 years his responsibility has been to troubleshoot and handle incidents and problems. Now he's working with changes and implementations where F5 plays a big part.

Steve

Steven Iveson, the last of four children of the seventies, was born in London and was never too far from a shooting, bombing or riot. He's now grateful to live in a small town in East Yorkshire in the north east of England with his wife Sam and their four children. He's worked in the IT industry for over 15 years in a variety of roles, predominantly in data centre environments.

Steve first encountered a BIG-IP Controller in 2004 and has been working with TMOS and LTM since 2005. Steve's iRules have been featured in two DevCentral 20 Lines or Less articles, he's made over 3000 posts on the DevCentral forums and he's been F5 certified since 2010.

Dedications

Philip

I would like to dedicate this book to my wife Helena and my family for their support throughout the writing of this book. A lot of late nights and spare time has gone into this book but she has never complained.

Steve

For Linda Iveson; her strength and bravery facing and overcoming so many great obstacles, for so long, still inspires me. The capacity for love, resilience and tenacity you've passed to my siblings and I is beyond compare.

Acknowledgements

Philip

First off I would like to thank Holger Yström for making this eBook possible. With his help, the original study guide was acknowledged by many F5 representatives and made it all the way to the corporate headquarters in Seattle. Without his help the original Study Guide would not have become this big and I'm forever grateful.

I would also like to thank my bosses Mathias Åberg and Mats Borgström for giving me the opportunity to widen my knowledge and experience of F5 products.

Thanks to my department for the encouragement and support throughout the writing of this eBook.

A special thanks to Sharon McGlinn for helping me proof my material and making sure that my material does not contain any grammar or spelling mistakes. Hopefully we haven't missed anything!

Thanks to the Designerz who created the cover and the design of the eBook, you did a great job!

Thanks to F5 for making this possible and for all the help we've got in making this eBook. Two honourable mentions are Kenneth Salchow and Suzanna Litwin. You have both been great to work with and have always provided us with great input and assistance.

Finally I would like to thank Steven Iveson for wanting to participate in this collaboration. Your contribution to this eBook has truly raised its value and it has been a pleasure working with you.

Steve

Most of the information found in this book is available elsewhere, I've mostly just searched for it, gathered it up, put the pieces together and presented it in what I hope is a useful format and organised structure. That being the case, I'm keen to acknowledge those that have produced the materials which have formed the basis of this book.

Thanks to the many who've taken the time to contribute to DevCentral (DC) to inform, educate and assist others, myself included.

A special mention to the following F5 staff members and DC contributors: Colin Walker, an iRules guru, Joe Pruitt (username: Joe) who created DevCentral and now manages F5's Facebook pages amongst other things, Aaron Hooley (username: hoolio) who's made over 12 thousand posts on DC, Nitass Sutaveephamochanon (username: nitass) and Kevin Stewart.

Finally, thanks to Philip for making this book happen in the first place.

Feedback

Philip

If you have any comments, corrections or feedback regarding this book, feel free to send me an email on Philip.r.jonsson@gmail.com. You're also very welcome to connect on Linkedin. You can find my public profile at: https://www.linkedin.com/pub/philip-j%C3%B6nsson/3a/680/810.

Steve

Feedback, comments and corrections are more than welcome at: sjiveson@outlook.com. You can follow me on Twitter: @sjiveson, read my blogs at http://packetpushers.net/author/siveson/ and you're welcome to connect on http://uk.linkedin.com/in/steveniveson/en.

You can also join this book's Linkedin group by searching Linkedin for: 'All Things F5'. This is an independent group that is not associated with F5.

1. Introduction

The Book Series

This is the fourth book in a planned series covering the complete range of BIG-IP and related module features and concepts, core TMOS technologies and relevant fundamental topic areas, the others (in an unconfirmed order of likely publication) are;

- An Introduction to F5 Networks LTM iRules (published and on its second edition)
- An Introduction to the F5 Networks HMS v11 (published and on its second edition)
- An Introduction to F5 Networks, BIG-IP, TMOs and LTM v11 Volume One (published)
- The F5 Networks Application Delivery Fundamentals 101 Study Guide (this book)
- An Introduction to F5 Networks, BIG-IP, TMOS and LTM v11 Volume Two (due next)
- The F5 Networks BIG-IP Administration 201 Study Guide
- F5 Networks BIG-IP Advanced Firewall Manager
- F5 Networks BIG-IP LTM Advanced Configuration & Design
- F5 Networks BIG-IP & TMOS v11 Security
- F5 Networks BIG-IP & TMOS v11 Operations & Troubleshooting

Suggestions and ideas from readers on other topics and subjects for new or existing books are always welcome; refer to the Feedback section in the Preface for contact details.

Who is This Book For?

This book is designed to provide the reader and student with everything they need to know and understand in order to pass the F5 Application Delivery Fundamentals 101 exam. All generic networking, application, protocol and F5 specific topics and elements found in the exam blueprint are covered in full and in detail.

No prior knowledge is assumed and the book includes review summaries, over 90 diagrams and over 40 test questions to aid understanding and assist in preparing for the exam.

Even those attending official F5 training courses will find this book of benefit as those courses only cover the F5 specific elements of the curriculum.

How This Book is Organized

Most readers should read and study this book from start to finish, front to back. As with the official F5 blueprint, things move from the simple and abstract to the more complex and detailed and each topic builds upon the knowledge gained in earlier ones. We've ordered the book's chapters and sections to mostly reflect the order of that exam blueprint, although in a few cases where we've felt it's more appropriate we've ignored it.

Obviously if you feel you already fully understand a particular subject area you're free to skip past it (this is most likely with the OSI Model chapter we'd imagine) but at least take a look at the topics it covers to ensure you're not missing something. You may think you know TCP/IP inside out but what about IPv6? When was the last time you thought about TCP error correction?

Each chapter starts with a brief overview of the topics that will be covered and many end with a useful review summary as well as some simple questions to test your understanding. The chapters of the book and their contents are as follows;

- This chapter, **Chapter 1 – Introduction** provides the background; overviews of load balancing and Application Delivery Controller technologies and benefits, F5 Networks the company and its history and the hardware and software products.

- **Chapter 2 – The Application Delivery Fundamentals Exam** describes the wider technical certification program, the exam, the topics covered and offers a list of useful additional study resources.

- **Chapter 3 – The OSI Reference Model** steps through the first subject detailed in section one of the exam blueprint; the OSI model, and provides an overview of each layer.

- **Chapter 4 – The Data Link Layer in Detail** covers layer two of the OSI model in depth; CSMA/CD, MAC addressing, collision and broadcast domains, ARP, VLANs and LACP are all explored.

- **Chapter 5 – The Network Layer in Detail** moves on to layer three of the OSI model and IP host and network addressing, address classes, subnetting, fragmentation, TTL and IPv6.

- **Chapter 6 – The Transport Link Layer in Detail** provides an in-depth review of layer four of the OSI model, covering subjects such as TCP, UDP, retransmission, MTU, flow control, ports and services and many more.

- **Chapter 7 – Switching & Routing** describes these fundamental layer two and three network functions and how they interact in detail as well as NAT.

- **Chapter 8 – The Application Layer in Detail** covers layer seven of the OSI model, the application layer and some of its most popular protocols; HTTP, DNS, SIP, FTP and SMTP.

- **Chapter 9 – F5 Solutions & Technology** offers information on all the subjects detailed in section two of the exam blueprint; the numerous TMOS feature modules, core TMOS features, proxy modes of operation and high availability.

- **Chapter 10 – Load Balancing Essentials** moves on to section three of the exam blueprint; fundamental load balancing functions, methods and persistence.

- **Chapter 11 – Security** explains subjects detailed in section four of the exam blueprint; core security concepts, and takes a look at some of the most common security solutions in use today for performing authentication and authorisation, as well as VPN and IPsec technologies.

- **Chapter 12 – Public Key Infrastructure** further expands on this specific area of security and subjects such as encryption, digital signing and certificates.

- **Chapter 13 – Application Delivery Platforms** takes a close look at blueprint section five; BIG-IP hardware and virtualised software solutions and compares and contrasts the two. TCP Optimisations and more advanced HTTP features are also explored

F5 Networks the Company

Created as F5 Labs in 1996* by Michael D. Almquist** (aka Mad Bomber and Squish,) a technical entrepreneur and programmer and Jeffrey S. Hussey, an investment banker. F5 released its first HTTP web server load balancing device: the BIG-IP Controller, in 1997. The company, head-quartered in Seattle, Washington since its inception, has grown rapidly to date (barring a lull during the dot.com collapse between 1999 and 2001) and has expanded its product offerings significantly. They now produce a wide range of dedicated hardware and virtualised appliance ADCs. As well as load balancing these can provide SSL offload, WAN acceleration, application acceleration, firewalling, SSL VPN, remote access and much more.

Michael Almquist left the company in May 1998 over a year before the company went public on NASDAQ (symbol: FFIV) in June 1999 and was renamed F5 Networks. By mid-2005, industry analyst firm Gartner reported F5 had captured the highest share of the overall ADC market and by late 2013*** the company earned more than $1.5 billion in annual revenue and employed over 3,400 people in 59 locations around the world. The company has no long term debt and assets of over $2 billion. Services earned 46.1% of revenues and products 53.9%, with the largest sales market being the Americas, followed by EMEA, APAC and Japan. Research and development expenses for the financial year were $209m.

According to Netcraft®, in May 2009, 4.26% of all websites and around 3.8% of the top million sites were being served through F5 BIG-IP devices. A look at this Netcraft page: http://uptime.netcraft.com/up/reports/performance/Fortune_100 shows that on 7th February 2014, 20% of the US Fortune 100's public websites were served through F5 BIP-IP ADCs including those of Bank of America, Dell, Disney, Lehman Brothers, Lockheed Martin, Wachovia and Wells Fargo.

The company's Scottish born President and CEO, John McAdam has held these roles since July 2000.

The company name was inspired by the 1996 movie Twister, in which reference is made to the fastest and most powerful tornado on the Fujita Scale: F5.

Significant technical milestones and business events in F5 Networks' history include;

- **1895** – Nortel® is founded (as Northern Telecom Limited)
- **1995** – Brocade® is founded
- **1996** – F5 is incorporated (February)
- 1996 – Cisco® launches LocalDirector; technology based on its acquisition of Network Translation Incorporated that same year (the PIX® firewall platform also sprung from this acquisition)
- 1996 – Foundry Networks® is founded (originally called Perennium Networks and then StarRidge Networks, renamed Foundry in 1997) (later to be acquired by Brocade in 2008)
- 1996 – Alteon Networks® is founded (later to be acquired by Nortel in 2000)
- **1997** – F5 Launches its first BIG-IP Controller (July)
- 1997 – ArrowPoint Communications® is founded by Chin-Cheng Wu (later to be acquired by Cisco in 2000)
- **1998** – F5 Launches the 3DNS Controller (September)
- 1998 – Reactivity is founded

- 1998 – NetScaler is founded
- 1999 – F5 Goes public on NASDAQ (June)
- **2000** – Cisco acquires ArrowPoint Communications (at a cost of $5.7b) for their content switching technology which they release as the Content Services Switch (CSS) range the same year but fails to develop the product further
- 2000 – Redline Networks® is founded (later to be acquired by Juniper in 2005)
- 2000 – FineGround Networks® founded (later to be acquired by Cisco in 2005)
- 2000 – MagniFire Websystems® founded (later to be acquired by F5 in 2004)
- 2000 – Peribit Networks® (WAN optimisation) founded (later to be acquired by Juniper® in 2005)
- 2000 – Nortel acquire Alteon Networks (at a cost of $6b in stock) (the Alteon application delivery assets later to be acquired by Radware® in 2009)
- **2001** – The iControl XML-based open API is introduced by F5 with v4
- **2002** – v4.5 Released and includes the UIE and iRules
- **2002** – Acopia Networks® founded by Chin-Cheng Wu (who also founded ArrowPoint Communications in 1997) (later to be acquired by F5 in 2007)
- **2002** – Crescendo Networks® founded (later to have its IP acquired by F5 in 2011)
- **2003** – F5's DevCentral Community and technical reference website launched
- **2003** – F5 Acquires uRoam (at a cost of $25m) for its FirePass technology (SSL VPN, application and user security)
- **2004** – F5 Acquires MagniFire Websystems (at a cost of $29m) for its web application firewall (WAF) technology TrafficShield, which forms the basis of the ASM product
- 2004 – F5 releases TMOS v9 and TCL-based iRules
- 2004 – Zeus Technology® releases Zeus Traffic Manager
- **2005** – F5 Acquires Swan Labs® (at a cost of $43) for its WAN optimization technology (WANJet)
- **2005** – Juniper Networks purchases Peribit Networks (WAN optimisation) and Redline Networks (ADCs) at a cost of $337m and $132m respectively
- **2005** – Cisco acquires FineGround Networks (at a cost of $70m) and integrates its technology with the Catalyst switch line to create the ACE product
- **2005** – Cisco launch numerous Application-Oriented Networking (AON) products to support the convergence of 'intelligent networks' with application infrastructure
- **2005** – Citrix acquires NetScaler (at a cost of $300m)
- **2006** – Lori MacVittie joins F5
- **2007** – Don MacVittie joins F5
- **2007** – A10 Networks® launches its AX Series family of ADC appliances
- **2007** – F5 Acquires Acopia Networks (at a cost of $210m) for its file virtualisation technology, which is later re-branded as its ARX range
- **2007** – Cisco acquires Reactivity (at a cost of $135m) for its XML gateway technology, which they launch as the ACE XML Gateway product the same year
- **2008** – F5's VIPRION modular, blade based hardware is released
- **2008** – Juniper discontinues it's DX line of load balancers based on the Redline Networks technology acquired in 2005
- **2008** – LineRate Systems® is founded
- **2008** – Foundry Networks is acquired by Brocade (at a cost of $2.6b (Brocade originally offered $3b))
- **2009** – Nortel ceases operations
- **2009** – Radware acquire Nortel's Alteon application delivery assets (at a cost of $18m)
- **2009** – F5 Releases TMOS and LTM v10
- **2010** – Cisco ACE XML Gateway sales end

- 2010 – Cisco Application-Oriented Networking (AON) products sales end
- **2011** – F5 Releases TMOS and LTM v11
- 2011 – F5 Acquires Crescendo Networks intellectual property (at a cost of $5.6m) for its application acceleration technology
- 2011 – Riverbed® acquires Zeus Technology (at a cost of $110m) for its software based ADC product Zeus Traffic Manager and rebrands it as Stingray (rebranded again as SteelApp™ in 2014)
- 2011 – Cisco CSS sales end
- **2012** – F5 Acquires Traffix Systems® (at a cost of $140m) for its mobile/cellular 4G/LTE and Diameter signalling protocol switching technology
- 2012 – Riverbed and Juniper form a partnership in WAN optimisation and application delivery products, with Juniper licensing the Riverbed Stingray (later renamed SteelApp™) software ADC and Riverbed integrating Steelhead Mobile technology into Juniper's JunOS Pulse client
- 2012 – Cisco end development of their ACE load balancing products and partner with Citrix to recommend NetScaler as their preferred product
- **2013** – F5 Acquires LineRate Systems (at a cost of $125m) for its layer seven and application delivery software defined networking technology
- 2013 – F5 Acquires Versafe® (at an unknown cost) for its mobile and browser security and monitoring products (the TotALL suite)
- 2013 - The iControl REST open API is introduced by F5 with TMOS v11.4
- 2013 – F5 Becomes an OpenStack corporate sponsor
- 2013 – F5 Launches the Synthesis frame work and introduces SDAS: Software-Defined Application Services™
- 2013 – F5 Reduces the price of the 10Mb limited Lab Edition of BIG-IP VE (including LTM, GTM, AFM, ASM, AVR, PSM, WAM and WOM) from around $2000 to just $95, in a gutsy move to capture market share
- **2014** – Riverbed rename Stingray (formerly Zeus Traffic Manager) to SteelApp™
- 2014 – F5 Acquire Denfense.Net® (at an unknown cost) for its cloud-based DDoS mitigation technology and services

Having gained a leading market share in the load balancing and local traffic management enterprise market for some time F5 is now targeting and looking for growth in additional markets, supported and evidenced by their ever expanding product range. These markets include; security (AFM, ASM and APM), cloud (AWS etc.), mobile signalling (Traffix) and acceleration, virtualisation, WAN optimisation and SSL VPN and RAS.

*This article suggests it was actually late 1995: http://www.udel.edu/PR/Messenger/98/1/cyber.html although it was indeed early 1996 when the company was incorporated.

**You'll find in many sources that Michael Almquist has effectively been written out of the company's history.

***Data taken from the company's September 2013 financial year end 10K annual report found here: http://www.sec.gov/Archives/edgar/data/1048695/000144530513003079/ffiv10k9-30x2013.htm.

F5 Terminology

Before we get into the exam specifics I think its worthwhile exploring the terminology surrounding F5 Networks' products. This isn't tested on the exam in any way but without an understanding of the terms you'll find in this book and elsewhere and particularly how they relate to F5's hardware and software, things will be harder for you than they need to be. To that end, the next three sections will explore the primary marketing term for the overall product range and then move on to the terms used in relation to the hardware and software (some of which are the same!)

What Is BIG-IP?

So, just what is BIG-IP? It's confusing; back in the day, BIG-IP was the single name for everything and all you had was the BIG-IP Controller. Now, things are a bit different and you have the application switch hardware, virtual edition, TMOS, TMM, LTM, GTM and all the rest. To add to the confusion BIG-IP is quite often used interchangeably with TMOS or even just F5. As specific and well, simply pedantic I can be I still catch myself saying things like "check your F5's logs…" or "what's the CPU load on this BIG-IP."

So, back to the question, what is BIG-IP? Well, simply put it's all of the things I've mentioned so far; it's an all-encompassing term for the hardware, the Virtual Edition container, TMOS (the software components), TMM (a component of TMOS), LTM (which runs within TMM), GTM and all the other modules.

BIG-IP Hardware

When discussing BIG-IP hardware, things become rather more specific but keep in mind that for many hardware components there will be a related software component that runs on top of it, which has the same name. The primary hardware elements and their purpose are as follows;

- **Traffic Management Microkernel (TMM)**; traffic processing hardware components as follows;
    - A L2 switch module (possibly using network processing NICs)
    - Packet Velocity ASIC(s) (PVAs) or Embedded PVA (ePVA) using FPGAs
    - FPGAs providing ePVA, SYN check and other functions in hardware
    - Dedicated SSL encryption or FIPS hardware
    - Dedicated compression hardware (in some models)
    - TMM uses all CPUs (although one is shared with the HMS) and almost all system RAM, a small amount being provisioned for the HMS.

- **Host Management Subsystem (HMS)**; responsible for system management and administration functions and runs a version of CentOS (Community enterprise Operating System) Linux (which includes the SELinux feature). The HMS uses a single CPU (shared with TMM) and is assigned a dedicated provision of the overall system RAM, the rest being assigned to TMM.

- **Always On Management (AOM)**; provides additional 'lights out' management of the HMS via a Management processor as well as layer 2 switch management and other supporting functions for TMM.

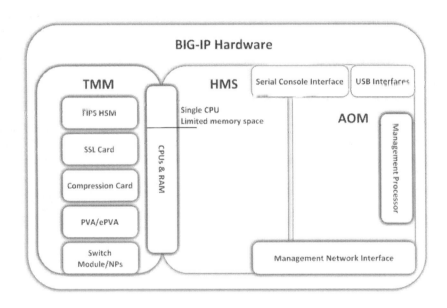

BIG-IP Software – TMOS

F5 Network's Traffic Management Operating System (TMOS) is, first and foremost and for the sake of clarity, NOT an individual operating system. It is the software foundation for all of F5's network or traffic (not data) products; physical or virtual. TMOS almost seems to be a concept rather than a concrete thing when you first try to understand it. I've struggled to find a truly definitive definition of TMOS in any manual or on any website.

So, what is TMOS? It's not too tough after all, really; TMOS encompasses a collection of operating systems and firmware, all of which run on BIG-IP hardware appliances or within the BIG-IP Virtual Edition. BIG-IP and TMOS (and even TMM) are often used interchangeably where features, system and feature modules are concerned. This can be confusing; for instance, although LTM is a TMOS system module running within TMM, it's commonly referred to as BIG-IP LTM. I suspect we have the F5 marketing team to thank for this muddled state of affairs. See the comments section for some clarification from F5 but some debate too.

TMOS and F5's so-called 'full proxy' architecture were introduced in 2004 with the release of v9.0. This is essentially where the BIG-IP software and hardware diverged; previously the hardware and software were simply both referred to as BIG-IP (or BIG-IP Controller). Now, the hardware or 'platform' is BIG-IP, and the software TMOS. Anything capable of running TMOS and supporting its full proxy counts as a BIG-IP so the virtualised version of TMOS is called BIG-IP Virtual Edition (VE) rather than TMOS VE. Where the VE editions are concerned, just the TMM and HMS software components of TMOS are present (more details next).

The primary software elements of BIG-IP, collectively known as TMOS, encompass all of these things;
- **TMM**;
    - Software in the form of an operating system, system and feature modules (such as LTM), other modules (such as iRules) and multiple network 'stacks' and proxies; FastL4, FastHTTP, Fast Application Proxy, TCPExpress, IPv4, IPv6 and SCTP.
    - Software in the form of the interface to and the firmware that operates the dedicated SSL and other cards and hardware.
    - A 'native' SSL stack.
    - Interfaces to the HMS.

- **HMS**; this runs a modified version of the CentOS Linux operating system and provides the various interfaces and tools used to manage the system such as the GUI Configuration Utility, tmsh CLI, DNS client, SNMP and NTP. The HMS also contains an SSL stack (known as the COMPAT stack): OpenSSL, which can also be used by TMM where necessary.

- **Local Traffic Manager (LTM)**; this and other 'feature' modules such as APM, ASM and GTM expose specific parts of TMM functionality when licensed. They are typically focussed on a particular type of service (load balancing, authentication and so on).

- **AOM**; lights out system management accessible through the management network interface and serial console.

- **Maintenance Operating System (MOS)**; disk management, file system mounting and maintenance.

- **End User Diagnostics (EUD)**; performs BIG-IP hardware tests.

Traffic Management Microkernel (TMM)

TMM is the core component of TMOS as it handles all network activities and communicates directly with the network switch hardware (or vNICs for VE). TMM also controls communications to and from the HMS. Local Traffic Manager (LTM) and other modules run within the TMM.

TMM is single threaded until TMOS v11.3; on multi-processor or multi-core systems, Clustered Multi-Processing(CMP) is used to run multiple TMM instances/processes, one per core. From v11.3 two TMM processes are run per core, greatly increasing potential performance and throughput.

TMM shares hardware resources with the HMS (discussed next) but has access to all CPUs and the majority of RAM.

FastL4

Utilised via a FastL4 profile assigned to a Performance (Layer 4) Virtual Server. The FastL4 profile essentially provide the original (first generation load balancer) packet-based (packet-by-packet) layer-four transparent forwarding half-proxy functionality used prior to TMOS and LTM v9.0. On hardware platforms this is mostly performed in hardware (providing very high performance); with VEs this is done in software but still significantly faster than a standard L7 Virtual Server.

Host Management Subsystem (HMS)

The Host Management Subsystem runs a modified version of the CentOS Linux operating system and provides the various interfaces and tools used to manage the system such as the GUI Configuration Utility, Advanced (Bash) Shell, tmsh CLI, DNS client, SNMP and NTP client and/or server.
The HMS can be accessed through the dedicated management network interface, TMM switch interfaces or the serial console (either directly or via AOM).
HMS shares hardware resources with TMM but only runs on a single CPU and is assigned a limited amount of RAM.

Always On Management (AOM)

The AOM (another dedicated hardware subsystem) allows for 'lights out' power management of and console access to the HMS via the serial console or using SSH via the management network interface. AOM is available on nearly all BIG-IP hardware platforms including the Enterprise Manager 4000 product, but not on VIPRION. Note AOM 'shares' the management network interface with the HMS.

Maintenance Operating System (MOS)

MOS is installed in an additional boot location that is automatically created when TMOS version 10 or 11 is installed. MOS, which runs in RAM, is used for disk and file system maintenance purposes such as; drive reformatting, volume mounting, system reimaging and file retrieval. MOS also supports network access and file transfer.

MOS is entered by interrupting the standard boot process via the serial console (by selecting TMOS maintenance at the GRUB boot menu) or booting from USB media.

The grub_default -d command can be used to display the MOS version currently installed. Note, only one copy of MOS is installed on the system (taken from the latest TMOS image file installed) regardless of the number of volumes present.

End User Diagnostics (EUD)

EUD is a software program used to perform a series of BIG-IP hardware tests – accessible via the serial console only on system boot. EUD is run from the boot menu or via supported USB media.

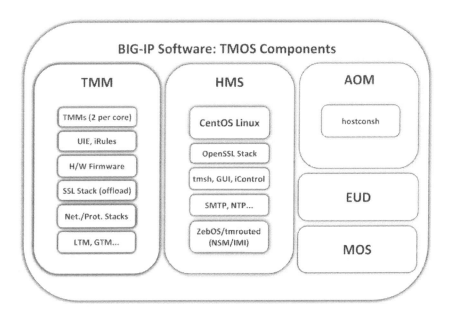

And another that demonstrates the different 'planes';

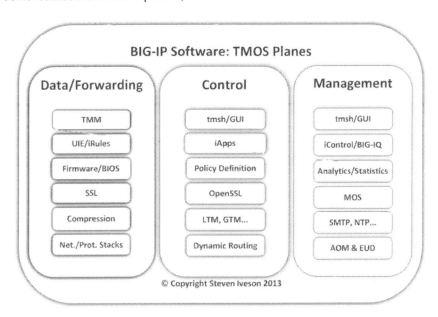

2. The Application Delivery Fundamentals Exam

The Application Delivery Fundamentals exam is the first within the F5 Professional Certification Program and is based on TMOS v11.1. Passing this exam is a prerequisite for the TMOS Administrator certification which is itself a prerequisite for all further certifications and exams.

In this chapter we'll discuss the wider Professional Certification Program, explorer the exam topics and detail additional resources that you might find useful as you work through this guide and plan for the exam.

The F5 Professional Certification Program

The F5 Professional Certification Program (F5-PCP), as it is now known, has been undergoing radical transformation since the second half of 2012. Prior to this transformation, there were a limited set of exam subjects at two certification levels.

With the new program there are now five levels of certification and six levels of exams or labs (there's a difference as the first level exam (covered by this book) does not result in any certification or credential award.) The first three of the exam levels (two certification levels) are shown below (the higher levels are still under development);

Exam Level	Exam Name	Certification Level	Skillset
101	Application Delivery Fundamentals	None	Basic network, protocol and ADC concepts and operation, TMOS architecture and modules.
201	TMOS Administrator	C1: F5 Certified BIG-IP Administrator (F5-CA)	Basic troubleshooting, day to day maintenance and management of devices and configuration objects.
301a	LTM Specialist a	C2: F5 Certified Technology Specialist (F5-CTS)	Architect, Setup, Deploy
301b	LTM Specialist b		Maintain and Troubleshoot
302	GTM Specialist	C2: F5 Certified Technology Specialist (F5-CTS)	DNS administration, GSLB, multiple data centres, configuration and administration

303	ASM Specialist	C2: F5 Certified Technology Specialist (F5-CTS)	Web application security and operation, configuration and administration
304	APM Specialist	C2: F5 Certified Technology Specialist (F5-CTS)	RAS, AAA, configuration and administration

In case you're wondering why this exam doesn't result in a certification; this is designed to encourage greater candidate commitment and deter 'casual' candidates who might normally take an 'easy' entry level exam simply to bulk out their CV. This, along with the wider network, protocol and application knowledge requirements increase the value and quality of the program and hopefully reduce the likelihood of accelerated training programs being formulated.

Further information on the PCP can be found here: https://www.f5.com/services/certification/faqs.html.

Why Become Certified?

Before embarking on any certification path, this is a worthwhile question to ask of yourself. There are many benefits to certification (and debate on the entire subject) but most of them must be qualified based on factors such as; which vendor, the program's reputation, the employment market, employer attitudes, certification relevance and more. Remember that most vendors will make money from a certification program regardless of its benefits or value to you. Also keep in mind that a certification doesn't prove you are competent. Here my view on the typical benefits;

- Certification involves study, learning and the acquisition of knowledge – these are all good things but remember you'll learn and benefit more if you go for something that isn't an everyday part of your job. It's still of benefit to certify in skills you already possess and this will help fill any gaps in your knowledge, but studying something outside of your everyday will be more rewarding and hopefully open more avenues of opportunity in the future, especially if you chose something in demand or likely to be soon.

- Certification will improve your understanding, knowledge and self-confidence.

- Certification proves to others you can study, read, take notes, work alone, follow through, do research and organise yourself in general – assuming it hasn't taken too long to achieve isn't considered an easy certification.

- Certification can help you keep your job, gain a pay rise or a promotion although what you choose and it's perceived value will be critical here.

- Certification gives you an advantage over other candidates without it although, again, what you choose and it's perceived value will be critical.

Choosing a Certification

All of the benefits detailed above will vary in 'weight' depending on the certification program (or programs) you chose to embark on. When deciding, you should consider the following;

- Forget the vendor; will you learn something useful about technology?
- Does the certification carry any weight in the market, how is it perceived by employers/hirers?
- Do too many people have it?
- Is this certification alone good enough to achieve your goals?
- Is there demand for the certified skills?
- What benefits of certification does the vendor supply, if any?

Getting Started/First Steps

If you haven't already, you should take a quick look at the certification pages on the F5 website that can be found here: https://www.f5.com/education/certification/. Along with the overview provided at the start of this chapter this should tell you all you need to know about the certification program. Should you be really stuck, you can always email the F5-PCP team at: f5certification@f5.com.

Next, we'd suggest you register for an F5.com account here: https://login.f5.com/resource/registerEmail.jsp which will give you access to a number of resources exclusive to registered users.

A DevCentral account will also likely be very useful and provides access to F5's community support and documentation site. Register here: https://devcentral.f5.com/register.

Then, before you can even think about booking an exam, you are required to register with the F5 Credential Management System (CMS) and complete the various agreements found there – you can't sit an F5 exam otherwise. The CMS also provides program updates and some useful downloads; you can find it here: https://i7lp.integral7.com/durango/do/login?ownername=F5&channel=F5&basechannel=integral7.

This account is entirely separate to an F5.com and DevCentral account.

Finally, once you've confirmed you are eligible to take an exam, you'll need one more account, this one with Pearson VUE, F5s examination provider. When you're ready to sit this exam (or any other) you'll need to book it through Pearson VUE here: https://www2.pearsonvue.com/f5/.

Taking Exams

As already mentioned, you must register with the F5 CMS in order to be eligible to take this exam and book it through Pearson VUE.

The number of questions, time allowed, and passing score are provided when you book the exam, however, there are normally 70 questions over 90 minutes with a required passing score of 69%. All questions are scored equally.

Exams are typically $135 USD in the Americas, $145 USD in EMEA, and $155 USD in APAC.

You must wait at least 15 days before you can retake a failed exam the first time, 30 days the second time, 45 days the third time and finally 730 days the fourth time. You have to wait 730 days before you can attempt an exam for the fifth time to decrease the possibility of cheating and question recording. The extended delay ensures you face a rewritten exam as exams are updated every two years.

Certifications expire after two years; re-certifying your highest certification achieved recertifies all lower level certifications, as is the norm for most certification programs.

Note that F5 Training courses only cover the F5-specific elements of each exam as you are expected to already have (or gain) knowledge and experience of general networking and network and application protocols. Don't worry, this book, of course, covers everything.

Additional Resources

The following will be of particular interest to students studying for this exam;

AskF5

Available at: https://support.f5.com/ (previously https://ask.f5.com/ which still works too) AskF5 is the F5 Networks technical knowledge base and self-service online support site – no account is required.

AskF5 provides knowledge base articles related to; support, known issues, solutions, best practises and security advisories. You can also obtain release notes, manuals and guides.

DevCentral

F5 DevCentral (DC), available here: https://devcentral.f5.com/ is a community website featuring forums, blogs, tech tips, wikis, code sharing for iRules, iControl, iApps templates, tutorials and more. An account is required to access some content or contribute.

Created as CodeShare in 2003 by Joe Pruitt, the architect of iControl (Joe is still with the company) DevCentral now has over 122,000 members in 191 countries. Membership grew over 25% in 2012 alone.

F5 University

Free, self-paced web-based training related to basic technologies and concepts, changes in new software versions and basic LTM configuration are available via the F5 University available here: https://universlty.f5.com/. An F5.com account is required to access the site.

You can also gain lab access to an F5 running TMOS v11.4.0 (plus two Linux hosts) for two hours at a time; an invaluable tool for those without access to their own device.

Exam Blueprints

These can be found on the F5.com website and in the Downloads section of the CMS and provide a comprehensive list of the exam objectives and the skills and knowledge required to pass the exam. The blueprint for this exam can also be found here: https://www.f5.com/pdf/certification/exams/blueprint-app-delivery-fundamentals-exam.pdf.

BIG-IP LTM Virtual Edition (VE) Trial

An LTM VE 90 Day Trial can be obtained from here: https://www.f5.com/trial/ - you'll need an F5.com account to obtain it. You've probably already got one right and if not, it'll be useful going forward. Prior to April 2014 you could only trial v10.1 but that has now changed to v11.3.0 which is great, but for the purposes of this exam either is good enough for you to get your hands on the product and have a look around. Don't think it's an essential requirement; the 101 exam doesn't require any practical knowledge of actually using or configuring BIG-IP.

BIG-IP VE Lab Edition

You can now purchase the latest BIG-IP VE Lab Edition for the very, very cheap price of $95 (it used to be around $2000). It's limited to 10Mb total throughput but includes LTM, GTM, APM (10 user limit) AFM, ASM, AVR, PSM, WAM and WOM. It's an incredibly cost effective tool for getting hands on experience using F5s products, testing and building an understanding of how things work and interact. As mentioned in the previous section, don't think it's an essential requirement; the 101 exam doesn't require any practical knowledge of actually using or configuring BIG-IP. Only the 2xx and 3xx exams do.

BIG-IP VE on Amazon Web Services (AWS)

It takes more time, effort and research to get started but I can highly recommend AWS as an alternative to the VE Trial and Lab Editions, especially if you don't have a lab server or powerful PC/laptop with the right software. As an added benefit you also get to learn about and gain practical experience with AWS (and the cloud) itself.

The recently introduced Free Usage Tier (details here: https://aws.amazon.com/free/) makes building a small, private lab environment very cheap. You can create a Virtual Private Cloud (VPC) and a number of EC2 Linux server 'micro instances' for purposes such as running a web server or other services, all for free.

Then you just need to add an LTM VE EC2 instance. It isn't free but you can create and run one, charged hourly, with any of the Good, Better or Best license bundles, at a very low cost. Those costs are constantly changing and depend on a number of factors (including taxes) but to give you an example, I can run a VE with the Good license for around $0.50 an hour. You only need to run your instances (and thus only get charged) as and when you need to.

Of course, there is a steep learning curve to overcome and it's probably not worth tackling for the purposes of this exam but particularly if you plan on pursuing the higher level certifications it's something I'd recommend you do at some point.

Understanding the Open System Interconnection reference model is critical to those working in the networking field. It was published by the International Organization for Standardization (ISO) in 1984 and was originally intended to be the basis for the implementation of a new network protocol stack, most of which never materialized.

3. The OSI Reference Model

Understanding the Open System Interconnection reference model is critical to those working in the networking field. It was published by the International Organization for Standardization (ISO) in 1984 and was originally intended to be the basis for the implementation of a new network protocol stack, most of which never materialized.

The model consists of seven logical layers, each of which describes one or more functions that, when combined as a whole, represent a fully featured network environment (or system) capable of providing everything needed for two or more hosts to communicate with each other.

So, why is this old, seemingly unused network model still around? Well, logically dividing network functions in this way provides an abstraction useful for a few reasons;

- It eases learning; rather than attempting to tackle the subject of networking as a whole, the functions of each layer, from the lowest to the highest can be taught and understood one at a time
- The same benefit applies when discussing, designing and implementing networks; each layer can be dealt with (or perhaps ignored) as necessary, one at a time
- Again, this benefit of segregation and layer 'independence' also applies to network hardware and software development and protocol design
- Changes to or the introduction of additional functionality at one layer does not require change in the other layers (although in reality that's not always the case)

Of course, the reality of this conceptual, theoretical model is not as simple as it may seem. The layers of the model are not entirely independent as most layers rely on functions provided by the layer underneath and provide functions to the layer above. Some are very tightly coupled and cannot be dealt with as independent entities in any practical way.

The model's structure and layers, each layer's functions and the actual real-world protocols that provide them are displayed in the following diagram;

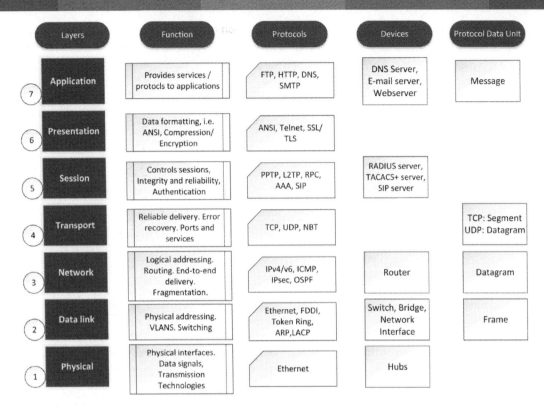

Please keep in mind at this point that this is a theoretical model (and also not the only one) and each layer represents a set of functions, not an actual protocol or standard. In the real world (as we'll see later) the data link functions can be performed by Ethernet for instance, the network functions by IP. Neither Ethernet nor IP are OSI compliant protocols or an official part of the OSI model; they simply perform functions that are described by layers two and three.

When sending data from one host system to another, it is processed by the top layer (the application layer) on the sending host and then every other layer down to the bottom layer (the physical layer). Each layer adds information to and/or transforms the data as necessary as it performs its functions; this is known as encapsulation. The physical layer actually translates the data into electrical signals that are transmitted to the receiving host.

Following is a table detailing some of the different PDU encapsulation names used depending on the protocol and OSI model layer involved;

OSI model:	Protocol:	Protocol data units:
Data-Link	Ethernet	Frame
Network	Internet Protocol	Datagram
Transport	User Datagram Protocol	Datagram
Transport	Transmission Control Protocol	Segment
Application	Various	Message

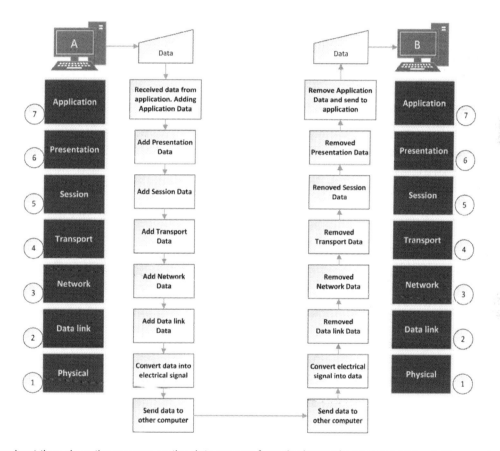

The receiving host then does the reverse as the data passes from the lowest layer to the highest. The previously added (by the sending host) encapsulation data is used as required at each layer and then removed as the data is passed up to the next.

We'll only cover the physical, data link, network, transport and application layers in greater detail in the following chapters as they are the most common ones you'll come into contact with and knowledge of them is essential for the exam.

Layer 1 – Physical Layer

This is the simplest layer (in theory at least); it defines the specification of the cables and other physical (and wireless) network mediums, the connectors, signaling and other parameters. Some examples of mediums are coaxial cable, twisted-pair copper cables and fiber optic cables (which use light rather than electrical signals).

The following table describes the different functions of the physical layer;

Function	Description
Data Encoding	This modifies the binary values (digital signal) that are used by the host to suit the physical medium and also how the receiving host detects when a transmission begins.
Physical Medium Attachment	This describes the physical medium's cabling, for example how many pins the connector has and which pin does what. For example, which pin will receive data and which will send it.
Transmission Technologies	There are two types of transmission technologies that can be used to transfer data, baseband (digital) or broadband (analog). This function determines which technology is used and how.
Physical Medium Transmission	This function defines the specification of the physical medium used (even wireless uses a physical radio interface). It determines how many volts should represent a certain signal state based on which physical medium is used.

Layer 2 – The Data Link Layer

Data link layer protocols are responsible for transferring data between hosts connected to the same network medium (two hosts on the same wireless SSID or connected to the same hub for instance). One of its many functions (in most cases) is to make sure that data is transmitted without error and collisions are detected and recovered from.

The data link layer is only concerned with communications between hosts connected to the same physical network. Communications between different networks are handled by protocols and mechanisms operating above layer 2.

At the data link layer we use the term *frames* to refer to the protocol data unit (PDU) which is created by encapsulating the network layer packet with a header and trailer containing necessary layer two information.

Here's a detailed description of common data link functions;

Function	Description
Identification of the Network Layer Protocol	The data link layer protocol header includes a code that specifies which network layer protocol is encapsulated within the frame. This helps the receiving system to determine which protocol to pass the encapsulated data to when it needs to be sent to the network layer.
Error Detection	The sending host runs the frame through a *cyclical redundancy check (CRC)* calculation on the data that the frame contains and adds the result to the frame. When the frame arrives at the receiving end, it can perform the same CRC check and determine if the transfer has been successful, without any errors.
Addressing	Both the data link and network layers have addresses but there is a huge difference between them. Data link layer addresses are known as hardware addresses and are used to transfer data within the local network. The address is expressed in hexadecimal and is 6 bytes (or 48 bits) long.

You can find the current list of MAC addresses and their allocations to vendors (known as Organizationally Unique Identifiers (OUIs)) at: https://standards.ieee.org/develop/regauth/oui/public.html. You can use this page to search for a MAC address and see which vendor it belongs to.

Layer 3 – The Network Layer

Network layer protocols are responsible for end-to-end communications between two hosts regardless of where they reside in relation to the physical network medium (unlike the data link layer which is only significant within the local network). Network layer protocols are unaware of the physical network medium and the path(s) between two hosts and rely on layer two protocols for delivery across physical networks.

The network layer uses addresses that are significant between and across multiple networks and that are not tied to a physical device in any way. A host can also have multiple network layer addresses. With the most common layer three protocol Internet Protocol (IP), addresses only change if Network Address Translation (NAT) is used to specifically do so (we'll discuss this later in chapter 7).

To help further clarify the difference between layer two and three, remember that a layer two MAC address is tied to a physical host whereas a network layer address, such as an IP address, can be assigned to and easily changed on any host.

Layer 4 – The Transport Layer

The major functions of transport layer protocols can include (not necessarily in combination); flow control, reliability, multiplexing, connection-oriented communications and congestion avoidance. The most common real-world protocols used at this layer are TCP (Transmission Control Protocol) and UDP (User Datagram Protocol) but there are many others.

Connection-Oriented and Connectionless

The major difference between the TCP and UDP protocols is that TCP is connection-oriented and UDP is not (its connectionless, the complete opposite). A *Connection-Oriented* protocol ensures that two hosts establish and agree a connection before transmitting any data between them; this process is called the "*Three-Way-Handshake*" where TCP is used. TCP also makes sure that if any packets are lost or dropped in transmission they are re-sent and also performs error checking.

A connectionless protocol like UDP doesn't perform error checking or guarantee data is delivered. However, in return for these apparent drawbacks, in some scenarios it provides one major benefit: better performance.

TCP is appropriate when you need to ensure the quality of the data that you receive. This could involve, for instance, an email, a webpage or a file. If you receive a file that is missing data it will be completely unusable. You probably think that this should be the case for all data transmissions but there are scenarios where speed is preferable and data loss can be tolerated.

Services that benefit from using a connection-less protocol like this include voice, video streaming services and DNS. With DNS all you really want is a simple answer and if the DNS server does not reply you can just resend the DNS query again very quickly. With voice and streaming services current data is more valuable than correct and complete data. For example, if you are watching a soccer game online and a packet gets corrupted or lost on the way to you it is pointless resending it. The data it contains is no longer relevant; it contains 'stale' information from the past and there is no point in displaying old data on a live streaming service.

TCP Packet Segmentation

When an application generates data that is going to be transferred over the network, the application does not consider that the data may be too large for the network. The TCP protocol is responsible for splitting up the original data into several smaller pieces in order to successfully transmit it over the network. The protocol assigns numbers to each segment that is about to get transferred and keeps track of them in order for the recipient to reassemble the data once it has received all of the packets.

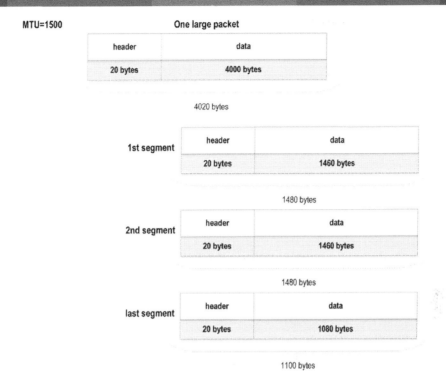

TCP Segmentation can be quite CPU intensive and is often offloaded to a network interface card; a feature known as TCP Segmentation Offload (TSO) or Large Segment Offload (LSO).

Layer 5 – The Session Layer

As a network technician, the layers you will come into least contact with are the session layer and the presentation layer, which is why we will not explore these layers in any detail.

The session layer is the first layer where efficient transmissions over the network are not considered. Functions such as addressing, routing and error correction are all managed by the lower layers.

The session layer is concerned with how hosts exchange their data which is called *dialog* and maintain a healthy exchange between the two systems which is much more difficult than it may seem. Requests and replies may cross each other on their way to the recipient that can cause errors in communication and protocol operation.

Layer 6 – The Presentation Layer

This is the simplest layer of them all. In most cases the presentation layer acts as a pass-through connecting the session layer with the application layer. The application layer accesses the session layer by sending the request to the presentation layer. It will then pass it on to the correct session layer function.

The presentation layer also translates the various data syntaxes between layers; this enables functions like compression and encryption. The translation occurs in two stages, the *abstract syntax* and the *transfer syntax*. The sending host translates the data from the abstract syntax into the transfer syntax and the receiving system translates the transfer syntax back into the abstract syntax. After that it is passed on to the application layer.

Layer 7 – The Application Layer

The application layer is often confused with the actual software application that users run on their computer. This is not the case; all the software applications that a computer runs have a corresponding service (or protocol) which is called when the application wants to transfer data.

For instance, if you use a web browser and want to visit a website the web browser calls the HTTP service so it can pass its request and data to it. The HTTP service will then perform its functions and pass the (possibly modified) encapsulated data to the layer below, the presentation layer. This process is repeated at each layer until the data is finally transmitted onto the network to the destination web server.

Some of the most common protocols that operate at layer seven are;

- ❖ HTTP – Hyper Text Transfer Protocol
- ❖ SMTP – Simple Mail Transfer Protocol
- ❖ DNS – Domain Name System
- ❖ FTP – File Transfer Protocol
- ❖ SSH – Secure Shell

Chapter Summary

* The OSI reference model consists of seven logical layers, each of which describes one or more functions that, when combined as a whole, represent a fully featured network environment (or system) capable of providing everything needed for two or more hosts to communicate with each other.

* The Physical Layer defines the specification of the cables and other physical (and wireless) network mediums, the connectors, signaling and other parameters.

* The Data link layer protocols are responsible for transferring data between hosts connected to the same network medium (two hosts on the same wireless SSID or connected to the same hub for instance).

* The Network layer protocols are responsible for end-to-end communications between two hosts regardless of where they reside in relation to the physical network medium (unlike the data link layer which is only significant within the local network).

* The major functions of transport layer protocols can include flow control, reliability, multiplexing, connection-oriented communications and congestion avoidance. The most common real-world protocols used at this layer are TCP (Transmission Control Protocol) and UDP (User Datagram Protocol) but there are many others.

Chapter Review

In order to test your knowledge and understanding of this chapter, please answer the following questions. You will find the answers and explanations of the questions at the end of this chapter.

1. What OSI model layer is responsible for logical addressing, routing and end-to-end communication?
    a. The Network Layer
    b. The Data Link Layer
    c. The Session Layer
    d. The Application Layer

2. What Protocol data unit is used in the Data Link layer?
    a. Segment
    b. Message
    c. Frame
    d. Datagram

3. Is the TCP protocol Connectionless or Connection-Oriented?
    a. Connection-Oriented
    b. Connectionless

4. Can the UDP protocol guarantee that the traffic sent, reaches the destination and is in good health?
    a. Yes
    b. No

Chapter Review: Answers

You will find the answers to the chapter review questions below:

1. The correct answer is: A

    a. **The Network Layer**
    b. The Data Link Layer
    c. The Session Layer
    d. The Application Layer

2. The correct answer is: C

    a. Segment
    b. Message
    c. **Frame**
    d. Datagram

3. The correct answer is: A

    a. **Connection-Oriented**
    b. Connectionless

The major difference between the TCP and UDP protocols is that TCP is connection-oriented and UDP is not (its connectionless, the complete opposite). A *Connection-Oriented* protocol ensures that two hosts establish and agree a connection before transmitting any data between them; this process is called the "*Three-Way-Handshake*" where TCP is used.

4. The correct answer is: B

    a. Yes
    b. **No**

A connectionless protocol like UDP doesn't perform error checking or guarantee data is delivered. However, in return for these apparent drawbacks, in some scenarios it provides one major benefit: better performance.

4. The Data Link Layer in Detail

In order to communicate with other devices on the same network you need an address to identify each device on the physical network. This is one of the core functions of the Data Link Layer. It is responsible for identifying the host's physical address on the network using what is known as a Media Access Control (MAC) address. This addressing scheme is also called Ethernet Addressing.

The data link layer can be subdivided into two layers, the Media Access Control (MAC) Layer and the Logical Link Control (LLC) layer. The LLC is responsible for frame synchronization and provides a degree of error checking. In the Data Link Layer you find many different technologies that have a special purpose; these include Address Resolution Protocol and VLANs, which we'll cover shortly.

The header (and trailer) fields added to encapsulate the data (the variable length layer 3 payload) are as follows;

- Destination MAC Address – six Bytes
- Source MAC Address – six Bytes
- An optional 802.1Q tag if VLAN tagging is used – four Bytes
- Length of the frame – two Bytes
- Frame check sequence – four Bytes

We'll explore the purpose of some of these headers over the course of this chapter.

Ethernet Access Method CSMA/CD

Have you ever been to an event or party with a lot of people and everyone is talking loudly and over the top of each other and you are trying to make sense out of what everyone is saying? This was an issue during the early days of network computing since hosts on a network shared the same medium and would frequently transmit at the same time as each other, causing collisions. With an increased numbers of hosts on the network this problem only got worse. In order to tackle this *Carrier Sense Multiple Access / Collision Detection* (CSMA/CD) was invented. CSMA/CD was developed by Robert Metcalfe and Dave Boggs together with their team at Xerox Palo Alto in 1973. Initially it was used on the network connecting the islands of Hawaii, called ALOHAnet.

In 1980 the Institute of Electrical and Electronics Engineers (IEEE) began work on an international standard to define Ethernet networks. CSMA/CD is one of the technologies that was eventually included and standardized in 1985's IEEE published standard called "IEEE 802.3 Carrier Sense Multiple Access with Collision Detected (CSMA/CD)". To fully understand CSMA/CD, let's break it down and analyze each component in turn.

Carrier Sense Multiple Access

When a host needs to send out frames on an Ethernet interface, it always begins by listening on the interface and sensing if there is any traffic being transmitted; this is *carrier sense*. This is necessary as each host on the network shares the same medium; this is *multiple access*. If it turns out that the network is busy, the host waits for a random period of time and then listens again. This is to prevent a collision from occurring. A host will not transmit until the network is idle.

Collision Detection

The most essential part of CSMA/CD is the *collision detection* phase. Without it, hosts on a network could not detect that there has been a collision and the hosts could receive corrupted data.

With collision detection, when a collision occurs the sending hosts detect it, immediately stop sending data and sends out a jam signal to alert other hosts on the network that a collision has taken place. When a receiving host gets the jam signal it drops all partial frames it has received. After a host has transmitted the jam signal it waits for a random period of time before attempting to retransmit any data (and repeats the carrier sense phase). This is sometimes called a *back off period*. Both hosts involved in the collision have their own random time to wait before attempting to send the data again.

Almost all of the prior CSMA/CD information is no longer relevant in today's switched networks. But it is still necessary to know how the technology has evolved over the years. Hopefully you can appreciate how much better things are today.

In the following diagram you can see CSMA/CD in action;

1. Host A is trying to send data to Host C but the transmitted signals haven't reached Host D when it starts listening on its interface. At the same time Host D is trying to send data to Host B. Therefore both Host A and Host B are transmitting at the same time, causing a collision.
2. When the hosts detect a collision, a jam signal is sent out on the network to inform everyone that a collision has occurred.
3. Thereafter, both transmitting hosts wait for a random period of time and starts listening on the network again.
4. The host who firsts starts to listen on the network and detects that its idle gets to retransmits its packets. In our case this is Host A.

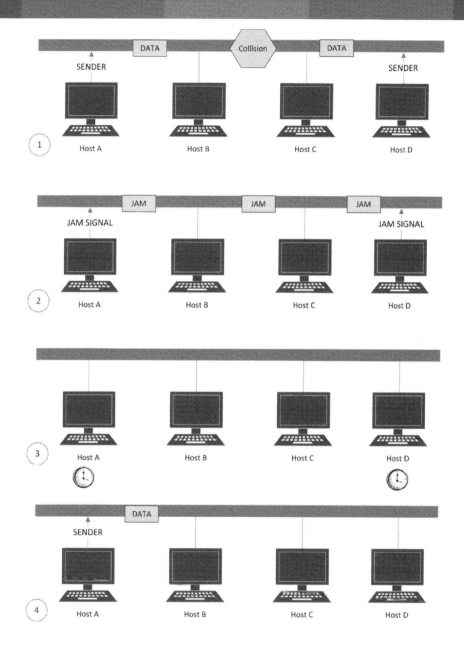

The more traffic you have on your network segment, the more collisions are likely to take place. Collisions are normal in Ethernet but if too many occur, it will cause delays. This will be covered in more detail shortly.

Collision Domains

Back in the eighties and nineties a hub (or even a single long piece of cable) was typically used to connect several hosts together creating a LAN and a so-called collision domain. A collision domain encompasses a layer two network and the hosts attached to it, those hosts having the potential to communicate at the same time, causing a collision.

In this collision domain every host can talk directly with every other using the hub. The hub simply receives a frame and sends it to each host connected to every port (you can see why hubs were originally called repeaters). If a host connected to the hub is the intended recipient it will accept the frame. If not, the frame is dropped. A hub cannot send frames to a specific host; instead it floods the network (and every host on it) with every frame to ensure it is received by the correct host.

Hubs and other shared network media devices (be it Ethernet based, Token Ring or something else) are obviously outdated technologies. However, we've described them to help you understand why and how things have changed over time.

As more hosts are added to the network, the more collisions that occur (as described previously), eventually leading to an unusable network. In a network experiencing a high collision rate, little can be transmitted as the network is constantly flooded with jam signals. This is why switches were introduced; a switch divides every port on the switch into a separate collision domain which significantly reduces or even eliminates collisions. Effectively every port on the switch is a dedicated layer two network (and collision domain) and there is no longer a shared network medium.

MAC Addressing

MAC addresses are also known as hardware (or physical) addresses and every Ethernet network interface has one. They are assigned by the IEEE and written in a colon separated hexadecimal format (at least, they should be). A MAC address consists of 48bits (6 bytes) where the first 24 bits are used to identify the vendor and the last 24 bits are used to identify the device (or device interface) manufactured by that vendor. Here's an example: 00:50:56:C0:00:08; note that leading zeroes can be omitted, resulting in 50:56:C0:8.

The good thing about the standardization of MAC Addressing is its compatibility. When data frames pass across differing physical layer interfaces such as Ethernet onto Fast Ethernet and vice versa, there is no need to change the Ethernet frame addressing format. But some changes may be needed when bridging between different media types like FDDI and Ethernet or Token Ring and Ethernet.

Pretty much every network attached device builds a table for each MAC address it 'sees' on the LAN segment; this is called a MAC Address Table. This is used in conjunction with a protocol called Address Resolution Protocol to map logical (network layer) IP addresses to physical MAC addresses on a local network. This will be covered in more detail shortly.

You can find the current list of MAC addresses and their allocations to vendors (known as Organizationally Unique Identifiers (OUIs)) at: https://standards.ieee.org/develop/regauth/oui/public.html. You can use this page to search for a MAC address and see which vendor it belongs to.

MAC Address Table

Unlike a hub, when a switch is used on the network and hosts are attached and transmit data across the network the switch starts to learn every host's MAC address. This process is unsurprisingly called **learning**. This information is stored in what is called a MAC address table. The MAC address table will contain the MAC address of the host and the port that it is connected to. Therefore when the switch receives a frame from a host it will look through its MAC address table for the destination and if the entry is found in the MAC table it will forward the frames out of the corresponding port. This provides considerable benefits over hubs which 'repeat' or flood every frame out of every port (except the receiving one) all the time, as fewer frames are transmitted and hosts do not need to deal with frames that are not destined for them.

When the switch receives frames with a destination MAC address that it does not have a MAC address table entry for, the switch *does* send out the frame on every port *except* the one the frame arrived on. This process is called flooding – this is what a hub does with every frame all the time. When (and if) the unknown host replies to the frame, the MAC address is stored in the switch's MAC address table so when frames are destined for that host again the switch will know on which port it should send out the frames. Below you will find an example of a MAC address table.

```
root> show arp
MAC Address        Address         Name                         Interface        Flags
00:1b:0d:e7:00:40  2.248.168.1     gw-n8-m-rg-a13.ias.bredba    fe-0/0/0.0       none
00:1b:0d:e7:00:40  2.248.168.57    h57n8-m-rg-a13.ias.bredba    fe-0/0/0.0       none
74:d0:2b:25:ca:d9  192.168.1.2     192.168.1.2                  vlan.0           none
60:67:20:95:a2:ec  192.168.1.4     192.168.1.4                  vlan.0           none
78:a3:e4:c4:6b:c3  192.168.1.9     192.168.1.9                  vlan.0           none
54:72:4f:6d:8b:66  192.168.1.17    192.168.1.17                 vlan.0           none
00:11:32:0c:71:dc  192.168.1.200   192.168.1.200                vlan.0           none
Total entries: 7
```

As mentioned previously, a switch divides every port on the switch into a separate collision domain which means that every port acts as a dedicated layer two network, which significantly reduces, or even eliminates collisions. This is very important to remember.

Routers also separate collision domains but in a different manner to a switch; they do so because they operate at layer three, the network layer and do not forward layer two frames between networks.

Broadcast Domains

Broadcasts are necessary in an Ethernet network to support a number of technologies such as ARP (discussed shortly). A layer two broadcast frame is sent to the destination MAC address of: FF:FF:FF:FF:FF:FF and is accepted and inspected by every host in a broadcast domain. A broadcast domain is defined as *the group of hosts that will receive a broadcast message transmitted by any one of the group's members*. In other words, a broadcast domain consists of all the hosts connected to and that can communicate with each other on the same physical or virtual layer two network. A broadcast domain can contain multiple collision domains – more soon.

Whilst required, broadcasts can cause host and network performance issues if the network is constantly flooded with broadcast packets. Since Ethernet relies on CSMA/CD, if we have a lot of network traffic this will increase the amount of wait time and collisions hosts on the network experience (ignoring for a moment the benefits of switches). For these reasons it is desirable to divide large broadcast domains into many smaller broadcast domains to reduce unwanted network traffic and unnecessary host frame processing. In order to do this a layer three device called a router is introduced. A router helps decrease broadcasts in the network because it does not forward layer two (or for that matter layer three) broadcasts between networks.

Issues with Dividing Broadcast Domains

Even if creating multiple broadcast domains has its benefits, there are some downsides too. For example, DHCP is a protocol that automatically assigns IP addresses to devices on the network and it uses broadcasts to operate. If you have two separate broadcast domains and one of the domains has a running DHCP server and the other does not, you have a problem. Since routers do not forward broadcasts, the DHCP server in one broadcast domain cannot assign IP addresses to the hosts in the other broadcast domain.

There are ways to solve this but it is worth keeping in mind when you are setting up your network topology.

The Difference between Collision Domains and Broadcast Domains

A collision domain is created when multiple hosts are connected to a networking device like a hub. As we previously discussed a hub transmits data to all hosts which are connected to it. Therefore there is a chance a collision will occur between the clients and that is why it is said to be a collision domain.

Collision domains can be divided using a switch which divides every port on the switch into a separate collision domain and transmits data according to MAC address information, as shown next;

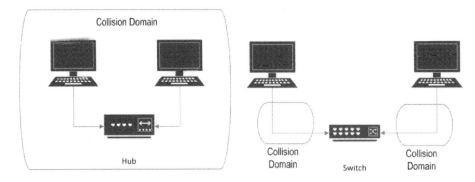

Whether connected to a hub or a switch hosts on the same physical layer two network (or VLAN) are still part of a broadcast domain. Large broadcast domains are divided into smaller ones to reduce the amount of traffic that is seen on the network. A router or other layer three device is used because they do not forward broadcast frames between networks, as shown;

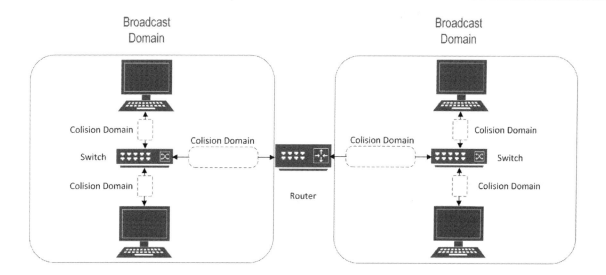

Exam Tip: It is very important to understand the difference between collision domains and broadcast domains and why it is important to minimize the size of them. Make sure you fully understand this.

Address Resolution Protocol (ARP)

ARP's purpose is to glue together (or map) layer three IP addresses to layer two MAC addresses. Remember that layer three addresses are logical and layer three has no understanding of the underlying physical network topology. Equally, layer two has no understanding of layer three addressing. When layer two is passed a packet from layer three, how does it know where to send it? What MAC address should layer 2 use?

This is where ARP comes into play, by providing layer two with the information it needs in order to transmit frames to the correct destination layer two address that is currently associated with the logical address layer three provided.

When a host wishes to send a packet to an IP address, layer two needs to know the MAC address of the destination host. In order to get it, the host sends an *ARP request* for the IP address, a broadcast to all the hosts on the local layer two network. If the IP address is a remote address (on a different logical, layer three network) it will instead send an ARP request for the default gateway's MAC address because that will handle the traffic.

The ARP request contains the source host's IP and MAC addresses and the IP address of the system it wishes to communicate with. The ARP request is sent out using a layer two broadcast which means that the request is received by all of the hosts in the same broadcast domain. When the requesting host receives the MAC address of the destination system in an ARP response, it saves it in its *ARP cache* for a period of time. The whole process is described in the following diagram;

The ARP Process

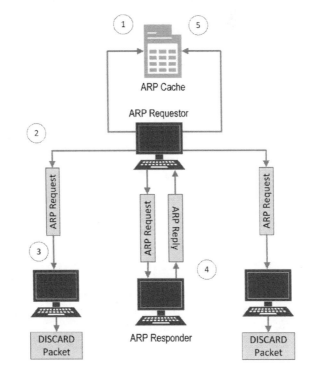

1. The host sending data checks its own ARP table and if the address does not exist it generates an ARP request containing the following;:
    a. Its own (source) IP address and MAC address.
    b. The IP address of the receiving host
    c. Destination MAC address: FF:FF:FF:FF:FF:FF

2. The sending host sends out the ARP request as a broadcast within its broadcast domain.

3. The hosts within the broadcast domain that receive the ARP request examine it and check if it is requesting their own IP address and MAC address. If it isn't, it discards the packet silently.

4. When the correct host picks up the packet it will send a reply back to the sender. This packet is called an *ARP Reply (or response)*. The host will use its own IP address and MAC address in the reply and send the ARP reply back to the original sender.

5. When the sending host receives the MAC address of the requesting host, it stores this information in its ARP cache and then proceeds with sending the intended packet using the MAC address it just received.

There is some confusion as to where ARP should be placed in the OSI reference model. Some say that it should belong in the network layer because it helps the Internet Protocol (IP) with resolving hardware addresses and some say that it should belong to the data link layer since its messages are carried within data-link layer frames.

ARP is not accounted for in the original OSI Model: ISO 7498-1 created in 1984. An appendix to the standard, the Internal Organization of the Network Layer (IONL): ISO 8648 created in 1988 specifies a structure for ARP like protocols (subnetwork dependent convergence facilities) but still isn't specific on a layer. However, considering ARP's use of MAC addresses for communication (IP addresses are the payload, not the means of communication) and inability to cross layer three boundaries we think it's pretty safe to consider it a layer two protocol. [The ISO charges for its standards documents but RFC994 contains most of the draft text that formed ISO 8648 if you fancy a read]

 If the destination is located on another logical network then ARP will not request the IP address of the ultimate destination. It will instead use the IP address of the default gateway and send the data to the default gateway which passes the traffic on to the next-hop address until it reaches its final destination.

VLANs & VLAN Tagging

A VLAN or a *Virtual LAN* is a virtual network that has the technical properties of a physical layer two network without the physical constraints. All hosts in the same VLAN can communicate with each other, as hosts connected to the same physical LAN can. As with physical networks, hosts in one VLAN cannot communicate with hosts in another without using a router or some other layer three device to route traffic between the two. A VLAN, like any physical network also represents a single broadcast domain.

Unlike physical networks formed using a hub, multiple VLANs can exist on a single switch and each port on a suitable switch could be assigned a different VLAN. As with any virtualization feature, this provides a great deal of flexibility and independence from physical considerations. For instance, if you have two departments that must be on different networks, rather than using a dedicated hub per department you can use a single switch with two VLANs and still maintain the required separation.

This is illustrated in the following diagram;

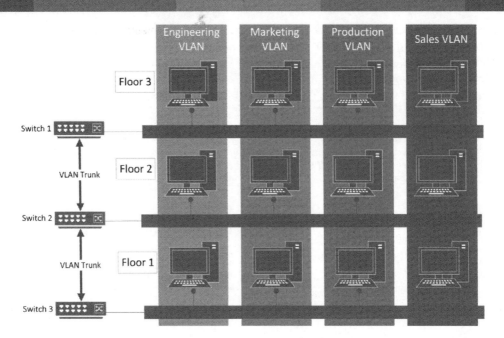

In the diagram you can see that we have four VLANs, Engineering, Marketing, Production and Sales. The network is divided into different floors and each floor contains four hosts that are physically connected to the same switch. Each port on the switch is assigned to one of these VLANs and each host connected to one of those ports will therefore belong to that VLAN.

This means that even though the hosts have different physical locations they are still part of the same logical network, the same VLAN. Even though the hosts in each VLAN are on different floors and connected to different switches, they can still communicate with each other. Hosts on the same floor but in different VLANs cannot, at least not without the aid of a router.

 Most modern day switches support layer 3 switching which means they have the ability to route traffic between VLANS. Thus, you do not actually have to attach a router to the network.

Using VLANs adds a 32-bit (4 byte) sub header to Ethernet frames where necessary; typically internally within a switch and across switch to switch links (trunks) that carry multiple VLANs. This header is called a *VLAN tag* and it identifies which VLAN the frame belongs to. How this works is specified in the IEEE 802.1Q standard. Unfortunately the standards document is not free; it can be purchased for a rather high price at the following URL: http://standards.ieee.org/findstds/standard/802.1Q-2014.html.

 When the frames travels over what is called a trunk port the tag is not removed. We will discuss trunk ports in more detail in this chapter.

Since VLANs are not dependent on network dedicated physical connections, member hosts can be located on any switch where that VLAN is available and trunked and a host can even belong to several VLANs. However in order to use more than one VLAN on a single port you need to enable VLAN trunking.

VLAN Trunking

When configuring VLANs on a switch port you can use one of two modes; access mode (also known as untagged mode) or trunk mode (also known as tagged mode). Access mode means you use a single VLAN on a port (or interface) and a tag is not used, at least when sending and receiving frames to and from the connected host (a tag may still be added if the frames cross a trunk port). Trunk mode however enables you to use multiple VLANs on a single port, with each frame being sent or received with a tag to identify the VLAN it belongs to.

This is beneficial when, for instance, you expand your network by adding more switches and you want to use the same VLAN(s) on the new switches. If you are using VLAN1, VLAN2 and VLAN3 on your current switch and you want to use those VLANs on the new switch, how are you going to connect them? If you just add the VLANs to the new switch and connect it to the existing one, hosts on the same VLAN connected to different switches will not be able to communicate.

You need to create a trunk port on each switch in order for the VLAN information to pass between the existing and new in the form of tagged frames. The trunk ports on each will serve as a passage between them, identifying every VLAN you use in your network. This is illustrated in the following diagram;

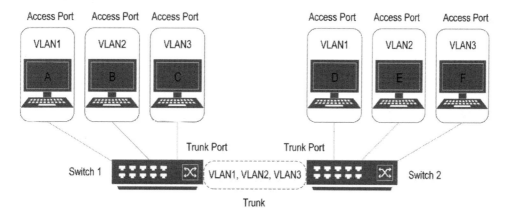

 You could actually not use a trunk (and therefore VLAN tagging) but instead you'd need to use a dedicated port on each switch for every VLAN used across the two which would be very wasteful. In the example above you'd use three ports per switch instead of just one per switch.

The Benefits of Using VLANs

VLANs are a great way to segment your network and reduce collision and broadcast domain size without using additional devices. You can use dedicated VLANs per business unit or the different floors of a building. For instance, if an organization has divided their VLANs based on departments and the IT department has been moved to another floor in the building. Instead of changing the cabling of the whole building, they could use VLANs and just change the VLAN tag of the relevant switch ports in the new location. This is just one of the advantages of VLANs; you can also implement VLANs if you have a lot of clients on the same network and want to lower the level of broadcasts.

Layer 3 Switching

When first introduced switches were limited to layer two functions; this meant routing traffic between VLANs required the involvement of a dedicated (and expensive) router. This is of course exactly the same as when using a physical LAN but is a significant drawback where VLANs are concerned as it negates the benefits of flexibility and physical independence. To overcome this, *layer three switching* was introduced.

This simply provides layer three router functions within a switch. As well as retaining the general benefits of using VLANs you also save money as you do not need to buy additional hardware to route traffic between VLANs. Since these devices are capable of both switching and routing, their cost is usually higher than that for just a layer two switch but still cheaper than purchasing both a layer two switch and dedicated layer three router.

VLANs in Real-Life Scenarios

Some people ask, *"Why can't I just subnet my network? Wouldn't that give me the same result?"*. The benefit that VLANs provide over a subnet is that devices that are in two different physical locations can be on the same network and two devices in the same physical location can be on different ones.

Another common question is, *"How large does my network have to be in order to gain the benefits of a VLAN?"*. Your network does not really need to be a certain size to be able to gain the benefits of VLANs. As mentioned before, you can divide your VLANs based on physical floors or departments or any other way you might like without purchasing dedicated hardware. If you experiencing performance problems within your network, creating VLANs can decrease broadcasts and therefore increase performance. VLANs will also help you apply security policy as you can segregate hosts into separate VLANs. You can then limit the traffic between the two. The possibilities are endless.

Exam Tip — In configuring and managing an F5 device, you need to fully understand what a VLAN is and what it used for. When configuring interfaces on a F5 device you associate one or more VLANs with each interface and may also configure tagging.

Link Aggregation Control Protocol (LACP)

Link Aggregation Control Protocol is a protocol that combines (or bundles) several physical Ethernet interfaces into a single logical link that operates using one MAC address, as if it were a single physical interface.

This technology is known by many different names depending on which vendor provides it. For instance Cisco has called their link aggregation technology *EtherChannel* (but note, use of LACP is optional) and other vendors use the names *teaming* or *trunking*. LACP is standardized under the IEEE standard, *802.3ad* or *802.1ax*.

Exam Tip

In the F5 world several combined Ethernet connections are called a trunk. This can be very confusing since VLAN tagging is also described as trunking by Cisco and other vendors.

The two main advantages of using LACP (or any similar technology) are *improved reliability* and *aggregated throughput*.

If one of the physical links in a bundle suffers from a failure, the device keeps transmitting and receiving both outgoing and incoming frames on the other physical links that are still active. This technology is so seamless that a user or an application will not usually experience any issues.

Chapter Summary

- One of the core functions of the Data Link Layer is the MAC-addressing. This is responsible for identifying the host on the network using what is known as a MAC-address.

- Carrier Sense Multiple Access: Collision Detection or CSMA/CD is the access method of Ethernet networking. It was introduced in 1985 and is part of the IEEE 802.3 standard.

- A switch makes it possible to decrease collisions by separating each port in the switch into separate collision domains.

- A broadcast domain is a group of hosts that will receive a broadcast message transmitted by any one of its members. A broadcast domain can be divided into several broadcast domains by using a router.

- ARP stands for Address Resolution Protocol and it is responsible for keeping track of what MAC address is connected to a specific IP address and vice versa.

- VLANs or Virtual LANs are logical network segments that help manage the network by grouping certain ports together over one or more switches. Since VLANs work above the physical layer it does not matter that the hosts are connected to different ports over multiple switches, they can still talk to each other.

- Link Aggregation Control Protocol is a technology that combines several Ethernet connections into one logical link that operates under one MAC address. In the F5 world combining several Ethernet connections is called a trunk. This can be very confusing since VLANs also uses the concept of trunking ports in the Cisco and other vendor worlds.

Chapter Review

In order to test your knowledge and understanding of this chapter, please answer the following questions. You will find the answers and explanations of the questions at the end of this chapter.

1. What access method does Ethernet use?
    a. Carrier Sense Equal Access: Collision Detection
    b. Carrier Sense Multiple Access: Collision Avoidance
    c. Carrier Sense Multiple Access: Collision Detection
    d. Carrier Sense Single Access: Collision Detection

2. How many bits does a MAC address have?
    a. 24 bits
    b. 32 bits
    c. 48 bits
    d. 64 bits

3. What device can be used to divide a collision domain into several smaller collision domains? (Choose the most correct answer)
    a. A switch
    b. A hub
    c. A router
    d. Both a switch and a router can be used.

4. What MAC address is used when an ARP request is sent out on the local area network?
    a. 255.255.255.255
    b. FF:FF:FF:FF:FF:FF
    c. The ARP request is addressed separately to each device on the LAN.
    d. It uses its own MAC address.

5. What are VLAN trunks used for?
    a. It is used to tag only one VLAN on a certain port on the switch.
    b. It is used to combine several Ethernet connections into one logical link that operates under one MAC address.
    c. It is used to enable several VLANs on one single port on the switch. This makes it possible to connect several VLANs between multiple switches.
    d. It is used to enable several switches to be connected together for configuration synchronization and hardware redundancy.

Chapter Review: Answers

You will find the answers to the chapter review questions below:

1. The correct answer is: C
    a. Carrier Sense Equal Access: Collision Detection
    b. Carrier Sense Multiple Access: Collision Avoidance
    c. **Carrier Sense Multiple Access: Collision Detection**
    d. Carrier Sense Single Access: Collision Detection

Option b is the access method of the wireless Ethernet standard 802.11 and option a and d do not exist.

2. The correct answer is: C
    a. 24 bits
    b. 32 bits
    c. **48 bits**
    d. 64 bits

Option b is the number of bits an IP-address contains and option d is the amount of bits the new host operating system kernels operates on.

3. The correct answer is: D
    a. A switch
    b. A hub
    c. A router
    d. **Both a switch and a router can be used.**

Both a switch and a router are able to divide collision domains but the router also has the ability to divide broadcast domains. A hub does not have the ability to divide collision domains.

4. The correct answer is: B
    a. 255.255.255.255
    b. **FF:FF:FF:FF:FF:FF**
    c. The ARP request is addressed separately to each device on the LAN.
    d. It uses its own MAC address.

When an ARP request is sent, the sending host uses the broadcast address of the MAC address which is FF:FF:FF:FF:FF:FF. This ARP request will therefore be sent out to every host on the local segment and the host with the correct IP-address will respond back with its MAC address.

5. The correct answer is: C
    a. To tag only one VLAN on a certain port on the switch.
    b. It is used to combine several Ethernet connections into one logical link that operates under one MAC address.
    c. **It is used to enable several VLANs on one single port on the switch. This makes it possible to connect several VLANs between multiple switches.**
    d. A VLAN trunk enables several switches to be connected together for configuration synchronization and hardware redundancy.

VLAN trunks are used to send several VLAN IDs over a single connection. This is configured by the network administrator on a specified port on the switch. This enables the VLAN to span over several switches using the trunk port.

Remember that an F5 device also uses trunk ports but it means something completely different. In F5, a trunk port is the same as Link Aggregation Control Protocol (LACP) which means that you combine several Ethernet connections into one logical link that operates under one MAC address.

5. The Network Layer in Detail

Internet Protocol (IP) is only one of many real world protocols that operate at the network layer. However, as it is used almost universally it's what the exam and therefore this book focuses on solely in relation to the network layer. This section will almost entirely focus on addressing; later chapters will cover other layer three related subjects such as routing and NAT, which will build upon on your understanding of this subject.

The header fields added by this layer to encapsulate the data (the variable length layer 4 payload) are as follows;

- Version – four bits
- Internet Header Length (IHL) – four bits
- Differentiated Services Code Point (DSCP) – six bits
- Explicit Congestion Notification (ECN) – two bits
- Total Length – two Bytes
- Identification – two Bytes
- Flags – three bits
- Fragment Offset – 13 bits
- Time to Live (TTL) – one Byte
- Protocol – one Byte
- Header Checksum – two Bytes
- Source IP Address – four Bytes
- Destination IP Address – four Bytes
- One or more optional Options headers – variable length

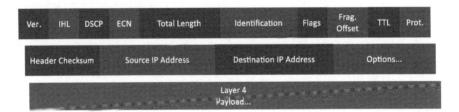

We'll explore the purpose of some of these headers over the course of this and the Switching & Routing chapters.

Understanding IP Addressing

An IP address is a logical, physically independent address, very different to a MAC address which relates to a specific physical device interface. An IP address is used to identify a network interface on a logical IP network (a MAC address identifies a network interface or device attached to a physical network). Multiple IP addresses can be assigned to a physical interface.

The IP protocol and IP addresses make it possible for any host to communicate with any other, regardless of location or physical network type, as long as they have an IP address and a subnet mask to identify which network they belong to (and those networks are connected in some way).

An IPv4 (the predominant version) address is composed of 32-bits (4 bytes) and has both a *host portion*, which identifies a specific host and a *network portion* which identifies which network the host belongs to. This 32-bit address can be broken down into four decimal parts with each composed of 8 binary bits (an octet); four times eight is thirty-two bits (4*8=32). A subnet mask is used to differentiate what portion of the address is the host portion and what portion is the network. This will be described in detail shortly.

Structure of an IP Address

Each decimal value in an IP address has an 8 bit binary equivalent. The decimal IP address is converted into a binary format which the host understands (as with all data eventually). Decimal values are used when expressing IP addresses only for our own convenience and speed; binary expression would be longer, more time consuming and more prone to error.

Each octet (8 bits, 1 byte) of an IP address is converted to a decimal value and separated by a period (dot). For this reason, an IP address is said to be expressed in dotted decimal format (for example, 192.168.0.1). The value in each octet ranges from 0 to 255 decimal, or 00000000 - 11111111 binary.

Here is an example if all the binary values in an octet are set to one (with the decimal calculation and value in brackets);

Binary values	1	1	1	1	1	1	1	1	
Decimal values	128	64	32	16	8	4	2	1	128 + 64 + 32 + 16 + 8 + 4 + 2 + 1 = 255

Here is an example of the first octet in the address, 192.168.0.1 expressed in binary (with the decimal calculation and value in brackets);

Binary values	1	1	0	0	0	0	0	0	
Decimal values	128	64	32	16	8	4	2	1	128 + 64 + 0 + 0 + 0 + 0 + 0 + 0 = 192

Here is the whole IP address presented in both binary and decimal values.

Decimal Format	192.	168.	0.	1
Binary Format	11000000.	10101000.	00000000.	00000001

Converting Between Binary & Decimal

In order to fully understand IP addressing we need to be able to convert an IP address from its decimal form to a binary one and vice versa. We do this for several reasons. For instance when you are calculating subnets or when you are calculating how many hosts a network can contain. We will go through some of these common tasks in the following sections.

Converting between binary and decimal formats can be difficult. The key to learning this is to use and practice many different examples until you fully understand how it works.

Converting from Binary to Decimal

First of all, each binary bit (digit) in an octet has its own value. These values start at 1 and double for every step you make to the left until you reach the final bit in the octet. Each octet holds a value of 2^0 (two to the power of zero) through to 2^7 (this is known as the base-2 numbering system). See the following example:

Binary values	0	0	0	0	0	0	0	0
Decimal values	128	64	32	16	8	4	2	1

This is one of the octets of an IP address expressed in binary digits. Each digit has a decimal value and in order to calculate it you will need to add together the base-2 value of each binary digit of 1, as follows;

Binary values	1	1	0	0	0	0	0	0	
Decimal values	128	64	32	16	8	4	2	1	128 + 64 + 0 + 0 + 0 + 0 + 0 + 0 = 192

In this example the decimal value is 192 because the first two (most significant) bits are activated (a 1 (one) rather than a zero). This will give the base-2 values of 128 and 64, the sum of which is 192 in decimal. This method is used for every octet in the IP address, both the host and network portions.

Converting from Decimal to Binary

There will be times when you need to convert an IP address from a decimal format to a binary format and the method used is similar to the binary to decimal method. Some examples of when you might do this would be when you are calculating how many available hosts a network can contain or when you're calculating the broadcast address of a network.

For instance let us use the decimal number of 168. We want to convert this into binary format. To do this we use our conversion table again.

Binary values	0	0	0	0	0	0	0	0	
Decimal values	128	64	32	16	8	4	2	1	168

Instead of adding the decimal values you subtract them. To simplify, ask yourself this; can you subtract 128 from 168? Yes, then we subtract 128 from 168 and add a 1 to the table (to represent the 128 value). See the following example:

Binary values	1	0	0	0	0	0	0	0	
Decimal values	128	64	32	16	8	4	2	1	168 − 128 = 40

 It is mathematically possible to subtract a bigger number from a smaller number but when calculating subnets the principal is that you cannot have any negative numbers. That is why it is important to only subtract if it is possible.

168-128 is 40 and we move on to the next value, can you subtract 64 from 40? The answer is no and therefore we do not add a 1 to the table. We proceed to the next value; can you subtract 32 from 40? Yes, then we subtract 32 from 40 and add a 1 to the table (to represent the 32 value), see the following example:

Binary values	1	0	1	0	0	0	0	0	
Decimal values	128	64	32	16	8	4	2	1	168 − 128 = 40 − 32 = 8

We proceed like this until we have reached a decimal value of 0 and when we are done it should look like this:

Binary values	1	0	1	0	1	0	0	0	
Decimal values	128	64	32	16	8	4	2	1	168 − 128 = 40 − 32 = 8 − 8 = 0

So the binary value of 168 is 01010100.

There are many tools and websites that can help you convert from decimal to binary and vice versa but it is necessary to know how to do this with pen and paper. Practice this with several different examples because it is essential to be able to do so.

Addresses Classes

IP addresses are divided into several different classes. These classes specify what portion of the IP address identifies the network portion and what identifies the host portion. The classes A, B and C are the most common ones.

Class A

First Octet	Second Octet	Third Octet	Fourth Octet
1 2 3 4 5 6 7 8	1 2 3 4 5 6 7 8	1 2 3 4 5 6 7 8	1 2 3 4 5 6 7 8
Network Identifier	Host Identifier		

Class B

First Octet	Second Octet	Third Octet	Fourth Octet
1 2 3 4 5 6 7 8	1 2 3 4 5 6 7 8	1 2 3 4 5 6 7 8	1 2 3 4 5 6 7 8
Network Identifier		Host Identifier	

Class C

First Octet	Second Octet	Third Octet	Fourth Octet
1 2 3 4 5 6 7 8	1 2 3 4 5 6 7 8	1 2 3 4 5 6 7 8	1 2 3 4 5 6 7 8
Network Identifier			Host Identifier

IP Address Class	Class A	Class B	Class C
First bit values (binary)	0	10	110
First byte value (decimal)	0-127	128-191	192-223
Number of network identifiers bits	8 - 1 = 7	16 - 2 = 14	24 - 3 = 21
Number of host identifier bits	24	16	8
Number of possible networks	126	16,384	2,097,152
Number of possible hosts	16,777,214	65,534	254

The reason we subtract 1 network identifier bit from Class A, 2 from B and 3 from C is because the first bit values are fixed for each class; this means that the number of uniquely identified networks is reduced.

However the total number of bits used to identify the networks is still the same. It is just the number of uniquely identified networks that decrease.

 There is also a Class D which is used for multicast and a Class E which is used for experimental purposes. We will not go into further detail on these as they are beyond the scope of this book.

In the previous diagram you can see that Class A identifies its network using the first 8 bits (the first octet or 1 byte) as/for the network mask. We use the subnet mask to identify which portion is the network and which portion is the host. To identify the network portion of a Class A address we need to use all of the bits in the first octet of the subnet mask, this results a subnet mask of 255.0.0.0 in decimal. This may also be displayed by using a so-called prefix of */8* which indicates that 8 bits are used to identify the network portion. This means that the other 24 bits are used for the host portion.

Since Class A ranges from 00000000 to 01111111 in binary (for the first octet), which is 0 to 127 in decimal, every time you see an IP address that begins with the number 1 to 127, you know it is a Class A address. Out of these networks there are actually only 126 usable networks. An address that starts with 127 is reserved for diagnostic and internal purposes; for instance the IP address 127.0.0.1 is used to diagnose the local TCP/IP stack and if you can successfully ping that address, then the local TCP/IP stack is working properly.

 Ping is a tool that all computer operating systems support and this tool sends out an Internet Control Message Protocol (ICMP) message to the IP address you defined. If you get a response from the destination then that system is up from an IP perspective. Unfortunately some Internet Service Providers and other companies may choose to deny ICMP packets so when you are trying to ping those systems you will not get a response. But that does not mean that the system is not actually up.

Even though you can only have 126 available Class A networks, each one of these can have up to *16,777,214* hosts in it. As Class B and C dedicate more bits to the network portion a wider number of networks are available but a lower number of hosts per network.

This is a balancing act to be performed based on how many networks and hosts you need in any particular situation and in each case the subnet mask may be different. This is the key feature in subnet masking, where you can take an IPv4 address network (or range) and subnet it into smaller networks. This will increase the amount of networks but decrease the amount of hosts per network. We will go into more detail on how subnetting works later in this chapter.

Private Addresses

The *Internet Assigned Numbers Authority (IANA)* has assigned special networks in each of the classes which can be used for addressing within private, internal networks (rather than on the public Internet). These ranges are specified in RFC1918. The main reason for this is that the number of available public (Internet routable) networks and addresses has declined significantly as more and more people and companies have connected to the Internet. Using public addresses on private networks is a great waste of what is now a precious resource. Instead, we use these private addresses and a technology called *Network Address Translation* (NAT) to translate between private and public addresses (typically provided by an ISP) where necessary, when connecting to the Internet.

Anyone can use an internal private network range and addressing; you do not have to ask for permission to do so from any central body. Note that as two hosts cannot have the same IP address on a network, issues can occur when two networks that happen to use the same private address range need to be connected. NAT can also be used to overcome this issue.

There are several private address ranges, one for each address class. In the following table you can see what the specified networks are and how many hosts each can accommodate. You'll note the class B and C ranges have a subnet mask/prefix which doesn't match the class; this is because multiple networks are provided.

In the case of class B, 16 classful networks are provided: 172.16.0.0/16 through to 172.31.0.0/16. With class C its 256: 192.168.0.0/24 through to 192.168.254.0/24.

Class	Network Range	Classful Networks	Hosts per network
Private Class A range	10.0.0.0/8	1	16,777,214
Private Class B range	172.16.0.0/12	16	65,534
Private Class C range	192.168.0.0/16	256	254

IP routing is a critical part of the Internet Protocol and it is responsible for ensuring that a packet gets to its specified location. This will be covered in detail in the Switching and Routing chapter.

Calculating Networks and Hosts

You now understand how an IP address is comprised of a network portion and host portion and that the number of networks and hosts are dependent on how many bits you use for each portion. Next, we need to be able to calculate how many networks and hosts we can use with a certain number of bits. By being able to calculate this we can allocate network ranges (or subnets) that are suitable for our needs.

To simplify this for mathematical purposes a Class C network will be used, for example 192.168.1.0.

Here is the question: *"How many hosts does this network address support?"*. It is actually quite simple. We know that an IP address consists of 32 bits in total. A Class C address uses 24 bits to identify the network portion leaving 8 bits to identify the host portion. To be able to calculate how many unique IP addresses we can have in this network, we use the following equation:

```
2^X-2 (Where X indicates the number of host bits you are using.)
```

In our case it will look like this:

```
2^8-2 = 254 hosts (256-2)
```

The reason we subtract two addresses is because there are two that we cannot use. The IP address of 192.168.1.255 is the broadcast address and the address 192.168.1.0 is the network address and these cannot be assigned to a host.

To easily identify which addresses cannot be used we have to look at the binary value of an IP address. When the host portion contains only 00000000 (0 in decimal) or 11111111 (255 in decimal) the address cannot be used. This however does not apply to every address because when we look closer at subnetting, an IP address can contain all ones or zeroes and still look valid and not end in either 0 or 255. We will examine this later in this chapter.

Here's a reminder of how we calculate the decimal figure from base two:

Binary values	1	1	1	1	1	1	1	1	
Decimal values	128	64	32	16	8	4	2	1	128 + 64 + 32 + 16 + 8 + 4 + 2 + 1 = 255

In case you are wondering why subtracting 2 results in a figure of 254, remember that 0 is also considered as an address. A decimal value of 255 represents 256 addresses: 0 through to 255.

To be able to calculate how many networks we get from a certain amount of bits we use almost the same equation. If we want to know how many networks Class B supports we use the bits of the network portion of the address to perform the calculation. A Class B uses 16 bits to identify its network portion but we have to remove two bits because they are reserved to identify the class. Therefore we need to use 14 bits.

However the total number of bits used to identify the networks is still the same. It is just the number of uniquely identified networks that decrease.

Let us use that in our equation:

```
2^14 = 16,384 networks
```

When calculating networks we do not remove two addresses because all of the addresses are valid network addresses. Remember this when calculating subnets.

Subnet Masking

If we were to only use the IP addresses in a specified class with its network identifiers and host identifiers we would not need a subnet mask. But as we mentioned before, you can divide a single address range into multiple subnets.

For instance if you were to use a Class B address, its default subnet mask would be 255.255.0.0 which would use the first 16 bits for networks and the last 16 bits for hosts. But if you instead use a subnet mask of 255.255.255.0 on a Class B address you would dedicate 24 bits to the network portion and the remaining 8 bits to the host portion.

By borrowing bits from the host portion to use in the network portions you decrease the amount of hosts per network but increase the amount of networks you can use. This is useful when you want to divide your network into smaller networks. For instance you could divide your network into a client network, server network, wireless network and so forth. This can also be useful for security reasons.

Variable Length Subnet Masking (VLSM)

Subnetting using the standard classes is quite easy to understand. However, in most real life scenarios you don't subnet using class-standard subnets but between (or within) and across class boundaries, since most companies are not assigned a Class A or Class B address. For instance, splitting a /24 subnets into two sub-networks or combining two /24 subnets into a larger single 'supernet'.

You can use as many bits of the host portion as you want *as long as* there are still bits left to represent the hosts. Remember the equation from before. For instance, in the scenario where we only reserve 1 bit to the host portion the equation would look like this:

```
2^X-2  (Where X indicates the number of host bits you are using.)

2^1-2=0
```

The reason why we subtract two addresses is because there are two addresses we cannot use. The IP address of 192.168.1.255 is the broadcast address and the IP address 192.168.1.0 is the network address and these are not valid addresses for hosts.

This would result in no addresses for the host portion.

Now let us look at how we use this method on a Class C network with an IP address of 192.168.1.0. This address uses 24 bits for its network portion (subnet mask 255.255.255.0) which means we can borrow up to 6 bits from the host portion for subnetting.

If we borrow more than 6 bits from the host portion we do not have enough bits left for hosts. If we borrow all 6 bits we can have 2 hosts on each network using the remaining 2 bits.

For the purposes of this example we will 'borrow' 4 bits. In binary the subnet mask will now look like this:

11111111.11111111.11111111.11110000

This results in a decimal value of 255.255.255.240 (the decimal value of 11111111 is 255; the decimal value of 11110000 is 240) and a prefix of /28.

Since we borrowed 4 bits from the host portion to use in the network portion, how many networks can we now have? Let us look at the usual equation again:

```
2^4 = 16
```

In order to calculate how many hosts this will support per network, we use the following equation:

```
2^4 - 2 = 14
```

All right! So we now have 16 subnets and each can have 14 hosts. Now we need to calculate each network and available host IP addresses. We do this by identifying the first available network: the subnetted IP address 192.168.1.0/28.

Original IP address

IP Address	192.	168.	1.	0
Binary Format	11000000.	10101000.	00000001.	00000000
Borrowed bits	11000000.	10101000.	00000001.	00000000
	Network Portion			Host Portion
Subnetmask	255.	255.	255.	0

Subnetted IP address

IP Address	192.	168.	1.	0
Binary Format	11000000.	10101000.	00000001.	00000000
Borrowed bits	11000000.	10101000.	00000001.	00000000
	Network Portion			Host Portion
Subnetmask	255.	255.	255.	240

The borrowed bits part indicates the octet from which we borrowed 4 bits and they are highlighted in the red color. You can see that there are four remaining bits, these are the bits that we have left for hosts. Below you can see some of the available networks we have created by borrowing 4 bits from the host portion:

Subnetted IP address

IP Address	192.	168.	1.	0
Borrowed bits	11000000.	10101000.	00000001.	00000000
	Network Portion			Host Portion
Subnetmask	255.	255.	255.	240

Subnetted IP address

IP Address	192.	168.	1.	16
Borrowed bits	11000000.	10101000.	00000001.	00010000
	Network Portion			Host Portion
Subnetmask	255.	255.	255.	240

Subnetted IP address

IP Address	192.	168.	1.	32
Borrowed bits	11000000.	10101000.	00000001.	00100000
	Network Portion			Host Portion
Subnetmask	255.	255.	255.	240

Subnetted IP address

	192.	168.	1.	48
	11000000.	10101000.	00000001.	00110000
	Network Portion			Host Portion
	255.	255.	255.	240

This list continues until all of the 4 bits have been turned on which gives the binary value 1111. Now we know what network addresses we can use, let's take a closer look at one of them and calculate the host address range.

To simplify things, let's use the first network address which is 192.168.1.0.

Subnetted IP address

IP Address	192.	168.	1.	0
Binary Format	11000000.	10101000.	00000001.	00000000
Borrowed bits	11000000.	10101000.	00000001.	00000000
	Network Portion			Host Portion
Subnetmask	255.	255.	255.	240

As we said before, we cannot use a host portion that contains all ones or zeroes because these are not valid addresses. Therefore the first active address would be the first bit in the host portion:

Subnetted IP address

IP Address	192.	168.	1.	1
Binary Format	11000000.	10101000.	00000001.	00000001
Borrowed bits	11000000.	10101000.	00000001.	00000001
	Network Portion			Host Portion
Subnetmask	255.	255.	255.	240

This is our first host address in this subnet and it results in the IP address of *192.168.1.1*. To be able to identify the last host address we have to turn on all bits except the last one because this is the broadcast address.

Subnetted IP address				
IP Address	192.	168.	1.	14
Binary Format	11000000.	10101000.	00000001.	00001110
Borrowed bits	11000000.	10101000.	00000001.	00001110
	Network Portion			Host Portion
Subnetmask	255.	255.	255.	240

Therefore the last address would be 192.168.1.14 so the address range would be 192.168.1.1 to 192.168.1.14.

Here is a collection of all the subnets with their host address range and subnet mask:

Subnet	Subnet mask	Host address range
192.168.1.0	255.255.255.240	192.168.1.1 - 192.168.1.14
192.168.1.16	255.255.255.240	192.168.1.17 - 192.168.1.30
192.168.1.32	255.255.255.240	192.168.1.33 - 192.168.1.46
192.168.1.48	255.255.255.240	192.168.1.49 - 192.168.1.62
192.168.1.64	255.255.255.240	192.168.1.65 - 192.168.1.78
192.168.1.80	255.255.255.240	192.168.1.81 - 192.168.1.94
192.168.1.96	255.255.255.240	192.168.1.97 - 192.168.1.110
192.168.1.112	255.255.255.240	192.168.1.113 - 192.168.1.126
192.168.1.128	255.255.255.240	192.168.1.128 - 192.168.1.142
192.168.1.144	255.255.255.240	192.168.1.145 - 192.168.1.158
192.168.1.160	255.255.255.240	192.168.1.161 - 192.168.1.174
192.168.1.176	255.255.255.240	192.168.1.177 - 192.168.1.190
192.168.1.192	255.255.255.240	192.168.1.193 - 192.168.1.206
192.168.1.208	255.255.255.240	192.168.1.209 - 192.168.1.222
192.168.1.224	255.255.255.240	192.168.1.225 - 192.168.1.238
192.168.1.240	255.255.255.240	192.168.1.241 - 192.168.1.254

Exam Tip — It is really important to know how to calculate IP addresses and subnets and to be able to know how many networks and hosts you can use with a particular subnet mask. Practice this until you fully understand it.

Classless Inter-Domain Routing (CIDR)

When address classes were introduced, organizations would get assigned one or several IP addresses from one of the different classes by their Internet Service Provider (ISP). This meant that you could get a class A, B or C address range and you would only work within that class and not subnet beyond it. For many companies, this was a real waste of IP addresses because companies and organizations would receive a very large network address range that could contain a large amount of hosts and they did not have anywhere near that amount of hosts in their network. For instance if a large company was assigned a class A address they would be able to use 16.7 million addresses but would perhaps only need as few as 100,000.

Therefore CIDR was introduced. As shown previously, we can subnet our networks exactly as we want to. You can use a class A address range with any mask of our choosing, 10.0.0.0/24 for instance. We are no longer limited to using the class defined mask; in short, CIDR makes it possible to subnet beyond the standard.

Broadcast Addresses

As we've already discussed, a broadcast address is an address that targets all systems on a specified network instead of just a single host. There is a relatively easy way to calculate what the broadcast address of a network is.

One method commonly used is a *bitwise OR calculation* which uses a reversed subnet mask. The reverse mask is the subnet mask but with the host bits all turned on rather than the network bits. If a system has the IP address of 192.168.1.240 and it uses the subnet mask 255.255.255.0 then what is the broadcast address of the system? To find this we have to convert the IP address into a binary format and then use the bitwise OR calculation. This works by comparing the reverse mask bits with the IP address bits; when at least one of the two bit values is set to 1, the results will be 1. Anything else will be a 0.

IP Address (Decimal)	192.	168.	1.	240
Subnetmask	255.	255	255.	0
IP Address (Binary)	11000000.	10101000.	00000001.	11011100
Reverse mask	00000000.	00000000.	00000000.	11111111
	Bitwise OR Calculation			
Broadcast (Binary)	11000000.	10101000.	00000001.	11111111
Broadcast (Decimal)	192.	168.	1.	255

Convert the binary values to decimal and you have the resulting broadcast address of 192.168.1.255.

We can apply this method to any IP address and subnet mask. Below you will find an example of using 192.168.1.35/27 (subnet mask 255.255.255.224).

IP Address (Decimal)	192.	168.	1.	35
Subnetmask	255.	255	255.	224
IP Address (Binary)	11000000.	10101000.	00000001.	00100011
Reverse mask	00000000.	00000000.	00000000.	00011111
	Bitwise OR Calculation			
Broadcast (Binary)	11000000.	10101000.	00000001.	00111111
Broadcast (Decimal)	192.	168.	1.	63

Fragmentation

When a host sends an IP packet onto the network it cannot be larger than a certain size. The size of the packet is determined by the *Maximum Transmission Unit* (MTU) and this is, by default, set to 1500 bytes. We'll cover MTU in detail in the next chapter.

Should a packet of this maximum size, being routed between two hosts, encounter a network with a lower MTU, we need to break it into pieces (fragments) that are equal to or smaller than the lower MTU before we can route it across that network. This is called Fragmentation, which is one of the functions of the IP protocol.

It is important to know that the fragments are not reassembled into their original state until they reach their final destination.

To be able to identify each packet at the receiving end, the sending host marks each packet with an ID called the *fragmentation ID*. The fragmentation ID is actually a copy of the ID field (IP identification number) that is located in the IP header.

There are three essentials pieces of information used to enable IP Fragmentation; each fragment must carry its "position" or "offset", it must state the length of the data that it is carrying and finally whether there are more fragments coming. The packet uses the *more fragments (MF)* flag to indicate this.

Time to Live (TTL)

There are many instances where a network can be misconfigured or routing protocols fail for some reason and routing loops occur. Here's a very basic example of a static routing misconfiguration that causes a rooting loop;

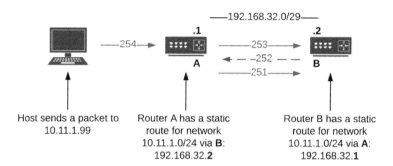

Host sends a packet to 10.11.1.99

Router A has a static route for network 10.11.1.0/24 via **B**: 192.168.32.**2**

Router B has a static route for network 10.11.1.0/24 via **A**: 192.168.32.**1**

A SYN packet destined for address 10.11.1.99 is sent by the host to its default gateway, which is router A. Router A is configured with a static route specifying packets for the 10.11.1.0/24 network should be routed to router B at 192.168.32.2. Router B is misconfigured with a static route specifying packets for the 10.11.1.0/24 network should be routed back to router A at 192.168.32.1.

The packet would then be endlessly routed back and forth between routers A and B, consuming bandwidth and both memory and CPU resources. When other packets are sent (retries for instance) the number of packets looping between the routers grows and eventually one or both routers will fail.

To prevent this, all packets have a TTL value which specifies a maximum number of layer three hops (typically routers) that can be traversed by that packet on the way to the final destination. Each time the packet passes through a layer three network device (a hop) the TTL value is decreased by one. When the TTL value eventually reaches one the packet is dropped by the device that receives it. Whilst this doesn't remove the routing loop it reduces its impact and avoids router failures.

This device may then also send an ICMP message back to the originating host saying, *destination host unreachable*. This alerts the sending host that something has gone wrong. The default TTL value varies between different operating systems.

TCP/IPv6

One of the problems with IPv4 is that publicly available addresses are starting to run out. Different technologies have been invented to slow this process down (CIDR and NAT for instance) but in the long run we need an IP address space which is much larger.

IP Version 6 is the solution to this problem; with its 128-bit address length, you have 2^{128} possible addresses available. This is a total of 340,282,366,920,938,463,463,374,607,431,768,211,456 addresses. This number of available addresses is staggering and can be quite hard to comprehend. To simplify, this means that you can give multiple addresses to every grain of sand that exists on the entire planet.

Implementing this new IP version is a tough task since old hardware and software often does not support it. You may have to invest in new equipment that many feel gives them nothing in return. You have already got a functioning IPv4 network and IPv6 will not enhance your network in any way. It really just adds support for those who cannot obtain an IPv4 address.

This has been the main problem with IPv6 and the reason why it is taking such a long time for everyone to implement it (it has been around for over 15 years now). Companies need to throw out or upgrade their old equipment and invest in new IPv6 equipment and for many this can be a very expensive investment.

There are however some technologies that can translate an IPv6 address to an IPv4 address and vice versa allowing the two versions to co-exist and negating the need for a wholesale 'rip and replace' approach. The implementation of IPv6 has started to expand because of this (among other reasons). For instance, in Sweden many government agencies have implemented IP v6 and all of them are recommended to use it by the end of 2013, by a board called Board of Mail and Tele or the *PTS (Post och Tele-styrelsen)*. Some government agencies were able to achieve the goal but unfortunately not all of them. The PTS has not published further recommendations as of this book's writing

The PTS argument for implementing IPv6 is to invest in the future of the Internet because we need to be able to communicate with countries where they use IPv6 addressing at a large scale.

Different IPv6 Addresses

Unicast Addresses

These addresses provide one-to-one transmission services to individual interfaces. This includes server farms that share a single address. IPv6 supports many different unicast addresses which includes global, link-local and unique local.

Multicast Addresses

Type of address	Description
Global unicast address	These addresses are used on the Internet and are routable. They are similar to the IPv4 public addresses in use today.
Link-local address	These addresses are similar to the private addresses used in IPv4 (10.0.0.0/8 etc.) They are not routable on the Internet and are intended to be used within internal, private networks.
Unique local address	These are also used for private addressing but they are unique so that joining two networks together will not cause a collision
Special addresses	These are similar to loopback addresses but are also used for 6-to-4 addresses for crossing from an IPv4 to an IPv6 network and IPv4-address mapped spaces.

Instead of flooding the network with broadcasts, each packet is sent to specified members of a multicast group, as is the case with IPv4.

Anycast Addresses

This address type was a late addition to IPv4 and is typically only implemented in relation to DNS with v4. Anycast addresses have a single address that can be assigned to multiple (normally geographically dispersed) hosts. This provides both location aware load-balancing and automatic failover.

The Structure of an IPv6 Address

The structure of an IPv6 address is a bit different from an IPv4 address. First of all it is represented in a hexadecimal, colon separated address format (similar to a MAC address) instead of the decimal, period (or dot) separated format. Secondly, it is a lot longer than an IPv4 address and has eight 16-bit sections instead of four 8-bit sections. The good news is that it can be shortened.

The IPv6 address is split up into three parts, the network identifier, the subnet and the interface identifier. If you are using a global unique address you will most likely receive addresses from your Internet service provider.

Provider-assigned network bits	Self-assigned subnet	Host bits
2001:0db8:3c4d:	:0015:	:0000:0000:abcd:ef12
48bit	16bit	64bit

The global prefix is the part you receive from your Internet service provider and the subnet and interface ID are set by the network administrator.

The Loopback Address

The loopback address or localhost address in IPv6 is as follows:

0000:0000:0000:0000:0000:0000:0000:0001

Since this is lengthy to write you can reduce the written size by representing one or more (if adjacent) group of four zeros with a double colon instead. You can only do this once with any single IPv6 address. This shortens the address and makes it much easier to write. So the loopback address will look like this:

::1

It is also possible to remove every leading zero in any 16 bit block wherever they appear. Here is one example:

2001:db8:00AC:F42C:00C4:F42C:09C0:876A:130B

Can be truncated and written as follows;

2001:db8:AC:F42C:C4:F42C:09C0:876A:130B

Here are some more examples:

Full address	Shortened address
2001:0db8:3c4d:0015:0:0:abcd:ef12	2001:0db8:3c4d:15::abcd:ef12
0000:0000:0000:0000:0000:0000:0000:0001	::1
0000:0000:0000:0000:0000:0000:0000:FFFF	::FFFF

There are no subnet masks in IPv6 so they use the same prefix (slash) notation as CIDR to identify which bits are used for the network portion, for instance;

2001:0db8:3c4d:15::abcd:ef12/64

That is the shortened version of the following IPv6 address:

2001:0db8:3c4d:0015:0:0:abcd:ef12/64

Chapter Summary

- An IP address is a logical address as opposed to a MAC address which is physical. This means that it is not uniquely assigned by the IEEE and can be changed.

- IP addresses are divided into several different classes. These classes specify what part of the IP address identifies the network and host portions. The most common classes are A, B and C.

- A broadcast address is an address that targets all systems on a specified subnet instead of just a single host.

- The loopback address or localhost address in IPv6 is ::1

Chapter Exercises

Below you will find various IP calculation exercises that will give you a greater understanding of calculating IP addresses.

Decimal and Binary Conversions

1. Complete the table below. It will provide you with practice in converting a binary number into a decimal format

Binary	128	64	32	16	8	4	2	1	Decimal
10110101	1	0	1	1	0	1	0	1	128+32+16+4+1 = 181
11001101	1	1	0	0	1	1	0	1	128+64+8+4+1 = 205
01001101	0	1	0	0	1	1	0	1	64+8+4+1 = 77
11101011	1	1	1	0	1	0	1	1	128+64+32+8+2+1 = 235
10100011	1	0	1	0	0	0	1	1	128+32+2+1 = 163

2. Complete the table below. It will provide you with practice in converting a binary number into a decimal format

Decimal	128	64	32	16	8	4	2	1	Binary
125	0	1	1	1	1	1	0	1	125-64-32-16-8-4-1 = 0 | 01111101
91	0	1	0	1	1	0	1	1	91-64=27-16=11-8=3 01011011
192	1	1	0	0	0	0	0	0	11000000
112	0	1	1	1	0	0	0	0	01110000
250	1	1	1	1	1	0	1	0	11111010

192 49
-128 -32 16
---- ---

3. Express the IP address 174.54.21.6 in binary format and identify which address class it belongs to. **Class B**

174(10101110) 54(00110110) 21(00010101) 6(00000110)

4. Express the IP address 212.126.47.98 in binary format and identify which address class it belongs to.

212(11010100) 126(01111110) 47(00101111) 98(01100010) = C

Subnetting

1. You have been assigned the network block 192.168.1.0/24. Now you want to split this network into several networks each containing at least 14 hosts. How many bits will you need to borrow from the host portion?

2. You have been assigned the network block 170.23.0.0/16 and you need to create eight subnets. Answer the following questions:

   a. How many bits do you need to borrow from the host portion to create 8 subnets?
   b. Specify the extended network prefix you need to use to create 8 subnets.
   c. Express the network addresses of the subnets you created.

Chapter Exercises – Answers

Below you will find the answers to the exercises.

Decimal and Binary Conversions

1. Complete the table below. It will provide you with practice in converting a binary number into a decimal format

Binary	128	64	32	16	8	4	2	1	Decimal
10110101	1	0	1	1	0	1	0	1	128+32+16+4+1 = 181
11001101	1	1	0	0	1	1	0	1	128+64+8+4+1 = 205
01001101	0	1	0	0	1	1	0	1	64+8+4+1= 77
11101011	1	1	1	0	1	0	1	1	128+64+32+8+2+1 = 235
10100011	1	0	1	0	0	0	1	1	128+32+2+1 = 163

2. Complete the table below. It will provide you with practice in converting a binary number into a decimal format

Decimal	128	64	32	16	8	4	2	1	Binary
125	0	1	1	1	1	1	0	1	125-64-32-16-8-4-1 = 0 | 01111101
91	0	1	0	1	1	0	1	1	91-64-16-8-2-1 = 0 | 01011011
192	1	1	0	0	0	0	0	0	192-128-64 = 0 | 1100000000
112	0	1	1	1	0	0	0	0	112-64-32-16 = 0 | 01110000
250	1	1	1	1	1	0	1	0	250-128-64-32-16-8-2 = 0 | 11111010

3. Express the IP address 174.54.21.6 in binary format and identify which address class it belongs to.

10101110.00110110.00010101.00000110 /16 or Class B

It belongs to the Class B address because the first octet starts with 10.

4. Express the IP address 212.126.47.98 in binary format and identify which address class it belongs to.

11010100.01111110.00101111.01100010 /24 or Class C

It belongs to the Class C address because the first octet starts with 110.

Subnetting

1. You have been assigned the network address 192.168.1.0/24. Now you want to split this network into several networks each containing at least 14 hosts. How many bits do you need to borrow from the host portion?

    Since you have been assigned a network with a 24 bit subnet mask this leaves only 8 bits left for the host portion. In order to obtain 14 hosts on each network you need to borrow 4 bits. This is because $2^4-2 = 14$. This will change the subnet mask from /24 to /28 instead and you will have 16 networks with each network containing 14 hosts.

2. You have been assigned the network block 170.23.0.0/16 and you need to create eight subnets. Answer the following questions:

    a. How many bits do you need to borrow from the host portion to create 8 subnets?

    We need to borrow three bits in order to create eight subnets because $2^3 = 8$.

    b. Specify the extended network prefix you need to use to create 8 subnets.

    We can express this using two methods and that is /19 or 255.255.224.0

    c. Express the network addresses of the subnets you created.

Subnet Number	Network Address	Binary value
Subnet #0	170.23.0.0/19	10000100.00101101.**000**00000.00000000
Subnet #1	170.23.32.0/19	10000100.00101101.**001**00000.00000000
Subnet #2	170.23.64.0/19	10000100.00101101.**010**00000.00000000
Subnet #3	170.23.96.0/19	10000100.00101101.**011**00000.00000000
Subnet #4	170.23.128.0/19	10000100.00101101.**100**00000.00000000
Subnet #5	170.23.160.0/19	10000100.00101101.**101**00000.00000000
Subnet #6	170.23.192.0/19	10000100.00101101.**110**00000.00000000
Subnet #7	170.23.224.0/19	10000100.00101101.**111**00000.00000000

Chapter Review

In order to test your knowledge and understanding of this chapter, please answer the following questions. You will find the answers and explanations of the questions at the end of this chapter.

1. How many hosts can a Class C network contain?
    a. 254 ←
    b. 16,384
    c. 65,534
    d. 255

2. How many bits does an IP address consist off?
    a. 24 bits
    b. 32 bits
    c. 48 bits
    d. 64 bits

3. What does MTU stand for?
    a. Maximum Transfer Unit
    b. Maximum Transmission Unit
    c. MAC Transmission Unit
    d. Minimum Transmission Unit

4. Which of the following subnet masks would you use when configuring a client with an IP address in the network address, 192.168.1.0/26?
    a. 255.255.255.0
    b. 255.255.255.128
    c. 255.255.255.192 ←
    d. 255.255.0.0

Chapter Review: Answers

You will find the answers to the chapter review questions below:

1. The correct answer is: A
   a. **254**
   b. 16,384
   c. 65,534
   d. 255

The correct answer is A because you use 8 bits for the host portion. When using the formula 2^X-2 (where X is the number of bits) you get the value of 254. $2^8-2 = 254$

2. The correct answer is: B
   a. 24 bits
   b. **32 bits**
   c. 48 bits
   d. 64 bits

The correct answer is B because the IP address is built up by 4 octets and each octet contains 8 bits. $8*4 = 32$. 48 bits are used in the MAC address.

3. The correct answer is: B
   a. Maximum Transfer Unit
   b. **Maximum Transmission Unit**
   c. MAC Transmission Unit
   d. Minimum Transmission Unit

4. The correct answer is: C
   a. 255.255.255.0
   b. 255.255.255.128
   c. **255.255.255.192**
   d. 255.255.0.0

We use 26 bits for the network portion of the address which means that we need to borrow two bits from the last octet. The first two bits of the last octet represent the values 128 and 64. Add these together and you get the value of 192.

6. The Transport Layer in Detail

When discussing computer networking, many people tend to associate it with the *TCP/IP protocol*. We have already talked about the IP part of the protocol suite (which operates at the lower network layer) and its importance; now it's time to talk about TCP and other protocols that are a part of the transport layer.

When one compares the network layer to the transport layer, you can say that the network layer provides the essential components to make it possible for two hosts on different networks to communicate. The transport layer on the other hand provides optional functions that help achieve a required quality of communication. Some of these functions are to make sure that the packet arrives at its destination, that the packet is not exceeding a suitable size and that the packets are exchanged at a speed that both hosts can handle. Every type of service has its specified requirements in order to perform at its best. This means that you will use different types of transport protocols depending on your needs (or the application's).

Transmission Control Protocol – TCP

TCP is a connection-oriented protocol that provides features like flow control and reliable data delivery, which overcomes issues such as packet loss and communication errors. TCP works very differently from the protocol UDP which is a connection-less protocol; we'll go into further detail on how UDP works shortly.

The application sends its data down the OSI model to the transport layer which encapsulates the data within a *TCP Header*. Very often the application layer will send data that is bigger than a single packet can carry; TCP will therefore split it up into smaller pieces called *segments*. A collection of segments that travel over the same connection is called a *sequence*.

TCP adds a separate TCP header to each segment, which it sends down to the appropriate network layer protocol (in this case IP). Each TCP header contains specific information like a source and destination port and a sequence number that specifies where the segment is within the sequence. That way the receiving host knows the correct order of the segments it receives and can reassemble the data within them successfully when the transfer is complete.

A diagram illustrating the TCP header and its fields follows:

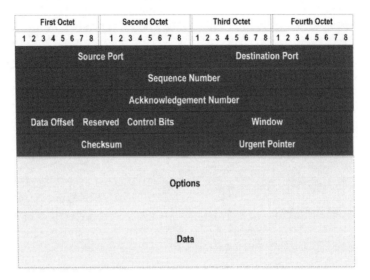

We'll explore the purpose of some of these headers over the course of this chapter.

TCP Options

In the previous diagram you can see that there is a header field which is called Options. This field provides extra, optional functionality to the TCP protocol and contains the following fields;

- Option Kind
- Option Length
- Option Data

Following you will find the most commonly used TCP Options:

Option Kind	Option Name	Description
0	End Of Options List	When using multiple TCP options, this Option Kind indicates the end of the options field.
2	Maximum Segment Size	Specifies the largest segment a host can receive
8	TSOPT – Timestamp	Adds time stamps to acknowledgment packets in order to measure the round trip time between two hosts

Exam Tip: You do not have to memorize all possible TCP Options but you need to understand what Options are used for.

The Three Way Handshake (3WHS)

As we mentioned before, TCP is a connection-oriented, reliable protocol which means that in order for it to send packets between hosts, they have to establish a connection with each other. This is called a *TCP Session*.

In a TCP session, every packet that is sent between each host is assigned a sequence number. An *Acknowledgement* or *ACK* has to be sent each time a system successfully receives a packet. If the sending system does not receive an ACK from the receiving one, the packet is resent.

Extensions exist to modify this ACK-per-packet behavior but right now we are only considering TCP's default, un-extended behavior.

In order to establish a TCP session, the hosts both have to participate in a process called *The Three-Way-Handshake*.

1. The initiating host sends a TCP packet called a *SYN packet*. With this packet the host is requesting a new session with the target host. This SYN packet contains an initial sequence number and other information such as the maximum segment size (MSS) which we'll explore shortly.
2. The target host sends back a SYN/ACK. The SYN/ACK packet contains the initiating host's sequence number plus 1. This has to be done in order to prove that it has received the initiating host's first packet.
3. The initiating host then responds to the SYN/ACK packet that the target host sent by sending a final ACK packet with the target host's sequence number plus 1. That way the target host can confirm the initiating host has successfully received the packet.

The packets in the Three Way Handshake are simply empty packets with the different TCP control bits activated. There are several different control bits other than SYN and ACK, as we'll see soon.

The whole process is shown in the following diagram:

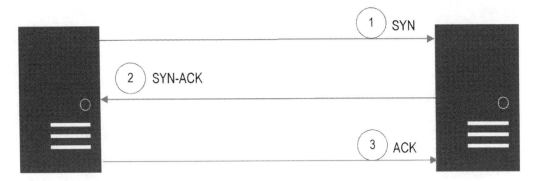

① SYN packet containing initial sequence number and other data

② SYN-ACK packet that contains target sequence number + ACK of initiating host's sequence number

③ ACK of target sequence number

When both hosts know which sequence numbers they will use, the session is established and they can start transferring data.

There is a similar process when TCP Sessions are terminated. Using this method ensures that both systems have completed their transactions. This process is shown in the following diagram.

1. The computer receives Close Signal from the application. Sends FIN

2. The recipient receives the FIN packet and replies back with an ACK. It also sends the Close Signal to its application

3. Computer sends back a FIN packet.

4. The sender replies back with an ACK packet.

User Datagram Protocol – UDP

Unlike TCP, the UDP is a connectionless protocol and provides no optional functions that will enhance the quality of the communication. The UDP packets can arrive out of order or not at all and UDP will not correct the order or request new packets. The reason we call this type of protocol connectionless is because the hosts do not established a connection with each other in advance of sending data and the state of the connection is not maintained.

There are no fields in the UDP header that contain information regarding which order the preceding or following packet will arrive in. It can be compared to sending a letter. You write the letter (the data you are sending) and you put it in an envelope (the UDP packet). Then you specify the recipient address (destination address and port) and the return address (the source address and port). You have no idea if the letter has been received and if you send another letter the day after, that letter may be received before the first one.

One question you might ask is *why would you use a protocol like this?* Even though UDP has no control over packet order or loss, there are scenarios where this is useful. UDP is simpler and thus can be processed by hosts at higher performance rates than TCP. This simplicity can also provide speed benefits as there is no initial delay experienced as there is with TCP, where a connection must be established before data is sent. For this reason, frequent used, relatively simple application layer protocols such as DNS use UDP as a transport.

DNS can also be used over TCP; however, it is not as prevalent.

Another situation could be if you send information that would be considered old if it arrived after a newer packet arrived. Examples of this are voice, video streaming, gaming and weather data – in other words, time sensitive traffic.

Following you will find a diagram of the UDP header:

First Octet	Second Octet	Third Octet	Fourth Octet
1 2 3 4 5 6 7 8	1 2 3 4 5 6 7 8	1 2 3 4 5 6 7 8	1 2 3 4 5 6 7 8
Source Port		Destination Port	
Length		Checksum	
Data			

Exam Tip — Just like the TCP header, you do not have to remember what fields comprise the UDP header.

TCP Device Communications

When the TCP three-way-handshake is complete and the hosts have established a connection, the following information is known by both systems:

- **Port number** – which port each host will use. We'll cover this in this chapter.
- **Sequence number** – each host uses the other's sequence number when acknowledging; confirming that the packet has been received.
- **MSS** – the maximum segment size of the packets sent between hosts.

The sequence and acknowledgment number fields form the core of reliable delivery in TCP. Since the hosts know the sequence number they last sent they also know the acknowledgment number they should receive next.

For example, if the sending host sends a packet with the sequence number 99, it knows that it needs to receive an acknowledgment number 100. If the sending host does not receive an acknowledgement of 100 it will retransmit the packet with the sequence number of 99. This is known as Retransmission, discussed next.

Retransmission

TCP is responsible for providing reliable data transfers between hosts. There are two common problems that can occur during a TCP connection; packets may arrive but in a corrupted state or fail to arrive at all.

To ensure packets are not corrupted in transit, before a host sends a packet, it performs a Cyclic Redundancy Check or CRC calculation on it and saves the resulting value in the packet's footer. When a host receives the packet, it compares the results of its own CRC calculation on each packet with the value in the footer. If the two values do not match the host discards the packet and withholds its ACK. This will trigger the sender to send the packet again.

When a host sends a packet it will wait for the retransmission timeout (RTO) to expire. This is the interval during which TCP expects to receive an ACK packet. The current default RTO is 3 seconds. If the host has not received an ACK, it will trigger a retransmission and no further data is sent.

Please note that during the Retransmission timeout the host will still send data. It is not until the RTO expires that the host stops sending any new data. It will instead retransmit the packets that it has already sent.

If an ACK still isn't received, further retransmissions occur; how many and the interval between them depends on the host's configuration. If this occurs over an extended period of time, the TCP connection will eventually time out and has to be re-established (if possible). This process ensures the sending host can be certain of what data the receiving end has received and what it has not, regardless of network conditions and reliability.

So what happens if the client does not receive a packet?

As an example, a client has established a TCP-3-Way handshake with a server and has requested some data. The server has created a response that contains 4 packets and all of these are sent to the client. However packet #2 does not reach the client.

In order to fully explain this scenario we have created a diagram and broken down each step in this process.

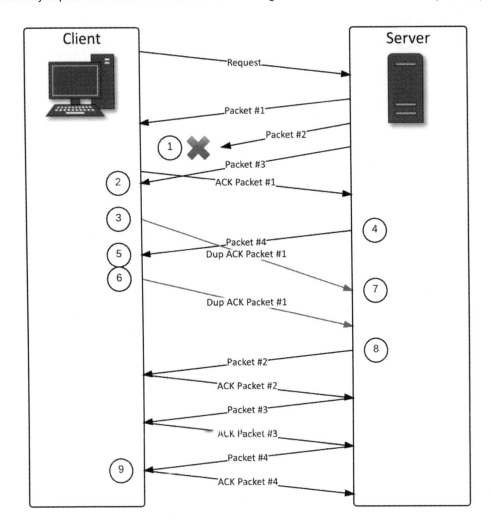

1. The server sends packet #2 to the client but the packet is lost in transit and never reaches the client.

2. The client receives packet #3 but when it examines the packet it realizes that the packet is out of order and that packet #2 is missing.

3. Even though the client successfully received packet #3 it has no way of telling the server. Therefore the client sends out a Duplicate ACK message to the server notifying it that has not received any good data beyond packet #1.

4. The server has not yet received the client's Duplicate ACK and therefore we see that packet #4 is sent from the server.

5. The client receives packet #4 but the client has no way of specifically telling the server that it has received both packet #3 and #4.

6. Therefore the client will again send out Duplicate ACKs stating that it still has not received any good data beyond packet #1. It will do this until the server retransmits all of the packets beyond packet #1 because the client has only sent back an ACK message for packet #1 and this means that once the server has received the Duplicate ACKs it will have to retransmit all of the packets again beyond packet #1 and this is very inefficient as packet #3 and #4 was received successfully.

7. The server receives the first Duplicate ACK message. The server will now retransmit packets #2 to #4 because the client has only confirmed the delivery of packet #1. The second Duplicate ACK message that the client has sent will be ignored.

8. The server retransmits all of the packets beyond packet #1 including packet #3 and #4.

9. The client successfully receives all of the packets that are being sent from the server and sends back an ACK to confirm the delivery for packet #4.

We have simplified the process in order to help you easily understand the concept.

Selective ACK – SACK

As mentioned in the previous section the original way of handling retransmissions is very inefficient. Although only one packet was lost on the way, all of the remaining packets of that window had to be retransmitted and this was because the client had no way of confirming the successful delivery of packet #3 and packet #4.

This problem was first highlighted in RFC1072 (published October in 1988) but only resolved with RFC2018 (published in October 1996) which introduced the TCP Option *Selective Acknowledgement* (SACK). Instead of just sending a Duplicate ACK of the previous ACK message, the client will now send a Duplicate ACK that has the SACK TCP option that tells which packets it has successfully received *after the one that is missing*.

The TCP SACK option is negotiated during the TCP 3-way handshake. Using a packet capture we can see that the TCP SACK option is enabled:

```
Transmission Control Protocol, Src Port: 58816 (58816), Dst P
    Source Port: 58816 (58816)
    Destination Port: 80 (80)
    [Stream index: 0]
    [TCP Segment Len: 0]
    Sequence number: 0    (relative sequence number)
    Acknowledgment number: 0
    Header Length: 40 bytes
    .... 0000 0000 0010 = Flags: 0x002 (SYN)
    Window size value: 5840
    [Calculated window size: 5840]
    Checksum: 0x9de2 [validation disabled]
    Urgent pointer: 0
    Options: (20 bytes), Maximum segment size, SACK permitted,
        Maximum segment size: 1460 bytes
        TCP SACK Permitted Option: True
```

Using our scenario from the earlier section, this means that the client can tell the server that it has received packet #1 but it has also received packets #3 and #4. In order to fully explain this process, let us use the diagram and scenario we used in the earlier section:

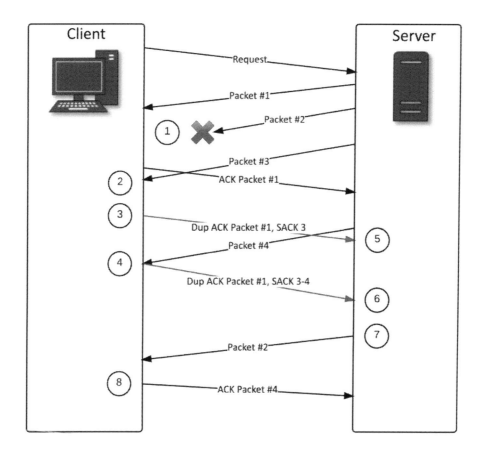

1. The server sends packet #2 to the client but the packet is lost in transit and never reaches the client.

2. The client receives packet #3 but when it examines the packet it realizes that the packet is out of order and that packet #2 is missing.

3. Therefore the client sends back a Duplicate ACK for packet #1 but this time it contains the TCP SACK option that contains the range of data that is has received successfully *after the packet that's missing*.

4. The client receives packet #4 successfully and sends another Duplicate ACK back to server but it will expand the range of data that it has successfully received.

5. The server receives the Duplicate ACK from the client. Since the Duplicate ACK contains the SACK for packet #3 it calculates that the client is missing packet #2 and it needs to be retransmitted.

6. The other Duplicate ACK that the client sent includes the SACK for packet #4 which indicates that the client has successfully received packet #4 and therefore there is no need to retransmit any more packets other than packet #2.

7. The server retransmits packet #2.

8. The client receives packet #2 and sends back an ACK packet for #4 to inform the server that is has successfully received all the packets up to packet #4.

 We have simplified the process in order to help you easily understand the concept.

As mentioned previously, SACK only defines the range of data that it has received successfully *after the packet that it's missing*. It will not print out the exact packets that it has received. In the following packet capture you can see SACK in action:

```
Transmission Control Protocol, Src Port: 58816 (58816), D
    Source Port: 58816 (58816)
    Destination Port: 80 (80)
    [Stream index: 0]
    [TCP Segment Len: 0]
    Sequence number: 461        (relative sequence number)
    Acknowledgment number: 17377      (relative ack number)
    Header Length: 44 bytes
    .... 0000 0001 0000 = Flags: 0x010 (ACK)
    Window size value: 318
    [Calculated window size: 40704]
    [Window size scaling factor: 128]
    Checksum: 0x34b6 [validation disabled]
    Urgent pointer: 0
    Options: (24 bytes), No-Operation (NOP), No-Operation (
        No-Operation (NOP)
        No-Operation (NOP)
        Timestamps: TSval 1545583, TSecr 2375917095
        No-Operation (NOP)
        No-Operation (NOP)
        SACK: 18825-20273
            Kind: SACK (5)
            Length: 10
            left edge = 18825 (relative)
            right edge = 20273 (relative)
        [TCP SACK Count: 1]
    [SEQ/ACK analysis]
```

In the packet capture we can see that the acknowledgment number is 17377. The left and right edges are the data range of the SACK so this means that the client has successfully received the packets containing the data bytes 18825 – 20273. So the SACK option is telling the server that it needs to retransmit the packets between 17377 and 18825.

In our scenario we have a Maximum Segment Size of 1448. In order to determine how many packets that needs to be retransmitted we can simply use the following equation:

(Left Edge Data - Acknowledgement Number) / Maximum Segment Size = Amount of missing packets.

If we use the data we have in our packet capture we get the following result:

(18825 - 17377) / 1448 = 1

This means that there is only one missing packet between 17377 and 18825 so therefore the server will have to resend that packet.

Exam Tip — It is important to remember Selective ACK for the exam. Make sure you understand its purpose and how it works.

MTU & MSS

This isn't an easy subject, it crosses the boundaries between three layers of the OSI model; data link, network and transport, which can be confusing. Whilst the TCP MSS is a transport layer setting, it can't be discussed alone as its value is dependent upon the network layer IP MTU. This, in turn, is dependent upon the data link layer MTU.

MTU

Before you can understand the transport layer MSS you need to understand MTU first. The MTU is the maximum size of a frame or packet that can be sent on the network at both the data link and network layers respectively. The network layer MTU cannot be larger than the data link layer MTU.

- The data link layer MTU is the maximum size of a **frame** including the data payload and all higher layer protocol headers (layer three and above) but *not* the layer two headers or trailer. The data link MTU is most often 1500 Bytes. In reality the MTU is actually higher; it must be to accommodate the Ethernet headers and trailer; an extra 18 to 22 Bytes depending on whether VLAN tagging is used. However, its value is typically expressed (and configured) as I've just described, hence the data link MTU value is the same as the network layer MTU. Non-Ethernet data link layers may of course have a different MTU.

- Where the network layer is concerned this is the maximum size of a **packet** including the data payload and all protocol headers (layer three and above). The IP MTU is most often 1500Bytes. In most cases the IP MTU is not specifically configured on a host or network device, it is automatically derived from the data link layer MTU. Clearly, the network layer MTU cannot be larger than the data link layer MTU.

MSS

Now both MTUs are clear we can finally discuss the transport layer MSS which is the maximum amount of data that can be carried within a TCP packet. To put it another way, it's the maximum value of the payload to be carried within a TCP/IP packet; it doesn't include the TCP and IP headers that the payload will be encapsulated with.

Thus, the MSS is typically 40Bytes smaller than the network layer MTU in order to accommodate the 20 Byte TCP headers as well as the 20Byte IP headers that the payload will be encapsulated with, giving us a typical value of

1460Bytes (1500-40). However, be very clear that this doesn't have to be the case; a host with an MTU of 1500 may have a MSS of 500Bytes for a potentially good reason.

It's worth noting that IP fragmentation (discussed in the previous chapter) has no influence on the MSS; fragmentation may allow a packet that exceeds the MTU to be broken into multiple parts but the MSS cannot be exceeded whether packets are fragmented or not. In other words, a 3000Byte packet can be fragmented by IP to overcome a 1500Byte MTU but if the receiving host has an MSS of 1460, the data will not be accepted. Despite the apparent direct relationship between MTU and MSS as most will match one closely to the other for maximum throughput, this is not always the case.

A host's TCP MSS is 'presented' to the other host during the TCP-Three-Way handshake using a TCP Option (discussed in an earlier section). If the MSS is not specified, a default value of 536Bytes is assumed.

Now we've covered both the MTU and MSS, let's use a useful analogy to describe and remember them. Picture a car, the passengers are the data payload (the MSS) and the baggage is the TCP and IP headers. The car itself is the MTU. Each road has a default value of cars it can contain simultaneously and therefore each car has to be a certain size. In networking terms that is 1500 bytes. Each car that drives onto the road has to match this value or be less or it will not work. We could also change the default value of every single road it drives on but this would be very hard to do. If we exceed the MTU we need to chop the car into smaller pieces. In order words, fragment the car.

Exceeding the MTU

There are scenarios where you have to add additional headers to a packet (encapsulate them further), for instance when using a VPN tunnel (we'll discuss this more in Chapter 11, Security). This results in IP fragmentation which generally causes poor performance and throughput due to the additional memory and CPU resources required of the fragmenting and receiving hosts or devices. This is ideally avoided by reducing the MSS as necessary, but often less appropriate MTU related methods are used.

Continuing with our earlier analogy, this means that if your car by default can hold 5 passengers, you will have to remove some passengers if you add more baggage (more headers). The removed passengers then need to be put in another car.

One common problem with VPN tunnels is fragmentation. If you use the MTU of 1500 bytes and have an MSS of 1460 bytes, if you add an additional VPN header you will exceed the MTU which will cause the packets to get fragmented. This may cause the VPN tunnel to perform poorly.

In order to solve this we decrease the MSS (the amount of passengers) to be able to fit the VPN header (the baggage) without exceeding the MTU (the car).

Flow Control & Window Size

The big difference between TCP and UDP is that TCP carefully keeps track of data that is being sent and makes sure that you get every single packet (and the data within). Flow control is one of the key technologies that assist with this. Flow control manages the rate data is sent so that the receiving host does not get overwhelmed with more data than it can handle.

In order to achieve this, TCP uses a *sliding window acknowledgment system*. As we know, TCP uses acknowledgments to signal to the sending host that is has received a packet successfully. Flow control and acknowledgements work together in order to avoid unnecessary packet loss where one host can transmit faster than the other can process the received packets. Acknowledgements are demonstrated in the following diagram;

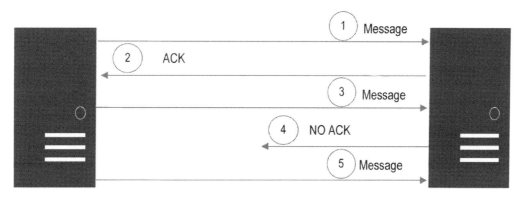

1. The computer sends the data to the recipient.

2. The recipient receives the message and replies back with an ACK.

3. Computer sends a new message.

4. The sender does not get an ACK back.

5. The sender do not receive the ACK and therefore re-sends the packet again.

Window Size in a very basic sense is the amount of data that a TCP host declares it can store in its memory buffer. On each side of a TCP connection there are buffers that store a certain amount of data that is either sent or received. This helps the network to work more efficiently. The window size is first negotiated during the TCP Three-Way-Handshake using the Window parameter in the TCP header, however this can be modified dynamically during the transmission. The window parameter defines the amount of data the host can receive before passing it on to the relevant application(s). This also applies when sending data from a host. When sending data it is called the *send window* and when receiving data it is called the *receive window*.

When a host receives data it needs to perform two tasks, *send back an acknowledgement to the sender* and *transfer the data to the application*.

The basic concept with sliding windows is that data is acknowledged when it is received but it is not necessarily transferred out of the buffer and passed on to the application immediately. This means that if the send window is greater than the receive window it will fill up the host's buffer faster than it can empty it. If this continues for too long it may lead to buffer overflow and the host may crash.

In order to prevent this we need to adjust the window size so that both hosts work at the same transfer rate.

In the following example, the server advertises that its window size is 2000 Bytes using the window parameter in the TCP header.

1. The client requests a file on the server and also specifies its current windows size (2000) using the window parameter in the TCP header.
2. The server receives the request and replies back with ACK packet.
3. The client replies back with ACK packet.
4. The server sends part 1/3 of the file which has the size of 1000 bytes.
5. The client replies with ACK packet and a new window size of 1000 bytes. The new window size is specified in the window parameter of the TCP header.
6. The server sends part 2/3 of the file which has the size of 1000 bytes.
7. The client receives part 2/3 and puts it in its buffer. Now the client has reached its limit and filled up the entire buffer. The client sends a reply back to the server stating that its window is currently 0 (known as a zero window) and acknowledges the data it has received.
8. Since the window is currently 0 the server will not send any more data.
9. When the client is finished processing the first 2000 Bytes of data, it requests the remaining part 3/3 from the server and specifies a new window of 2000 bytes. Since the receiver has processed all of its traffic in its buffer, the client can specify its window size as 2000 bytes again.
10. The server sends part 3/3 of the file which has the size of 1000 bytes.
11. Client receives part 3 of the file and replies back with ACK, and then terminates the connection.

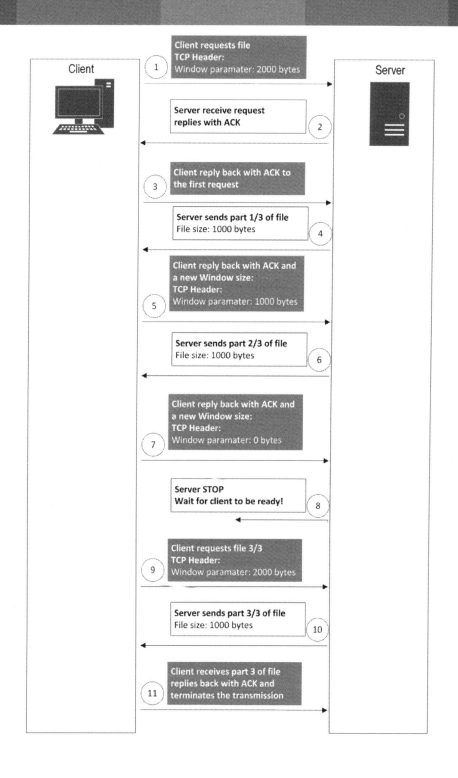

Silly Window

Even though flow control is a great way to manage traffic rates, it can cause some issues. When a server is not able to process data fast enough because the application is performing slowly, it is forced to decrease the window size accordingly. If the server is still suffering problems with data processing, the window size will decrease even further, to the point where the TCP and IP headers are bigger than the data. The TCP and IP header are 40 bytes so if the window size were to decrease below 40 bytes the communication becomes very inefficient, hence the name "silly window". This is like sending a package where the box itself weighs more than the contents inside.

Ports & Services

When a host is trying to access a server, you need a way to identify the services you are trying to access. Since most servers can run several different services, a method was required to identify both common and uncommon services and distinguish one service from another.

The solution was to assign each service a specific port number and use a specific range for common, well-known services and their related ports. These port numbers range from 0-1023, some familiar ones are:

- 80 - Web Server or HTTP (*Hyper Text Transfer Protocol*)
- 20 and 21 – FTP (*File Transfer Protocol*)
- 53 – DNS (*Domain Name System*)
- 22 – SSH (*Secure Shell*)
- 443 – HTTPS (*Hyper Text Transfer Protocol Secure*)

We will talk more about these applications and services later on in the book.

If we did not assign port numbers to services, it would mean that HTTP would be the only service a web server could provide and the client would have to know this somehow. Port numbers allow us to differentiate between the different services a server provides.

When accessing the server, the TCP header contains both the source and the destination port. The source port are used by the sending host to help keep track of existing connections but also make it possible to have multiple connections from a host. If we use HTTP as an example again, if you were to visit multiple HTTP sites, you would most likely always use port 80 as the destination port. But in order to visit multiple sites, you need to establish several connections, each with a unique source port that allows the HTTP servers to know which port to respond back to (and the client know which connection the data relates to).

When a host is communicating with a server it specifies a source and destination port, when the server replies back to the host the source and destination port will be reversed. Please see the following diagram for a more detailed description.

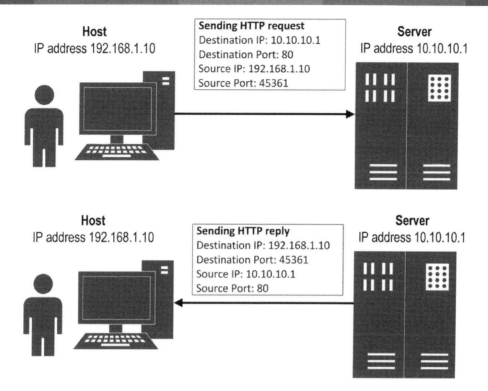

In the diagram we can see that the host with IP address 192.168.1.10 sends a HTTP request to the server with IP address 10.10.10.1 using destination port 80 and source port 45361. When the server responds to the host, the source and destination port are reversed.

The client host source port number is usually a random number between 1024 and the highest possible port number: 65535 (the highest possible number (in decimal) that can be achieved with 16bits). In order to specify which server and the service you are trying to access we use the destination IP address and port number. For example, *192.168.1.200:80 or 192.168.1.200:21*. In most cases, the service port is hidden from a user by the application and you only need to specify it when the default, standard port is not used. For instance, http://www.example.com will use well-known port 80, http://www.example.com:8080/ forces use of non-standard port 8080.

The combination of both an IP address and a port is often called a *socket*. In order to verify that a TCP service is up and running you can use telnet and specify the relevant port to see if the application is responding on that port. Please note that this is only possible when using the TCP protocol. The screen will normally be blank and you cannot input any commands but if the screen is up and running you know if the application is running on the specified port.

Port numbers are divided into three different ranges, as follows;

- Well-known: 0-1023
- Registered: 1024-49151
- Dynamic: 49152-65535

The well-known ports have been reserved for assignment by the Internet Corporation for Assigned Names and Numbers (ICANN). They are called well-known because they are mostly only assigned to standards-based open protocols that are likely to be in common use within the Internet community. For instance, HTTP uses well-known port 80 and SMTP port 25.

Registered ports on the other hand are ports that companies or organizations register with the ICANN in order to use them with their own proprietary application(s).

Dynamic ports are also known as private port numbers and can be used by any application, not just designated ones. Dynamic ports are used to avoid conflicts with applications that use well-known and registered ports; hence they are typically used as the source port by TCP clients.

TCP Reset Packets

TCP Reset packets are used when two hosts are communicating and one of the hosts wants to terminate the transmission quickly without expecting further communication from the other host. This can occur for several reasons, one of which is a TCP Half-Open connection (we'll explain these in the next section, *delayed binding*).

In a TCP session, each host in the transmission needs to both send and receive acknowledgements. The TCP protocol cannot work without this so when two hosts are communicating and one of them suddenly stops receiving acknowledgements it will cause problems. In order to solve this, the host that discovers the issue can send reset packet (RST Packets) to the non-responsive host in order to reset the transmission.

This is explained in the diagram.

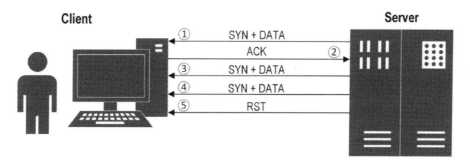

1. The server and client are communicating with each other successfully. The server sends some data to the client.
2. The client replies back with an ACK message stating that it has received the packet successfully.
3. The server sends another packet with some more data. But this time the client crashes and fails to respond with an ACK message.
4. The server expects to receive an ACK message but since the client did not respond, the server resends the packet.
5. The client is not responding to the packets so the server concludes that communication is no longer possible and therefore sends an RST packet to the client that will reset the transmission.

 There is a known exploit that hackers use regarding ACK messages. This attack is known as a TCP Half Open or SYN-Flood attack. An attacker will send multiple SYN packets to the server and when the server replies the client doesn't respond. If multiple clients do this it will eventually exhaust the server's memory resources and cause it to fail. We discuss this in detail in the next section.

Delayed Binding

There are some scenarios where the initial TCP request from a client to a server is not handled directly by the server. For instance when using a proxy, the initial request is terminated by the proxy and it then opens a new one to the server, on behalf of the client. This is used for several reasons including security. You'll find more details on proxy operation in the later F5 Solutions & Technology chapter.

A known DDoS (Distributed Denial of Service) form of attack is called a TCP-Half open or SYN flooding attack. The goal with this attack is to send so many SYN packets to the server that it will fill up the server's connection table. Each connection in the table consumes a small amount of memory and when the server's memory is exhausted it may cause the server to crash or will prevent it from responding to legitimate requests. Sending a SYN to the server is quite normal (it would be very difficult to communicate with it otherwise) so it isn't possible to deny these packets.

The server accepts the SYN, adds an entry to its connection table and sends back a SYN-ACK. However, the sending client(s) will not respond to the SYN-ACK which leaves the connection half-open. The entry in the server's connection table remains until it times out (normally taking up to a minute) and thus sending a large number of SYNs in a short time period can exhaust a server's memory.

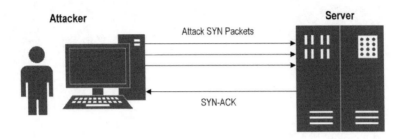

1. An attacker will initiate several SYN packets and send to the server. The server will see this as legitimate traffic and try to answer it by sending a SYN-ACK back. But the malicious user will not respond.

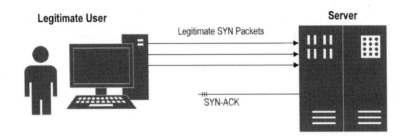

2. Then when a legitimate user tries to connect to the server, the server's connection table is full of illegal requests so that it can't answer the legitimate user. This is known as a SYN-Flood attack or TCP-Half Open.

Delayed binding can help protect real servers from this issue, where proxies are concerned, by ensuring a client-side connection is correctly established before establishing one server-side.

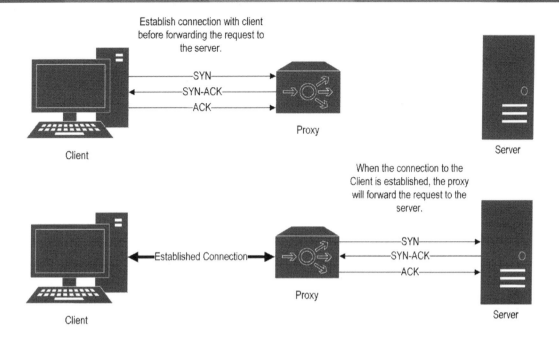

As you can see in the illustration, the proxy will establish a connection with the client. When the client and the proxy have a successful (fully open) connection, the proxy will open up the required connections towards the servers. This is called, *delayed binding*.

Exam Tip Knowing what delayed binding is and what it is used for is very important when taking the exam. Make sure you fully understand what it is and what it is used for.

Chapter Summary

- TCP is a connection-oriented protocol that provides features like flow control and reliable data delivery services that ensures that the packet arrive at the destination without any errors or packet loss.

- In a TCP session, every packet that is sent between each system receives a sequence number. An Acknowledgement or ACK has to be sent each time a system successfully receives a packet. If the sending system did not receive an ACK, the packet is resent.

- MSS is short for *Maximum Segment Size* and it is the maximum data each segment can contain. Segment size is the size of a packet if you remove the IP and TCP header.

- MTU is short for *Maximum Transmission Unit* and it is the default size of a packet that gets sent out on the network. In other words, how much total data a packet can contain.

- Delayed binding is used to prevent network attacks by having a proxy that handles the originating request and establishes a connection before the request is passed on to the server.

- Unlike TCP, the User Datagram Protocol or UDP is a connectionless protocol and provides no assurance that the packet arrives at the destination or that that it arrives without any errors.

Chapter Review

In order to test your knowledge and understanding of this chapter, please answer the following questions. You will find the answers and explanations of the questions at the end of this chapter.

1. True or false: TCP is a connection-oriented protocol?
    a. True
    b. False

2. Can you be certain that the packet arrives at the destination when sending a packet using the UDP protocol?
    a. Yes
    b. No

3. During the TCP Three-Way-Handshake, which packets are exchanged? Answer with the correct order.
    a. SYN, SYN, ACK
    b. SYN, ACK, SYN-ACK
    c. SYN-ACK, SYN, ACK
    d. SYN, SYN-ACK, ACK

4. What is the difference between MTU and MSS?
    a. MTU controls the size of the packets and MSS controls the speed of the transmission.
    b. MTU checks errors and MSS fixes those errors.
    c. MTU controls the speed of the transmission and MSS controls the size of the packets.
    d. MTU is the total size of a packet that gets sent out on the network and the MSS is the maximum size of a packet excluding the TCP and IP header.

5. Delayed binding: which statement is true?
    a. When using delayed binding, the initial request will not be handled directly by the server. A proxy or other device will first establish a connection and forward this to the server.
    b. Delayed binding is a great way to save bandwidth.
    c. Delayed binding cannot be used to increase security.
    d. When using delayed binding, a proxy will always forward the connection to the server.

Chapter Review: Answers

You will find the answers to the chapter review questions below:

1. The correct answer is: A
   a. True
   b. False

TCP is a connection-oriented protocol and it will make sure that the packet arrives at the destination uncorrupted. If a packet is dropped or lost, it will be resent until it has reached its timeout period.

2. The correct answer is: B
   a. Yes
   b. No

UDP is a connectionless protocol which means that it does not care if the packets arrive at their destination or if the packets get corrupted during transit. If a packet is lost UDP will not resend any packets.

3. The correct answer is: D
   a. SYN, SYN, ACK
   b. SYN, ACK, SYN-ACK
   c. SYN-ACK, SYN, ACK
   d. **SYN, SYN-ACK, ACK**

4. The correct answer is: D
   a. MTU controls the size of the packets and MSS controls the speed of the transmission
   b. MTU checks errors and MSS fixes those errors.
   c. MTU controls the speed of the transmission and MSS controls the size of the packets.
   d. **MTU is the total size of a packet that gets sent out on the network and the MSS is the maximum size of a packet excluding the TCP and IP header.**

5. The correct answer is: A
   a. **When using delayed binding, the initial request will not be handled directly by the server. A proxy or other device will first establish a connection and forward this to the server.**
   b. Delayed binding is a great way to save bandwidth.
   c. Delayed binding cannot be used to increase security.
   d. When using delayed binding, a proxy will always forward the connection to the server.

7. Switching & Routing

Switching

Early networks used multiple LANs that were connected to each other using a router. This formed a network that was larger than was possible with a single LAN. With a single LAN there was a limit to how many hosts could be connected and therefore you had to divide your network into multiple smaller LANs. When a single LAN got too big it caused the network to perform poorly and caused interruptions to traffic flow. Routers have been around for a much longer time than switches, but switches revolutionized network design.

As previously mentioned switches divide every port on the switch into a separate collision domain and decrease collisions drastically. They also forward the traffic out to the single port needed to reach the destination host instead of flooding the network (in most cases). This makes it possible to build very large LANs.

Routing

In previous chapters we have discussed layer three addressing, what a packet consists of and how communications between two hosts work. But we have not really explained how a packet gets from one host to another, step by step. Routing is not the only component that is responsible for making sure a packet arrives at the correct destination, but it is a fundamental technology.

In smaller environments, the router's job can be considered quite simple. It simply makes sure that traffic from one (layer three) network is transferred (routed) to another. When there are only two networks the only job the router has is to forward packets from one network to the other.

When the number of networks grows larger and more routers are added, things can get complicated quickly. When adding more routers, you may also add multiple paths between destinations and each router has to evaluate the available paths and choose the most effective one.

 A router does not have to forward every packet it receives. As we detailed previously, routers do not forward layer two or three broadcasts and other types of traffic.

In the following diagram you can see how complicated a network can be when using multiple routers (note each router has multiple paths to the others);

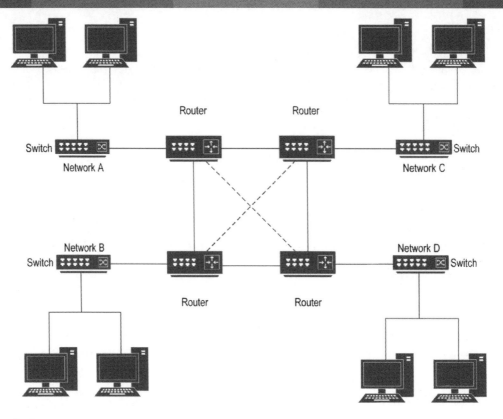

A Router's Role

The primary role of a router is to connect two or more networks together at layer three. There are many ways this functionality can be deployed, some examples are,

- Connecting several branch offices with each other over WAN links
- Minimizing network traffic by creating multiple broadcast and/or collision domains
- Connecting networks that are in different buildings or floors of a building
- Connecting networks that use different network technologies like FDDI

Different Types of Routers

A router can either be a stand-alone hardware device which is called an appliance or it can be software running on a server that has multiple network cards.

There are several UNIX/Linux distributions and Windows Operating systems that can function as a router. All you need to do is install at least two network cards that will connect to the different networks and configure the operating system to route traffic between the two.

Most companies (at present at least) choose an appliance solution because these offer vendor support and better functionality, which most software based routers do not. An appliance is a special-purpose computer which has several network interfaces, dedicated high-performance memory where it can store the routing table and an operating system that is custom built for the purpose. All routers must have at least two interfaces to be able to route traffic between networks. They also need to have an IP address assigned to each interface that participates in routing.

There are other router devices which allow you to share your Internet connection with other devices but this function is mostly deployed on consumer grade devices. These routers come with additional functions like firewalling, a DHCP server and switching functionality but generally much lower performance, security and reliability than enterprise grade routers.

The Routing Table

One of the core functions of an IP router is building a *routing table*. Without it, the router can only function as a packet forwarder. The routing table contains all of the information the router needs to make decisions about where to send the packets it has received. You can manually configure the routing table and this is known as *static routing* or you can automate the process using what is known as *dynamic routing*, using a Routing Protocol.

There are several different types of routes a router installs in its routing table, here are some examples:

- **Direct route** – The destination can be reached directly and is attached to a network one of the router's interfaces resides on
- **Default route** – When a router does not find a specific route in its routing table, it will send packets to the default route destination (if one is configured)
- **Static route** – A route that has been manually added to the routing table by an administrator
- **Dynamic route** – This route has been automatically added by a dynamic routing protocol such as OSPF or BGP

 We cover dynamic routing protocols in greater detail later in this chapter.

To be able to know where to send each packet, a router searches its routing table for the network containing the destination IP address and locates the longest (most specific) match. For instance, if the router has a whole network in the routing table and a single host address is being looked up, you may receive multiple matches. If we have the network addresses 192.168.0.0/16 and 192.16.10.0/28 in our routing table we will receive multiple matches when looking up the host 192.168.10.12.

The longest match is the most accurate match of the destination IP address. But the router does not look at the IP address in decimal format. It works like any other computer, with binary values. This means that the longest match refers to the binary value and not the decimal value. You will find an example of this below:

Route lookup

	Decimal	Binary
IP Address	192.168.10.12	11000000.10101000.00001010.00001100
Route #1	192.168.0.0/16	**11000000.10101000.**00000000.00000000
Route #2	192.168.10.0/28	**11000000.10101000.00001010.0000**0000

The router will use route #2 since it has the longest-match.

When it finds the longest match, the routing table data will indicate which interface the router should send the packet out on.

When a host sends packets to a destination outside the local network, it sends the packets to its *default gateway* (the default gateway is a router). It is as though the host is saying, "The destination host is not on the same network as I am" and asks the router to handle it. You could say that the default gateway is the host's door out of the network.

If the router finds the network in its routing table it can forward it to the next hop destination which forwards it to the next destination (if necessary) and this continues to occur until it reaches the final destination network and host.

When a packet travels through each network on the path to its ultimate destination, every layer three device it passes through is considered a hop. The next-hop address is simply the address to the next destination. In the routing table you will find the network or host address and the corresponding next-hop address which is the next destination.

If the router cannot locate the network an IP address resides on by looking into its routing table, it sends it to its *default route* (if one is configured). The default route is configured with the following IP address: 0.0.0.0/0

 If the router does not have a default route, the packet(s) will be dropped.

 The default gateway is typically a router which connects two or more networks together. A host will send packets to its default gateway when the network address is different from its own. A router does not have a default gateway since it is the door to other networks. Instead the router uses a default route (if configured) when it cannot locate a network in its routing table.

To summarize, a router uses its routing table to determine where to send packets and then forwards the packets to that destination (if it can) using the relevant interface.

In the table below you can see the output of a routing table from a router:

```
root> show route

inet.0: 5 destinations, 5 routes (5 active, 0 holddown, 0 hidden)
+ = Active Route, - = Last Active, * = Both

0.0.0.0/0           *[Access-internal/12] 00:00:45
                     > to 2.248.168.1 via fe-0/0/0.0
2.248.168.0/25      *[Direct/0] 12w0d 16:40:23
                     > via fe-0/0/0.0
2.248.168.108/32    *[Local/0] 12w0d 16:40:23
                      Local via fe-0/0/0.0
192.168.1.0/24      *[Direct/0] 12w0d 16:52:11
                     > via vlan.0
192.168.1.1/32      *[Local/0] 12w0d 16:52:22
                      Local via vlan.0
```

1. In this column there are multiple entries, these are the different routes that are installed in the routing table.
2. This column contains the type of route, and *sometimes* the address to which the traffic gets sent to if it matches one of these entries.
3. The third entry in the routing table contains the different interfaces (ports) that the traffic gets sent out on if it matches the route.

Note, in this example, traffic that is not destined to a specific network in the routing table is routed via the default route (0.0.0.0/0) and will get sent to next hop IP address 2.248.168.1 using interface fe-0/0/0.0.

Dynamic Routing Protocols

You can configure the routing table in two ways, either by manually entering the routes yourself, which is called *static routing* or automating the process using a *dynamic routing* protocol. If you have a small network, managing routing tables manually using static routes is easy but if you have a large network it is preferable to use dynamic routing protocols that will automatically build the routing table on every router.

A routing protocol operates through the exchange of network information between routers; each router then calculates the best path to each available destination network and dynamically 'builds' a suitable routing table. When there is a disruption or failure in the network environment, routers can advertise or detect this and recalculate the best path and related next hop address or interface.

Every routing protocol has its own unique method for exchanging network information between routers and determining the best path and related next hop address. There are three types of routing protocols:

- Distance-vector
- Link-state
- Path-vector

Distance vector protocols will only send full routing tables between neighboring routers and use simple metrics like hop count to determine the best routes.

Link state protocols on the other hand, build up a map of the entire network on each router by obtaining information from every other router on the network. Whenever there is a change or disruption in the network, relevant updates are flooded so that a recalculation of each route is made by each router. To speed up (and limit flooding by) this process, *hierarchical routing* is typically used. The network is divided into smaller regions and each router only needs to know how to get to the other networks within that region.

Path-vector protocols use path information instead and this gets updated dynamically, as with other protocols. Each entry in the path vector protocol contains the destination network, the next router and the path to it. Border Gateway Protocol is an example of a path-vector protocol and is used to route traffic across the Internet. Unlike link state protocols that build up a map of the entire network based on the information it has received, BGP receives a routing table from its neighboring peer at start up and then relies on updates that it receives. These route updates are stored in what is called a *Routing Information Base (RIB)* and a routing table will only store one route (the best one) per destination, however the RIB can contain multiple paths to a destination.

BGP divides each routing domain into what is known as autonomous system or AS.

 A routing domain is a collection of networked systems that operate common routing protocols and are under the control of a single administration.

When a host is trying to access a resource across the Internet, BGP chooses the best path through the Internet and most of the time it chooses the path that has the least number of autonomous systems, also known as the shortest AS path.

Here are a few examples of commonly used dynamic routing protocols:

- **Routing Information Protocol (RIP)** – This is a distance vector protocol that uses hop count as a metric to determine the best next hop. The most recent version is RIP version 2 which makes it possible to carry subnet information. This is necessary to support CIDR and VLSM. The maximum hop count is 16.
- **Intermediate System – Intermediate System (IS-IS)** – This is a link-state protocol; it creates a full network topology on every router and uses Dijkstra's algorithm to calculate the best next hop. It is commonly used by Internet Service Providers (ISP).
- **Open Shortest Path First (OSPF)** – This is one of the most commonly used protocols. OSPF is also a link-state protocol which creates a map of the entire network on each router. This protocol also uses the Dijkstra's algorithm and is used within both enterprise and ISP networks.
- **Border Gateway Protocol (BGP)** – This protocol is used to make routing decisions on the Internet and is used by ISPs. Instead of using a certain algorithm or a hop count, BGP bases its routing decisions on paths and network policies.

IP & MAC Address Changes - Routing In Action

To summarize everything so far regarding MAC and IP addressing, switching and routing let's look at what happens when a TCP/IP packet is sent from one host to another between two networks. Note that a shortened version of the MAC address is used in the following examples for the sake of brevity.

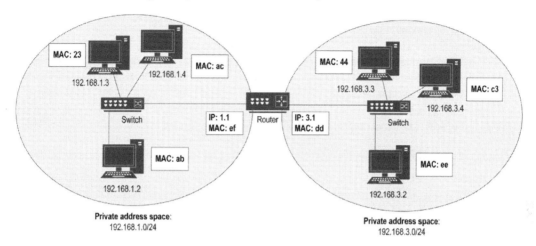

In the following illustrations you can see how both layer 2 and layer 3 addressing works and how these technologies enable the packet to travel from one destination to another. The difference between switches and routers becomes very clear.

In this example the host with IP address 192.168.1.2 wants to send data to the host with the IP address 192.168.3.2, which resides on a different network.

 Since we are only interested in viewing layers 2-4 we will combine layer 5-7 and call this the Application layer.

If we go through this process by looking at the OSI model, the Application layer will pass the data down to the Transport layer and the TCP protocol which will add a source port number and a destination port number.

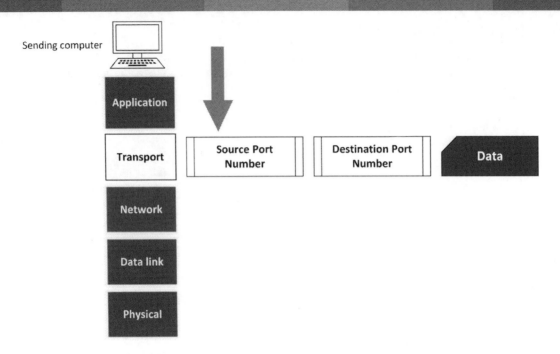

When the transport layer has added the port Information and encapsulated it within the TCP header fields, the transport layer passes the packet down to the Network layer and the IP protocol which then adds the source and destination IP addresses. The source and destination IP addresses are encapsulated within the IP header. During the entire transmission, these addresses will not change.

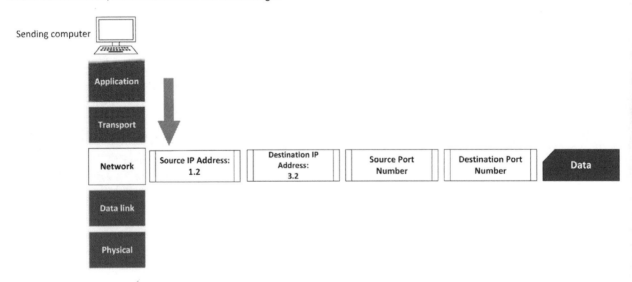

The next layer to process the data is the Data Link layer which adds the source and destination MAC addresses in the header fields which is encapsulated in the packet. But before it can do so, it needs to figure out if the destination host is on the same network as itself or not. If the host is *not* on the same network, it needs to send the data to the MAC address of the default gateway. It determines whether the destination host exists on the local network or not by comparing the network portion of the IP address to its own. Obviously in this example the destination is on a remote network.

If the PC does not know the MAC address of its default gateway, it will use ARP to send out an ARP request to all the hosts on its broadcast domain to determine the MAC address.

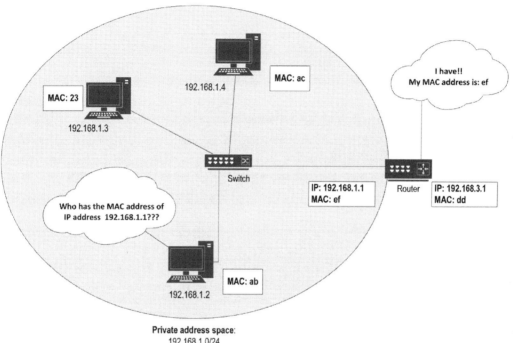

Once the host has the relevant MAC-address, it can correctly address the layer two frame and send it to the default gateway. The router will then do a routing table lookup to select a next hop to route the packet towards network 3.

It is important not to confuse the *default route* with the default gateway. To repeat what we explained earlier, the default gateway is a router which connects two or more networks together. Hosts will send packets to their default gateway when the network address is different from their own. A router does not have a default gateway since it is the door to other networks. Instead the router uses a default route when it cannot locate the specified network in its routing table.

You may ask how does a host know the IP address of its default gateway? This is configured either manually by the administrator or through DHCP.

The destination IP address is the final destination of the packet and the MAC addresses are the stops the packet makes along the way across each network medium until it reaches the correct host. So at each stop, the source and destination MAC-addresses will change.

After layer 2 has added the MAC addresses and a CRC checksum to the packet, it then passes it on to the physical layer which converts the ones and zeroes into electrical signals that can be transmitted on the wire.

The first device to receive the request is the Ethernet switch. The switch will look through its MAC address table to find a match for the destination MAC-address. A MAC address table on a switch is commonly known as a forwarding table. If no match is found it will broadcast the packet to all ports except the one it arrived at.

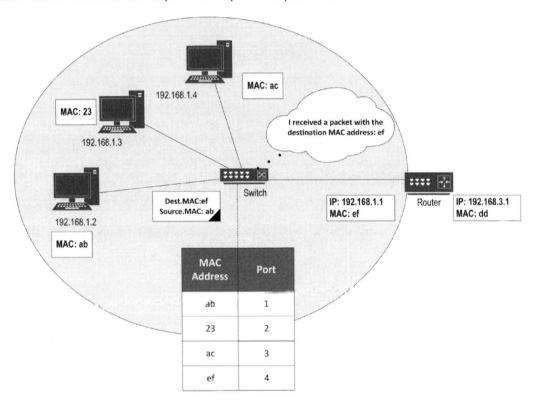

The switch finds a match in its forwarding table and sends the packet to the router via port 4. The switch will not change the MAC address or the layer 3 IP address; it will just forward the frame as necessary.

Now the router has received the packet at port 1 and looks at the destination MAC address to verify that it is the intended recipient.

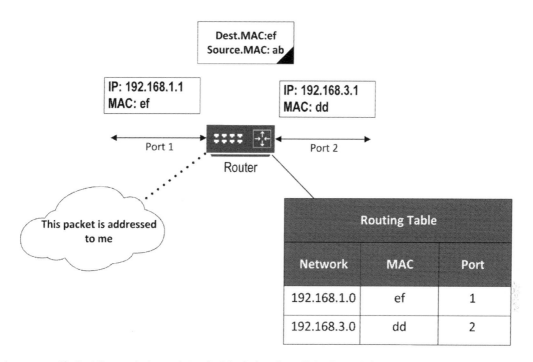

If the router can verify that the packet was intended for it, it strips off the layer 2 frame headers and examines the layer 3 destination IP address. By comparing the destination IP address against the networks in its routing table, the router can determine which port it should send the packet to. In our case the PC 192.168.3.2 belongs to network 192.168.3.0 which is a direct route on the router. Even though we know which port the router should forward the packet to, the router does not know the MAC address of the recipient. Therefore the router needs to perform an ARP request.

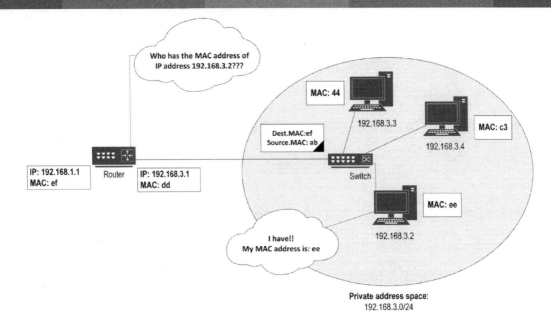

Next, the router adds a new destination and source MAC address. The source will be the MAC address of its own interface, port 2. The destination will be the MAC address of the destination host.

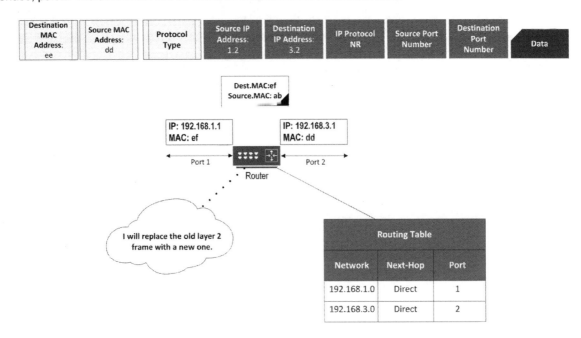

Since the router is a layer 3 device, it can remove the layer 2 frame and examine the layer 3 one. This is one of the big differences between switches and routers. The router cannot change the destination or source IP address but it will change the MAC address; each router will do so at each hop. A switch reads the layer 2 addresses but doesn't change these values. Now the packet has reached the switch in network 192.168.3.0.

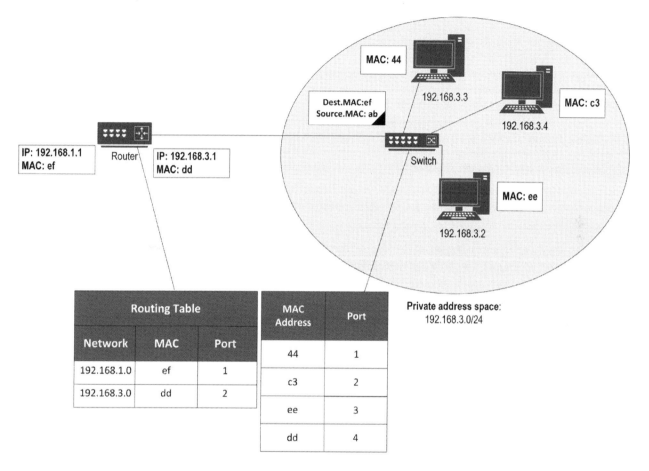

The switch now looks at its forwarding table to find the MAC address. If this address is not in the forwarding table, the switch will flood the packet on every port except the one it arrived on. In our case the MAC address of 192.168.3.2 exists in the forwarding table and the switch forwards the frame out of port 3 to the host.

When the packet arrives at the destination host it will examine the layer 2 address to verify that it is the intended recipient. Once it has done that, it will remove the layer 2 frame headers and look at the destination IP address. If the IP address matches, it will send the packet to the transport layer which will look at the destination and source ports. It will continue like this until the data reaches the correct application.

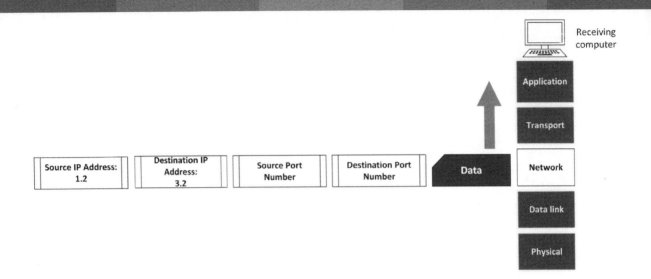

Network Address Translation (NAT)

We've previously discussed IP addressing and the fact public IPv4 addresses are running out. *Network Address Translation* (NAT) is a technique that helps minimize public address usage. We also mentioned that IANA reserved three private IP address ranges that cannot be routed on the Internet and they are used for internal purposes.

Commonly, NAT takes these private IP addresses and translates them into public IP addresses and vice versa, but it can be used with all addresses no matter if they are private or public. All the internal client requests appear to come from one device when in reality they come from several different clients and servers. This is also known as hide NAT. This technology provides a means of obscurity (often confused with security) by enabling users to hide their internal IP addresses behind one or more public ones. Not everyone agrees on this and it's a highly debated subject.

NAT is not only available on routers; it's also available on several other devices such as firewalls and load balancers. In all the following examples we will show a router.

There are several different types of NAT technologies with each one serving a specific purpose.

Static NAT

A static NAT is a one-to-one mapping between two addresses. It includes both a destination address translation in one direction and a source address translation in the other direction. The translation can occur in either direction (as discussed shortly in the Destination and Source NAT sections) but it is limited to translating only one address to another. Here is an example:

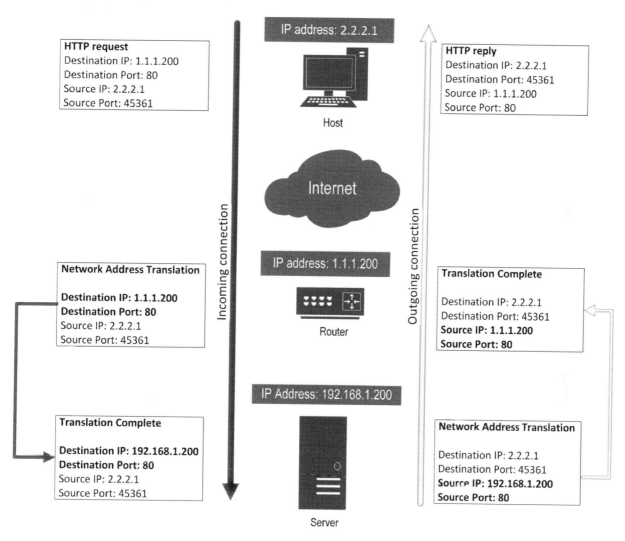

Destination NAT

This is a translation of the destination address of an inbound packet that enters a router's interface and translates the destination address before sending it out on the egress interface. The router knows where to send the packet based on the translated address that has been configured (not the original one). In the destination NAT 'rule' you define the original destination IP address and possibly a destination port as well as the translated address (and perhaps port) that packets will be routed to. Destination NAT can only be used with inbound traffic that enters a router's interface.

Here is an example of two destination NATs operating on a per port basis;

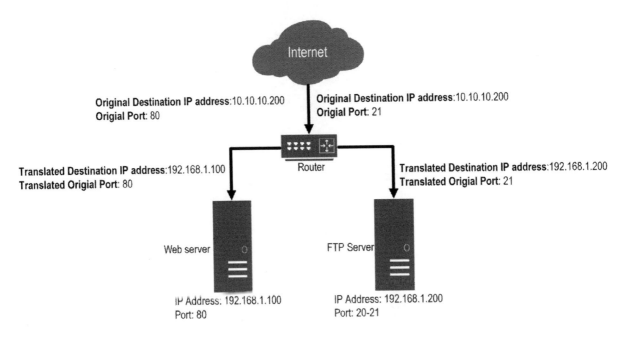

The most common use of Destination NAT is when you have a service on your internal network that you want to allow access to from the Internet. As the diagram shows above, clients can access both the web server and the FTP server by using the IP address 10.10.10.200 and the address will be translated to the internal addresses depending on which TCP port the user uses in its request.

Source NAT

Source NAT is used to (you guessed it) translate the source address of outbound packets that leave a router's interface. It does not matter if it is internal or external traffic. One common use of Source NAT is the translation of private IP addresses into a smaller number of (or just one) public IP address. This is something most networks use both in home and enterprise environments. Here is an example of Source NAT:

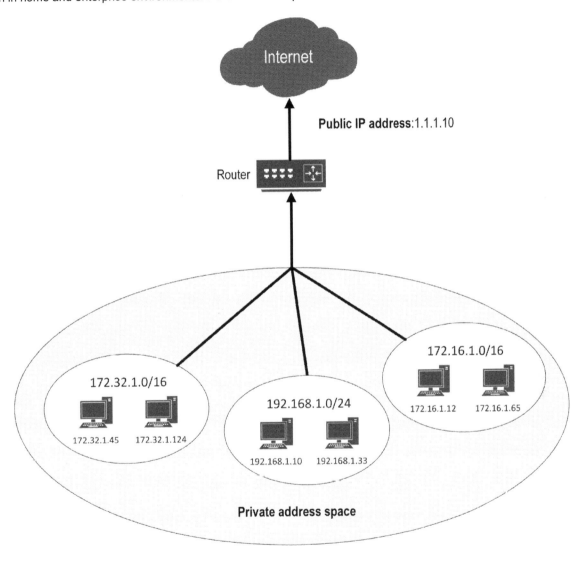

What happens with return traffic?

As you might have noticed in the Destination and Source NAT sections, we have only described the traffic flow in one direction. But what happens when a host replies back? When traffic is first passed through the router it will create a session. This session will continue to stay open as long as the communicating applications are actively exchanging packets. The router will monitor traffic traveling back and forth. This is called Stateful Packet Inspection (SPI).

A session record contains information such as the source and destination IP addresses, port numbers and the current sequence number of the last packet. A stateful router stores all of the active and permitted session records in a session table. The session table is stored in RAM and each record also contains a timeout value. If no communication occurs within the timeout period, the session will be closed and removed from the table. If the router also receives a FIN or RST packet the connection will be closed. SPI also enables the router to check each incoming packet and confirm that it actually belongs to a valid session and this increases security since the traffic passing through is expected traffic.

To use Destination NAT as an example. We have a client on the Internet that is trying to access a server on the internal network. When the SYN request has been received by the router, it will first create a session so it can track the state of the session along with the IP addresses, ports and sequence numbers. After that it will translate the destination address to the internal IP address of the server. When the server replies back to the client with a SYN-ACK, the packet will pass through the router and it will recognize that the traffic belongs to a valid session. If a FIN packet was received, this would be dropped as it would not be valid as the three way handshake has not yet completed. With the servers reply, the router translates the server's internal IP address to the relevant external IP address and forwards it to the client. The client will have no knowledge of the server's internal IP address. The whole scenario is described in the diagram below:

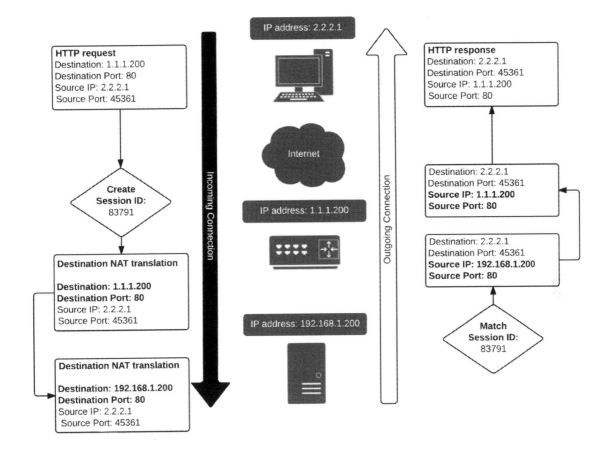

The difference between Destination NAT and Static NAT is that Destination NAT is not a one-to-one mapping, which means it only translates for connections initiated in one direction (inbound).. So if an internal server with the IP address 192.168.1.200 wanted to initiate an outbound connection to a host on the Internet there would be no translation and the connection would fail. This would have to be configured using a Source NAT in addition to the Destination NAT or by using Static NAT, which enables translation in both directions.

Chapter Summary

- The primary role of a router is to connect two or more networks together. But there are several other functions that a router can offer a network environment such as connecting several branch offices with each other over a WAN link or minimizing network traffic by creating multiple broadcast or collision domains.

- A direct route is a destination that can be reached directly and is attached to the LAN segment.

- A router does not have a default gateway since it is the door to other networks. Instead the router uses a default route when it cannot locate the specified network in its routing table.

- NAT stands for Network Address Translation and it is responsible for translating IP addresses. In most cases we translate an address from a public IP address to a private IP address and vice versa.

Chapter Review

In order to test your knowledge and understanding of this chapter, please answer the following questions. You will find the answers and explanations of the questions at the end of this chapter.

1. Which protocols are link-state protocols?
   a. RIP
   b. IS-IS
   c. OSPF
   d. BGP

2. True or false: Distance-vector protocols build a map of the entire network and make routing decisions based on this map.
   a. True
   b. False

3. In what direction is static NAT used?
   a. Incoming direction
   b. Outgoing direction
   c. Both incoming and outgoing

4. True or false: Destination NAT can be used for incoming and outgoing packets.
   a. True
   b. False

Chapter Review: Answers

You will find the answers to the chapter review questions below:

1. The correct answers are: B and C
    a. RIP
    b. **IS-IS**
    c. **OSPF**
    d. BGP

IS-IS and OSPF are both link-state protocols and they map the entire network based on the information they receive from other routers. RIP is a distance vector protocol and does not build up a map of the network. BGP is a path-vector protocol which makes decisions based on paths and network policies.

2. The correct answer is: B
    a. True
    b. **False**

Distance vector protocols do not build a map of the network, instead they use hop count to determine the best next hop.

3. The correct answer is: C
    a. Incoming direction
    b. Outgoing direction
    c. **Both incoming and outgoing**

Static NAT is a one-to-one mapping which means that it uses both source NAT and destination NAT. The communication is therefore both incoming and outgoing.

4. The correct answer is: B
    a. True
    b. **False**

Destination NAT can only be used for incoming connections.

8. The Application Layer in Detail

Many people get confused by the application layer and think that the application is an actual application like Microsoft Word or Internet Explorer; this is not the case. The application layer acts as a framework for the actual applications that run on top of it.

Some examples of application layer protocols are:

SSH	Secure Shell
FTP	File transfer protocol
HTTP	Hyper Text Transfer Protocol
DNS	Domain Name System

In this chapter we will examine the most common and fundamental applications that are used in an Application Delivery Solution.

Hypertext Transfer Protocol (HTTP)

HTTP is the application protocol which today forms the basis of a significant amount of the traffic on the Internet and probably within most business networks too. HTTP's primary purpose is to exchange content (web pages, images, files or just about anything else) between hosts, typically from a server to a client. HTTP Functions using a simple request and response messaging mechanism, with the client requesting a resource (some content) and the server responding with that resource. This basic functionality has been built upon through various means to provide today's sophisticated, dynamic websites. HTTP operates at the application layer (seven) of the OSI Model.

HTTP Is pretty old, with the first documented version appearing in 1991 (RFC2068 states it had been used since 1990) and the current version last being updated in 1999. V2.0 is currently in development and will likely be released in late 2014. HTTP was created by a team led by Tim Berners-Lee, who is credited with inventing the World Wide Web. F5 Networks itself was formed to create a product to specifically load balance HTTP traffic for sites on the World Wide Web.

HTTP is considered to be a stateless protocol in that the client and server do not store state data in any way. A request is sent and a response received; this 'transaction' has no impact on future ones, nor do earlier ones affect this one. This is why, for instance, the HTTP version number is sent in every request (and response) along with other data (in the form of headers – more on these shortly) such as User-Agent, Host, Cache-Control and Accept-Encoding. Cookies are used to provide a form of state when required (more on Cookies soon).

Here's what a simple HTTP request (for a part of the HTTP v1.1 RFC) looks like;

```
GET /Protocols/rfc2616/rfc2616-sec3.html HTTP/1.1\r\n  << The Request Line (Method, URL
& Version)
Host: www.w3.org\r\n           << The Server Hostname
User-Agent: Mozilla/5.0\r\n        << The User-Agent; information on the client browser
Accept: text/html\r\n
Accept-Language: en-US\r\n
Connection: keep-alive\r\n         << Indicates a Persistent Connection
```

And here's what the response could look like;

```
HTTP/1.1 200 OK\r\n                    << The Status Line (Version, Status Code &
Reason Phrase)
Date: Tue, 04 Feb, 2014 10:33:40 GMT\r\n      << The date and time on the server
Server: Apache/2\r\n                   << Information on the HTTP server
Content-Length: 35041\r\n              << The length of the content sent (minus any
Headers)
Content-Type: text/html\r\n            << The type of content sent
\r\n
[The content follows from this point...]
```

You'll note that each line of HTTP is terminated with the \r and \n metacharacters, indicating a Carriage Return and Line Feed respectively; essentially a new line. This is also used to insert a blank line between the last Header and the actual content body, to delimit the two.

These diagrams provide a visual representation of both a successful and unsuccessful HTTP request;

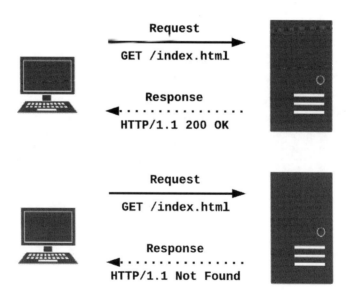

Multiple transactions between the same client and server, completed over the same established TCP connection are considered a session. A session may also comprise of multiple TCP connections (again between the same client and server) to improve performance. Sessions rely on HTTP Persistent Connections, discussed shortly.

A session over a single TCP connection looks like this;

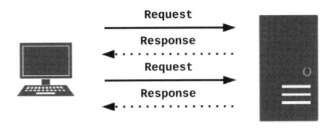

URLs – Uniform Resource Locator

Uniform Resource Locators (URLs) are (as the name suggests) a standard naming scheme used to identify the location of resources on the Internet. A resource is commonly content of some kind (a file or a web page) but can also be a service or process to be manipulated in some way.

URLs are not specific to HTTP and are a subset of Uniform Resource Identifiers (URIs). It's rather confusing but a URL is a type of URI which includes the access method and location of a resource, the resource itself is also specified as a URI, hence, a URL is a URI and also contains a URI (as you'll see). The HTTP v1.1 standard references the URI (and thus URL) syntax and semantics specified in RFC2396.

HTTP Related URLs are composed of the following components;

- URL Protocol Scheme – the protocol used to locate and access a resource, such as; `http://` or `https://`.

- Server Location (Host) – the Fully Qualified Domain Name (FQDN) aka the hostname of the server that holds the resource (where it can be located), for example: `www.google.com`. This includes any port specification following the hostname, such as `:8800` and is case insensitive. An IP address can be used but this should be avoided where possible.

- Path or Uniform Resource Identifier (URI) – the remaining part of the URL after the Scheme and Host, for example: `/test/index.html?username=test`. The most basic, shortest possible URI is '/'. The URI is composed of a Path and possibly a Query or other URI elements;

    o Path – the location of a specific resource on the Host, for example: `/test/index.html`

    o Query – a string (normally prefixed with (but not including) the `?` symbol) that provides information to the resource, for example: `?username=test`.

As you can see in the HTTP request example earlier in this section, the URL you type into a browser is designed to be user friendly and is 'converted' to meet the HTTP standard, with the URI being sent in the Request Line, the Server Location in the Host Header and the Protocol Scheme not appearing at all.

There are two types of URLs; absolute and relative. An absolute URL includes the three elements discussed previously, the Protocol Scheme, Server Location and URI. A relative URL contains only the URI, or possibly only part of the URI.

When a relative URL is used the browser client uses the protocol scheme of the current page or resource that contains the relative link. The browser will also include the Server Location (the hostname) and any missing parts of the URL based on the so called Base URL of the current page or resource that contains the relative link. For example if the URL of the page containing the relative URL is http://www.example.com/test/index.html and the relative URL is testpage.html the Base URL is http://www.example.com/test/ and the browser will dynamically build the URL as this: http://www.example.com/test/testpage.html.

Versions

There are currently three HTTP versions, the most recent being v1.1; within the protocol itself the version is expressed as: `HTTP/x.x` (`HTTP/1.1` for instance). The version is the third and last piece of data specified in the Request Line in a request and the first in the Status Line of a response. The Request Line is the first line of a HTTP request and the Status Line the first of response – take a look at the request and response examples earlier in this section to see what they look like. All responses should use the same version specified in the request. Details of each version are as follows;

HTTP v0.9

- Documented in 1991 here: http://www.w3.org/Protocols/HTTP/AsImplemented.html
- The first documented version
- The only supported method is GET (we'll cover methods shortly)
- The only supported response content format is HTML

HTTP v1.0

- Documented in RFC1945 in 1996
- Added support for;
    - HTTP Headers (which allows for most of the following features in this list)
    - Content encoding (compression)
    - Content types
    - User agents
    - The HEAD and POST methods
    - Basic authentication
    - Response status codes
    - Caching support features
    - Any mime compatible response content format is supported

HTTP v1.1

- Documented in RFC2068 in 1997
- Updated in RFC2616 in 1999
- Reworded and split into RFC7230, RFC7231, RFC7232, RFC7233, RFC7234 and RFC7235 in 2014
- The version in general use today
- Added support for;
    - The CONNECT, DELETE, OPTIONS, PUT and TRACE methods
    - The Upgrade request header (used by The WebSocket Protocol for instance)
    - Caching support improvements (for better performance)
    - Range requests (partial object requests allowing for pausing and restarting a download for instance)
    - The 100 Continue status code and 23 others for more accurate error reporting
    - Compression improvements (for better performance)
    - Persistence connections and Pipelining to improve performance
    - The Host header (allowing a single server to host multiple websites using a single IP address)
    - Digest and proxy authentication
    - Cookies
    - Content negotiation (preferred language etc.)

The HTTP/2.0 standard is current due to be ratified in late 2014.

Status Codes

HTTP Status Codes are used to indicate to a client (in a response), how the server has handled and fulfilled a request (or otherwise). They provide a form of status, success and error reporting for both the server, which includes these codes in its logs and the client that receives them. Status Codes are formed of a three digit numerical Status Code and a related Reason Phrase. The first of those three digits defines the Class of Response, those classes being;

- 1xx – Informational
- 2xx – Success
- 3xx – Redirection
- 4xx – Client Error
- 5xx – Server Error

The Reason Phrase is a brief, human readable description of the meaning of the Status Code. Note the RFC provides recommendations but allows for alternative text to be used. Here are a few examples of common Status Codes, the related RFC recommended Reason Phrase and their meaning;

- 200 – OK – The request was successful
- 302 – Found – Used to redirect to a different URL
- 400 – Bad Request – The client's request wasn't understood
- 401 – Unauthorised – Used to indicate authentication is required
- 404 – Not Found – The requested resource doesn't exist on the server

The Status Code is the second piece of data specified in the Status Line, the Reason Phrase the third and last; the first is the version. Take a look at the request and response examples earlier in this section to see what they look like.

Methods

The HTTP Method is specified in client requests and is the method (or action) to be performed on/with the resource specified by the URL. The two most common Methods are GET, which simply retrieves the resource and POST which is used to append data to a resource (posting a comment to a web page for instance).

The Method is the first piece of data specified in the Request Line, as shown in the request example earlier in this section. Other Methods include;

- **HEAD** – similar to GET but the server should not respond with the message body (the actual resource requested), only the Headers that would be sent if it did (as it would with a GET)
- **PUT** – a request for the server to store the resource sent by the client at the URI specified
- **OPTIONS** – a request generally used to ascertain the capabilities of a server in respect of the resource specified or in general (when used with a URI of *). Most servers will not respond to OPTIONS requests as this is widely considered a security risk
- **DELETE** – a request for the server to delete the resource at the URI specified. As you can imagine, this is rarely used
- **TRACE** – a request for the server to 'reflect' the request back to the client in the body of it's response; a loopback of sorts. Most servers will not respond to OPTIONS requests as this is widely considered a security risk
- **CONNECT** – used with proxies that can dynamically switch to being employed to establish a tunnel between a client and server, typically involving SSL

HTTP Header Features

Headers and their values (also known as Header Fields) are used for a wide and varied range of purposes within HTTP and are typically present in both request and response messages. In the majority of cases the Headers used in a response are different to those used in a request. Headers define the parameters that are used and exchanged in messages between client and server when using almost any HTTP feature (the obvious exceptions being the URL, Version, Status Code and Method). HTTP Headers were introduced in the HTTP/1.0 standard.

Headers are typically colon and trailing space separated name-value pairs; where multiple values exist those values are normally comma separated (no spaces). This is a general guide and is not always the case; each header type may have its own specific formatting. Headers appear directly after the Request or Status Line and before the content body; the \r and \n metacharacters are used to delimit between these and each Header.

Common v1.1 request Headers, example values and their functionality are described next;

- `Host: www.example.com\r\n` – required in a HTTP v1.1 request, this header contains the hostname of the server as specified in the Server Location element of the URL. This header allows a single server to host multiple websites using the same IP address but different hostnames, without requiring the use of a dedicated IP address or TCP port for each

- `User-Agent: Mozilla/5.0 (Windows NT 6.1; Win64; x64; rv:24.0) Gecko/20100101 Firefox/24.0 Waterfox/24.0\r\n` – provides details on the software used by the user or system when making the request. In many cases this will be a fairly long string indicated the version of the browser used

- `Accept: text/html,application/xhtml+xml,application/xml;q=0.9,*/*;q=0.8\r\n` – a comma separated list of Content Types (media formats) that will be accepted in the content body of the server response

  You'll note in this example and elsewhere that some values have a suffix like this `;q=x.x` – this is a **qvalue** used to indicate to a server a preference for some values over others, when multiple header values are present. If none is specified (and it's relevant) a value of 1 is assumed; 1 indicates the most preferred value (or values), lower preferences are expressed as decimal tenths of 1. In the above example `text/html,application/xhtml+xml` have a qvalue of 1 and are most preferred, `application/xml` is not as preferred and has a qvalue of 0.9 and `*/*` (any Content Type) is least preferred and has a qvalue of 0.8.

- `Accept-Language: en-US,en;q=0.5\r\n` – specifies the language(s) the client software would prefer are used in response content body

- `Accept-Encoding: gzip, deflate\r\n` – a comma and trailing space separated list of Content Encodings (compression methods) that will be accepted in the server response content body

- `Connection: keep-alive\r\n` – indicates to the server that a connection is persistent (see the next section for more information). The `keep-alive` value isn't actually a requirement of v1.1 (persistent connections are assumed) and was an unofficial extension of the HTTP v1.0 standard

- `Connection: close\r\n` – indicates to the server that a connection should be closed (see the next section for more information). Valid in the HTTP v1.0 and v1.1 standards

- `If-Modified-Since: Wed, 01 Sep 2004 13:24:52 GMT\r\n` – only satisfy the request if the resource has been modified after the specified date and time. If the resource hasn't been, the server will respond with a simple 304 Not Modified Status Code and Reason Phrase

Common v1.1 response Headers, example values and their functionality are described next;

- `Date: Wed, 01 Sep 2004 13:24:52 GMT\r\n` – nearly always required in a HTTP v1.1 response, the date and time a response was generated, in the format specified by RFC1123

- `Cache-Control: private\r\n` – specifies whether the response can be cached or not (and related parameters where necessary) by any caching mechanisms between and including the client and server (browser caches, network caches, proxies and the like). In this example, the response may not be cached by a shared cache but can be by a user specific one (such as the user's browser)

- `Connection: keep-alive\r\n` – indicates to the client that a connection is persistent (see the next section for more information). The `keep-alive` value isn't actually a requirement of v1.1 (persistent connections are assumed) and was an unofficial extension of the HTTP v1.0 standard

- `Connection: close\r\n` – indicates to the client that a connection should be closed. Valid in the HTTP v1.0 and v1.1 standards

- `Content-Encoding: gzip\r\n` – specifies the Content Encoding (compression method) that has been applied to the response content body (not the Status Line or Headers)

- `Content-Type: text/html; charset=UTF-8\r\n` – the Content Type (media format) of the response content body

- `Content-Length: 542\r\n` – the length of the response content body (this does not include the Status Line or Headers) in octets (an octet is eight bits or one byte)

HTTP Persistent Connections

More commonly known as HTTP Keepalives, Persistent Connections are a performance enhancement introduced in HTTP v1.1. They allow multiple requests and responses to be sent and received (one after the other) over the same persistent TCP connection, rather than a new connection being established for each request and response transaction. Without Persistent Connections, every single request results in a TCP connection being established and then closed, as follows;

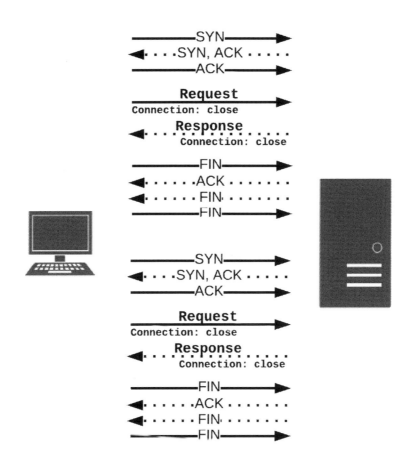

With Persistent Connections, multiple requests use the same TCP connection, as follows;

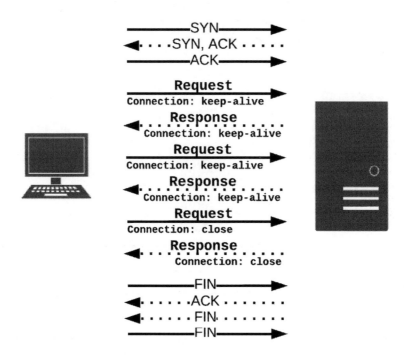

Not needing to perform the TCP three way handshake before sending each request and shutting down the connection after each response clearly saves both time and computing resources, particularly where SSL/TLS is used. It also allows for Pipelining (covered in the later Application Delivery Platforms chapter), reduces latency and congestion (a single TCP three way hand shake for multiple requests rather than one per request) and reduces server resource usage as fewer connection establishment and closure tasks need to be performed. Those connecting over lossy and/or high latency networks benefit the most.

Persistence support is assumed in HTTP v1.1; with v1.0 it is an unofficial extension not actually specified in the RFC and makes use of the Connection Header as follows;

- `Connection: keep-alive\r\n` – indicates to the client or server (depending on whether the header is contained in a request or response) that a connection is persistent

HTTP Persistent Connections are supported by all modern web browsers. Although it may seem similar to HTTP Pipelining, it is not as a request must be fulfilled before the next can be sent.

Despite the fact it's not needed, you'll often see this Header and value even in HTTP v1.1 requests.

Cookies

Cookies provide a mechanism to record state in relation to HTTP client connections to specific websites; this state information is stored by the client rather than the server (despite it being acted upon by the server). Cookies *are not* part of any HTTP standard and were first formalised in RFC2109 in 1997. This was superseded by RFC2965 in 2000 which in turn was superseded by the current standard RFC6265 created in 2011.

This state information can be used in many ways server-side including for session management (Persistence for instance), personalisation and tracking. The potential security and privacy risks associated with Cookies have been widely debated ever since their introduction and in the European Union websites are required by law to obtain user consent to store Cookies. Cookies may eventually be superseded by client fingerprinting and other methods.

Cookies are created on the client using the Set-Cookie HTTP Header in responses, the values and attributes of which depend on what information is being stored, although there are a number of 'standard' attributes such as Domain, Path and Expires. Here's an example of one of the Cookies Google sends when connecting to www.google.co.uk;

- ```
  Set-Cookie: PREF=ID=72d5f8d1334bd850:FF=0:TM=1391620617:LM=1391620617:S=OeYDjcs5bpS3ntMu;
  expires=Fri, 05-Feb-2016 17:16:57 GMT; path=/; domain=.google.co.uk\r\n
  ```

Cookies are returned to the Server using the Cookie Header; note the attributes are not included as they relate to the Cookie's storage and use on the client, not the state information the server requires;

- ```
  Cookie: PREF=ID=72d5f8d1334bd850:FF=0:TM=1391620617:LM=1391620617:S=OeYDjcs5bpS3ntMu\r\n
  ```

Further Reading

I'd highly recommend you simple read through the relevant parts of RFC2616 for further information on any of the subjects covered by the exam or to learn more in general about the protocol. The RFC is well written and fairly easy to understand compared to most. Even better, it was split into multiple RFCs and the language clarified in 2014, as follows;

- RFC7230 – HTTP/1.1: Message Syntax and Routing
- RFC7231 – HTTP/1.1: Semantics and Content
- RFC7232 – HTTP/1.1: Conditional Requests
- RFC7233 – HTTP/1.1: Range Requests
- RFC7234 – HTTP/1.1: Caching
- RFC7235 – HTTP/1.1: Authentication

If you'd rather something with better formatting and more explanatory text and context, I'd recommend this rather expensive but very comprehensive book;

- HTTP The Definitive Guide – David Gourley, Brian Totty et al. – O'Reilly

HTTPS (Secure HTTP)

Hyper Text Transfer Protocol Secure or HTTPS is just like HTTP except it is used together with Secure Sockets Layer (SSL) and Transport Layer Security (TLS). It provides a security layer on top of the HTTP protocol which encrypts data, ensures the identity of both devices and makes sure that data has not been modified during transit. HTTPS is a standard that is highly used by online banking and online shopping. When you use HTTPS, instead of the original http:// it uses the *https://* prefix. It also operates on port 443 instead of port 80.

Domain Name System (DNS)

One of the cornerstones in making the Internet work is the *Domain Name System* (DNS). Computers are not designed to communicate with natural language and understand what www.google.com is. These types of addresses have been designed to make it easier for people to remember the addresses of the different websites and hosts they usually visit or use. What DNS does is translate a domain name like www.google.com into the IP address corresponding to the server that hosts www.google.com.

DNS was designed in 1983 at the University of California by Paul Mockapetris. In November 1983, the Internet Engineering Task Force (IETF) published the first specification of the protocol in RFC 882 and RFC 883. The first update of the specification was in November 1987 by RFC 1034 and RFC 1035 and is still the most current version.

When the Internet was first developed it was so small that there was no need for a distributed, global DNS service. Instead every computer would have a local text file called "hosts". The hosts file would contain a simple list of the names and IP addresses of every host on the network (which was very small). When a new computer was added, every network administrator would have to update their version of the file on every relevant host. It was not until the Internet grew much larger that the need for DNS arose. DNS is part of the application layer and works on TCP and UDP port 53, with use over UDP the most common at present.

The domain name system is divided into domains that work in a hierarchical structure. This is very similar to what a directory tree looks like in a file system. This hierarchical namespace is beneficial because it allows each domain to be managed by a coparate organization, individual or administrator (if necessary). It also helps reduce the risk of duplicate names. If you had only a 'flat' namespace, the more clients you add to the network the greater the risk of users creating duplicate names grows. With the hierarchical structure every host or domain exists in a dedicated namespace and is unique. For instance, two hosts can have the same host name as long as they are in two separate namespaces. server1.toronto.com and server1.chicago.com have the same hostname but since they are in two separate namespaces (domains) they are still unique.

At the top of the namespace you have the root which is represented by a dot. Further down the namespace you have domains which are similar to directories and sub-domains which are similar to sub-directories and so on. Hosts are the smallest (least significant) piece of the namespace and represent a file in a file system. Below you will see an example of a small part of the Internet DNS.

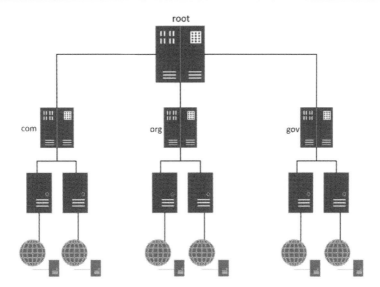

In order to maintain and keep updated records in the DNS namespace, administrators all over the Internet are responsible for updating DNS records when there has been some kind of change. Often it is an ISP or some another large organization that is responsible for this administration. Google for instance has its own DNS which uses the IP address 8.8.8.8.

 DNS is not only used on the Internet; it is also used extensively on internal networks by small, medium and large companies too.

When assigning a domain name that is going to be used on the Internet, you usually use the host portion to identify the role of a server although you don't have to do this. One example is to create a www record if the server is a web server. Here is an example of how it looks.

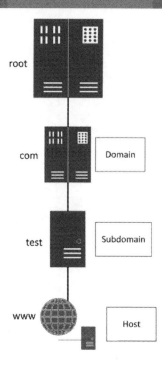

The full address (the Fully Qualified Domain Name (FQDN)) of the webserver would be www.test.com. The root dot (.) is hidden from the user, behind the scenes, where it is actually used.

Most companies and organizations use DNS in their internal environment as well, in order to map IP addresses to server names and internal resources. The name standards of internal resources vary and depend on the company, policy and/or how an administrator has designed things. This domain namespace is created for internal purposes only and is the "local domain"; it does not need to be globally unique. Every domain that has the .local namespace is only used for internal purposes and therefore cannot be used on the Internet.

Top-Level Domains

The name closest to the root dot (.) is called a top-level domain (TLD). There are a number of different TLDs; traditionally limited to country-specific allocations (such as .uk, .us, .es and so on) and a small number of 'global' or generic domains, such as;

- ❖ .com – Commercial Organizations
- ❖ .org – Non-commercial Organizations (charities etc.)
- ❖ .gov – Government institutions
- ❖ .net – Networking related organizations (although now 'general purpose')

Global domain names can typically be used by anyone. Others, such as .gov on the other hand are reserved and can only be used by suitably certified organizations. The Internet Corporation for Assigned Names and Numbers (ICANN) are responsible for the accreditation of domain name registrars as well as for any changes regarding the overall namespace such as adding more top-level domain names which, after a long period of stagnation, are rapidly growing in number. Registrars allocate domain names for (or within) a particular TLD on behalf of ICANN.

Second-Level Domains

To obtain a second-level domain you have to purchase the rights to it from a specific registry. For as long as you pay the fee for a domain you 'own' you have exclusive rights to that domain name. The registry is also responsible for publishing information on who owns the name and three contacts within the owning organization; an administrative contact, a billing contact, and a technical contact. The administrator who buys the name can create as many subdomains and host records within the second level domain without needing to inform the top-level domain registry. For instance, if you own testing.org you can create host records for www.testing.org, crazyserver.testing.org, www.madness.testing.org or whatever else you'd like.

Zones and Resource Records (RRs)

A lot of companies have branch offices in many different countries on several continents. Many of which have their own IT department which manages network devices and servers in that office. In order to easily manage DNS records related to them, we need to be able to divide domains so that we can delegate responsibility to the administrator of each office.

In order to do this we separate domains into *zones*. However this is only possible when we have a 3-level-domain namespace. In the following illustration example.com has delegated two subdomains and you can see that the New York site has its subdomains and hosts in one zone and Tokyo site is part of its own zone with its own subdomains. This means that the administrator in the New York site manages its subdomains and hosts and the administrator in Tokyo administrates their subdomains and hosts in Tokyo. Each zone must be represented by a DNS server (or more) that is the authority for that zone. One DNS server can maintain several zones which means that you will only theoretically need two (one master and one backup) but in terms of latency and delays you may want to set up a DNS server in for example Tokyo as well.

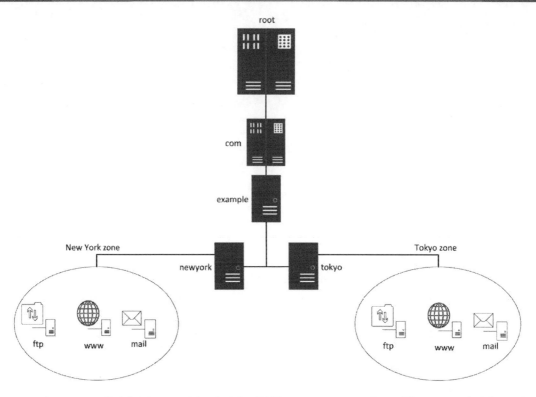

Resource records are so-called database entries that the DNS servers store and use. These contain information about the hosts in a domain and its subdomains. There are several different kinds of resource records, see the more common ones next;

- **SOA Record** (Start of Authority) – This is used to indicate that this DNS server is the authoritative source for information regarding the zone. Each zone has a SOA record and there can only be one per zone.
- **NS Record** (Name Server) – This record represents a DNS server in the zone and it does not matter if the server is a primary DNS server or a secondary. Each DNS server has to have a NS record.
- **A Record** (Host record) – This provides a name-to-address record that will convert a DNS name to an IP-address. In IPv6 the host record is represented by four As (**AAAA**)
- **PTR Record** (Pointer) – This provides an address-to-name mapping that supplies a DNS name for a specific address (a Reverse Lookup) in the in-addr.arpa domains. The main function for this record is for reverse lookups only (see the next section).
- **MX Record** (Mail Exchanger) – This record represents a host that can handle email traffic related to the domain. This can be a mail gateway or another mail server.
- **CNAME Record** (Canonical Name) – This record is used to create an alias for a host (A) record. You use CNAME records to provide alternative names for servers. If you have a server with the host record server1.test.com you can create a CNAME record called www.test.com and both records would be usable and 'point' to the same IP address.

Reverse Lookups

To explain how PTR records work we need to explain what the in-addr.arpa domain is and how it works. To be able to make efficient lookups on the Internet, DNS uses the domain in-addr.arpa. The in-addr.arpa domain is located beneath the root of the DNS tree and it has 256 subdomains which are named from the number 0 to 255. These numbers represent the possible values of the first Byte of an IP address. Each of these subdomains contains another set of subdomains that are also represented by the number 0 to 255 to represent the second byte and so on. These subdomains represent the full IP-address space of 4 bytes.

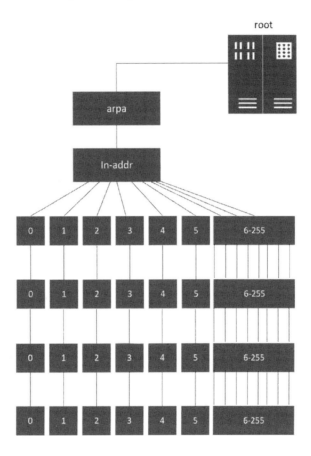

In other words, each host that has a DNS name also has a PTR record that represents its IP address. So if a system is configured with the IP address 172.32.144.21 and is listed in the DNS server for test.com with the host record www (so a full host name of www.test.com) then there is also a PTR resource record for *21.144.32.172.in-addr.arpa*. This means that there is a host record named 21 in the domain *144.32.172.in-addr.arpa*.

You might wonder why the IP address is reversed in the DNS namespace; this is because in DNS, the least significant word comes first.

How Does a Computer Resolve a DNS Name (To An IP Address)?

A user first enters the DNS name in their web browser; let's use www.google.com in this example. If the local cache on the computer does not already know the address, it sends the request to the local DNS *resolver*. The local DNS resolver is the component on the client computer that sends DNS lookups to remote DNS servers. It generates and sends queries to DNS servers, receives the answers and sends this information to applications. In our case this is the web browser. The local DNS resolver cache names and addresses for a short time but let's assumes there is no cached entry. The resolver sends the request to the configured remote DNS server.

The hosts file is still used in some environments and it can cause issues if it is configured incorrectly because the hosts file takes precedence over DNS.

 The hosts file is located in the following location on Windows XP and onwards
hosts: c:\windows\system32\drivers\etc\hosts

The process of DNS resolution is illustrated in the following diagram;

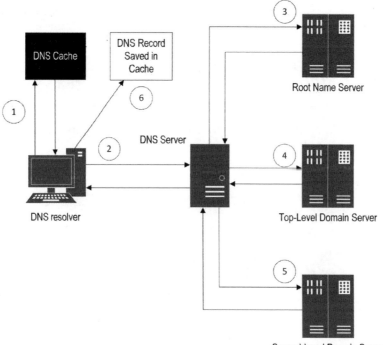

1. First the local DNS resolver checks the local DNS cache for a matching entry.
2. If an entry isn't found in the cache the resolver will send a request to a remote DNS server.

3. When the remote DNS server receives the request, it checks to see if it is responsible for the domain name. In most cases it is not, and the server generates a new request that it sends on to the root DNS server. The root server then checks its records for the top level domain which is com in our case. The root server will send a reply back to the original DNS server that it should ask the top-level domain com and provides the information required to contact it.
4. Now the DNS server knows the address of the top-level domain com and generates a new request to the com domain asking if it knows the IP address of google. The com domain looks through its records and sends a reply with the address of the DNS server for google.com.
5. The DNS server now knows the address of the google.com DNS server and sends a new request to it, asking for the address of www.google.com. The google.com server responds with an address and the original DNS server then forwards this to the client's local DNS resolver. The resolver then sends this information to the web browser.
6. The DNS record will also be stored in the computers local DNS cache for a short time to speed up the process next time the computer tries to access www.google.com.

Session Initiation Protocol (SIP)

SIP is a protocol used for voice and video calls over IP. The protocol specifies the messages that are sent between the two end point devices in order to establish maintain and terminate an IP based voice call. It is also used in video conferencing, streaming media, instant messaging and online gaming.

SIP was designed by Henning Schulzrinne and Mark Handley in 1996. In 1999 the protocol was standardized in RFC 2543. The latest version of the specification is RFC 3261 and was published in June 2002.

As with any Voice over IP (VoIP) technology, the need for dedicated PSTN, ISDN or multiplexed serial lines is removed; calls can be made over the Internet or any other IP based network. This decreases costs significantly particularly when used across existing internal or Internet connections.

SIP is mainly used to set up and tear down a session and typically uses TCP and UDP ports 5060 and/or 5061. If secure, encrypted communications are required *Transport Layer Security* (TLS) is available, this uses TCP port 5061.

File Transfer Protocol (FTP)

File Transfer Protocol is a very common protocol that commonly operates using both TCP ports 20 and 21. FTP is different to file sharing services that you access on your PC using "My Computer" or Windows Explorer. These file shares are locations on the network where you store your documents; they enable you to work with them as if they were stored locally on your computer. FTP's main purpose is to copy and transfer files from one system to another. Typically both systems are in different networks, one often remote.

Like HTTP, it is very important that the receiving computer receives the correct data without any errors, which is why FTP also uses the TCP protocol to communicate. FTP uses interactive CLI-based text commands to perform its various functions although use of a graphical interface (which hides this complexity from the user) is more popular.

FTP uses two ports to operate; when an FTP client connects to the server it uses TCP port 21 to establish the connection. This connection will remain open until the session is closed and is used to exchange commands (and responses) between the client and server. When the computer requests or sends a file to the FTP server, a separate connection is opened on port 20 to exchange the actual file. After the transfer is complete this connection is closed immediately. When you are using these ports you are most likely using what is known as Active FTP. It does not matter which connection method you use, FTP will always use one port for commands and another to exchange data.

The Difference between Active FTP and Passive FTP

There are two different ways for a client to connect to a FTP server and transfer files; Active FTP and Passive FTP. When setting up an FTP server (or load balancing FTP traffic) it is important to understand the difference between these modes and determine which will be best suited for your environment.

Active FTP

How Active FTP works is explained in the following illustration:

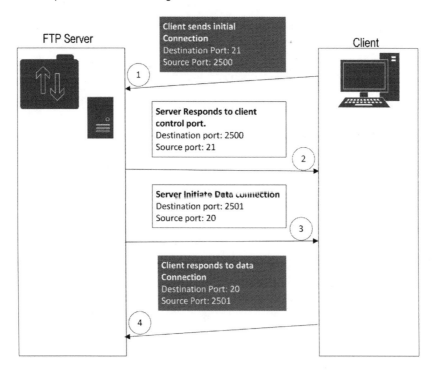

1. In our example, the client connects to the FTP server using source port 2500 and destination port 21.
2. The server responds to the request using source port 21.
3. The client then starts to listen on its data port 2501 (its source port +1) which it informed the server of in its initial request.
4. Thereafter the FTP server connects to the client on port 2501 from its source data port of 20, when transferring files.

One reason many administrators do not use FTP in Active mode is because the client is not responsible for establishing the data connection (it is initiated by the server). The client simply tells the FTP server what port it is listening on and expects that the server will open the connection to it. Since the second connection is a new outbound session, firewalls (and other security devices or software) may consider the connection as unwanted or hostile and block it.

Passive FTP

In order to solve the challenges when using Active FTP another method was created so that the client could initiate the connection to the server for both control *and* data traffic. This additional method is called *Passive mode* or *PASV*. PASV is actually the command that the client sends to the FTP server to indicate that it wishes to use Passive Mode.

In passive mode the client initiates both connections to the server which solves the firewall issue often encountered. How Passive FTP works is explained in the following illustration:

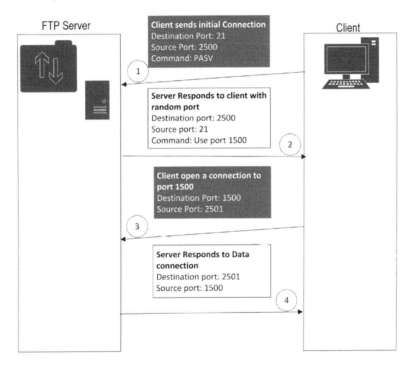

Let us use port 2500 as our source port again;

1. The client initiates a connection to the FTP server's destination command port 21, using the source port 2500 but instead of sending the server a data port to be used, it sends the PASV command instead.
2. This will trigger the FTP server to specify a destination port number (to be used by the client) and send this information back to the client in response to the PASV command. In our example this is 1500.
3. The client will then initiate a second connection to the server using destination port 1500 and source port 2501; this connection will be used to transfer data between the two hosts.
4. The server responds back to the client's request as required.

Even though passive mode solves many potential firewall problems it can result in issues on the server side. Since the FTP server is the one generating random ports you need to open up access on these ports on the server and firewall which leads to security problems. Fortunately most FTP server applications allow you to reduce the number of destination ports the server can generate and most firewalls can also monitor the control connection to dynamically permit the related data transfer connection.

Not all FTP applications support passive mode.

Simple Mail Transfer Protocol (SMTP)

There are three major protocols used for email transactions; these are Post Office Protocol (POP) v3, Internet Message Access Protocol (IMAP) and SMTP (easily confused with SNMP). The major difference between the three is that POP and IMAP are used to download or read email from an email server whereas SMTP is used to transfer (send) emails from both client to server and server to server.

SMTP was first defined in RFC 821 by Jonathan B. Postel in august 1982 but was updated in 2008. The 2008 edition added information regarding Extended SMTP which is also known as Enhanced SMTP. Extended SMTP is a definition of protocol extensions to the SMTP standard and the main identification method is that when clients open a tranmission they start with EHLO (Extended HELLO) instead of the regular HELO. You will read more about this later on in this chapter. Extended SMTP is documented in the RFC 5321.

Just like HTTP and FTP, SMTP is based on text commands that are sent between the two end-points and TCP is used for reliable transmission of the data. The default (or standard) TCP port used is 25 and communication is initiated by the sending system (which is called the sender-SMTP). Once the TCP session has been initiated, the sender-SMTP starts transmitting SMTP commands to the receiver-SMTP (the server). The receiver-SMTP responds with reply messages and three-digit numerical codes for each command that it receives. The most common code that you'll likely see is 250 which indicate the sender-SMTP command was successful. The groups of three-digit response codes are defined and divided as follows;

Three-digit Code responses

Three-digit code	Description
1xx	Success but requires confirmation
2xx	Complete success
3xx	Success so far. More input is expected
4xx	Temporary failures
5xx	Permanent failures

There are two commands that are used to initiate the connection, EHLO or HELO. EHLO is used when the client supports at least one of several possible extensions that are not part of the basic SMTP specification and HELO is used when it does **not**. Most of these extensions are supported by the majority of clients and servers these days and when the client has issued the EHLO command the server will reply with all of the extensions that it currently supports.

How SMTP works is explained in the following illustration:

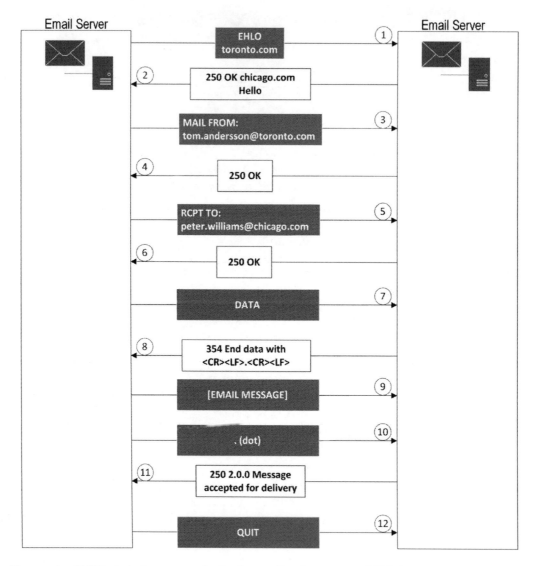

1. The sender-SMTP starts the communication by sending the command EHLO with its own hostname.

    EHLO toronto.com

2. The receiver-SMTP will log the senders IP address and respond back with the code 250, its own hostname and usually a greeting message.

    250 OK chicago.com Hello

Now the receiver-SMTP has identified the sender-SMTP and they are ready to continue.

3. The sender-SMTP will now send the individual sender's email address. This is the information that is located in the "From:" part of the email address. It could also be a mailing list or a redirector.

    MAIL FROM:tom.andersson@toronto.com

4. The receiver-SMTP replies back that the command was successful

    250 OK

It is very important that the email address is in the correct format and that the domain is valid. Otherwise the SMTP server will reject the email.

5. After that, the sender-SMTP will send the addresses of the receiving mail addresses. This could be a single recipient or multiple.

    RCPT TO:peter.williams@chicago.com

 The RCPT TO: command can only be used for a single address but it may be used multiple times where there are multiple recipients.

6. The receiver-SMTP replies back that the command was successful

    250 OK

7. Once all addresses have been added we can now go ahead and send the email. The email will include a header, a blank line, the message body and finally attachments, if there are any. The sender-SMTP will initiate the process using the command DATA.

    DATA

8. The receiver-SMTP will simply respond back with the status code 354 and tell the sender-SMTP to indicate the end of the data input using a single dot. As you remember from the table previously, the status code 3xx means success so far. More input is expected. We now wait until the sender-SMTP has sent all the data.

    354 End data with <CR><LF>.<CR><LF>

9. The sender-SMTP will now send all the data which is the header, message body and attachments.

   [EMAIL MESSAGE]

10. The sender-SMTP ends the data transfer by sending the dot.

    .(dot)

11. The sender-SMTP will receive a 250 message stating that the message was accepted for delivery.

    250 2.0.0 Message accepted for delivery

12. If the sender-SMTP does not have any more messages to send it will close the connection using the QUIT command.

    QUIT

Chapter Summary

- Domain Name System (DNS) is one of the keystones of making communication work. It operates at port 53 and it is responsible for resolving IP addresses into domain names.

- File Transfer Protocol (FTP) is responsible for copying and transferring a file from one system to another and it operates on both port 21 and 20. It can work in both active and passive mode.

- HTTP or Hyper Text Transfer Protocol is the network protocol that delivers resources on web pages on the World Wide Web and it operates on port 80. The commands used are GET, POST and HEAD.

- SIP or Session Initiation Protocol is a protocol used for voice and video calls over IP. The protocol controls the messages that are sent between the two devices such as the establishment of the session.

Chapter Review

In order to test your knowledge and understanding of this chapter, please answer the following questions. You will find the answers and explanations of the questions at the end of this chapter.

1. What port does DNS operate on?
    a. 80
    b. 53
    c. 3389
    d. 25

2. If you want to create a host record for a server you recently installed. What type of DNS record should you create?
    a. SOA Record
    b. PTR Record
    c. CNAME Record
    d. A Record

3. In FTP active mode, which entity will establish the data connection?
    a. The client
    b. The server
    c. Both

4. What is the main advantage of using passive mode FTP?
    a. The connection will not be blocked by the client's firewall
    b. The transfer speed is faster on passive mode
    c. The connection will not be blocked by the server's firewall
    d. Passive mode increases security

5. What does the HTTP status code: **404 Not Found** mean?
    a. The web browser could not resolve the DNS name.
    b. The requested resource does not exist.
    c. The server is offline and does not respond to the request.
    d. The resource has been permanently moved.

6. What is the purpose of the Connection: keep-alive header in HTTP v.1.0?
    a. Connection: keep-alive is used to keep the TCP session active
    b. Connection: keep-alive is used when new connections are open
    c. Connection: keep-alive is used to prevent a connection from timing out.
    d. Connection: keep-alive is used when you want the server to send all of the resources in one single segment.

7. What error code category indicates an error on the server's part?
    a. 2xx
    b. 4xx
    c. 5xx
    d. 1xx

8. You are trying to access a website on the Internet using your web browser and you receive an HTTP code of the category 4xx. Where does the problem reside?
    a. In the Web server
    b. In the Internet Service Provider (ISP)
    c. On the client computer
    d. In the DNS server

9. What is the main difference between SMTP, POP3 and IMAP?
   a. POP3 and IMAP use the UDP protocol; SMTP uses the TCP protocol
   b. SMTP is used to transfer email between end-points; POP3 and IMAP are used to download/access email.
   c. SMTP is only supported on Microsoft environments.
   d. SMTP has higher reliability than POP3 and IMAP

Chapter Review: Answers

You will find the answers to the chapter review questions below:

1. The correct answer is: B
   a. 80
   b. **53**
   c. 3389
   d. 25

DNS operates on port 53. Port 80 is used for HTTP. Port 3389 is used for RDP. Port 25 is used for SMTP.

2. The correct answer is: D
   a. SOA Record
   b. PTR Record
   c. CNAME Record
   d. **A Record**

The correct answer is to create an A record. An A record will provide a name-to-address record that will convert a DNS name to an IP-address.

SOA records are used to indicate the best DNS server in a DNS zone.

A PTR record is only used for reverse lookups.

A CNAME record is used to create an alias for a host record.

3. The correct answer is: B
   a. The client
   b. **The server**
   c. Both

When using FTP in active mode, the server will initiate the data connection and this may cause some problems. Since the data connection is a new connection and it is the server which initiates it, it is very likely that the client's firewall will block the request.

4. The correct answer is: A
   a. **The connection will not be blocked by the client's firewall**
   b. The transfer speed is faster in passive mode
   c. The connection will not be blocked by the server's firewall
   d. Passive mode increases security

In passive mode, both connections are initiated by the client so the connection towards the FTP server will most likely not be blocked by the client's firewall.

5. The correct answer is: B
   a. The web browser could not resolve the DNS name.
   b. **The requested resource does not exist.**
   c. The server is offline and does not respond to the request.
   d. The resource has been moved permanently

All 4xx codes mean that there is an error on the client's side. A 404 Not Found means that the resource that the client has requested does not exist so it is a user input error.

6. The correct answer is: A
   a. **Connection: keep-alive is used to keep the TCP session active.**
   b. Connection: keep-alive is used when new connections are open.
   c. Connection: keep-alive is used to prevent a connection from timing out.
   d. Connection: keep-alive is used when you want the server to send all of the resources in one single segment.

HTTP will always close the TCP connection once the client has received the requested resource. If the client applies the Connection: keep-alive header with every GET request, the HTTP server will keep the connection alive. This means that the TCP Three-way-handshake does not have to be made again and this saves CPU, memory and bandwidth.

7. The correct answer is: C
   a. 2xx
   b. 4xx
   c. **5xx**
   d. 1xx

5xx indicates an error on the server's part.

2xx indicates success of some kind

4xx indicates an error on the client's part

1xx indicates an informational message only

8. The correct answer is: C
    a. In the Web server
    b. In the Internet Service Provider (ISP)
    c. **On the client computer**
    d. In the DNS server

4xx indicates an error on the client's part

9. The correct answer is: B
    a. POP3 and IMAP use the UDP protocol; SMTP uses the TCP protocol
    b. **SMTP is used to transfer email between end-points; POP3 and IMAP are used to download/access email.**
    c. SMTP is only supported on Microsoft environments.
    d. SMTP has higher reliability than POP3 and IMAP

9. F5 Solutions & Technology

All available BIG-IP Modules and Features (or add-ons) simply expose and enable functionality that is already present in TMOS. Some of this functionality is provided by (or within) TMM and is consequently very high performance and some is not (the HMS is used instead) with the obvious result that performance and the throughput that can be maintained are lower.

The number of Modules (not Features) you can run on a hardware appliance is dependent on its specification and the TMOS version installed.

For full details of what Modules combinations are supported when running a TMOS version from 10 through to 11.3 see this matrix from F5: https://support.f5.com/content/dam/f5/kb/global/solutions/sol10288_images.html/big-ip-product-matrix-v35.pdf.

As a general rule of thumb only two Modules can be used on VE and lower end platforms, three or four can be used with middle and top end platforms. From v11.4 the number of supported modules (for both hardware and VE platforms) is mostly only limited by memory, as follows;

- 12Gb or more: any combination of modules
- 8Gb: up to three modules (or two if one is AAM) (GTM and LC do not count toward the limit)
- <8Gb, >4Gb: up to three modules (or standalone if AAM is used) (GTM and LC do not count toward the limit)
- 4Gb or less: up to two modules (or standalone if AAM is used, must be provisioned as Dedicated)

A combination of PEM and CGNAT is only supported on certain platforms.

Note that the following list of modules is unlikely to be definitive for long; F5 update, replace and merge Modules frequently as in the recent case where WAM and WOM are now no longer available separately and have been packaged together as the AAM Module. For the most up to date and detailed (yet biased) information on all available Modules, go here: https://www.f5.com/products/big-ip/.

Access Policy Manager (APM)

APM offers a unified, centralised access security solution for applications and networks, at typical TMM scale and performance; up to 1600 logins per second and 100,000 concurrent users. The module provides an increasing number of features and benefits;

- Dynamic, policy-based, context-aware access control
- Central control for diverse users and locations (remote, mobile, LAN and WLAN)
- Centralised, repeatable and consistent policy application
- Support for the CRLDP and OCSP dynamic certificate revocation protocols
- SSL VPN
- Authentication offload with support for RADIUS, LDAP, MS AD Kerberos, HTTP, RSA SecurID, OAM and TACACS+ authentication methods
- Single Sign On (SSO) features
- Java applet rewriting
- SAML support (from v11.3)
- Multi-vendor VDI support including VMware View, Citrix XenApp & XenDesktop, Microsoft RDP and Java RDP clients
- Enterprise Manager management
- High speed logging (HSL)

Access Policy Manager is available as an LTM or ASM add-on module for physical and Virtual Editions and VIPRION chassis platforms. It is also available as part of the BIG-IP Edge Gateway remote access product.

APM (in particular as part of the Edge Gateway product) is the successor to the FirePass product. APM and LTM or ASM are now the successor to the Edge Gateway product itself. APM also supersedes and vastly improves upon the 'legacy' Advanced Client Authentication (ACA) Module although it is still available.

Advanced Firewall Manager (AFM)

Introduced in early 2013 and available with TMOS v11.3 onwards, AFM simplifies and unifies the configuration and management of the Application Delivery Firewall (ADF) related features of TMOS, TMM and LTM. All relevant features are fully integrated into TMM and therefore provide very high performance; the figures are impressive. The ADF is defined as a combination of the AFM and LTM modules.

Other common TMOS, TMM and LTM features and benefits apply and are possibly even more relevant in a security context;

- Comprehensive DDoS mitigation features as described in the TMM and LTM chapters (and also including those previously available with the PSM)
- The full proxy architecture
- Flexible scaling options and ScaleN
- Full standard HA feature support
- Very high throughput and performance
- TCP Optimisations, reducing response times
- iRules and data and protocol manipulation
- Application awareness and context
- Function consolidation and further integration benefits when used with other modules (particularly ASM, APM and GTM) and features (such as IP Intelligence and Geolocation)
- AVR/Analytics integration
- ICSA Network Firewall Certification
- High speed logging (HSL)
- SSL Termination
- VPN Termination

This module is available for physical and virtual editions and VIPRION chassis platforms.

This LTM add-on Module is dependent on and can only be used in conjunction with LTM.

Application Acceleration Manager (AAM) Core Module

The AAM Core module is available for physical and virtual editions and VIPRION chassis platforms and is included with the base LTM license. AAM Core is a subset of the combination of features previously available in the WAM and WOM Modules. The Full version, detailed next, provides the full suite of features. Core includes;

- Symmetric Compression
- Dynamic Compression
- The SPDY Gateway Feature
- Bandwidth Controllers
- HTTP Caching
- HTTP Compression
- TCP Express
- OneConnect
- iSessions

This Module is dependent on and can only be used in conjunction with LTM.

Application Acceleration Manager (AAM) Full Module

The full AAM module is available for physical and virtual editions and VIPRION chassis platforms. A combination of the previously separately available WAM and WOM Modules, AAM provides the full set of features from those products. Features over and above the Core product include;

- Intelligent Browser Referencing (IBR) – increasing browser cache expiration dates (and other features) to reduce conditional GET requests
- Image Optimization – reducing image size to something appropriate to the requesting device
- Content Reordering – modifying the order of served content to optimise page load times
- Dynamic caching/deduplication
- Multi-protocol optimizations (HTTP, FTP, MAPI, UDP)
- Forward Error Correction (FEC) – provides recovery of lost packets to avoid retransmission and increase throughput on poor networks or links
- Parking Lot – GET request queuing for expired cache objects
- MultiConnect – performs client-side link modifications, which, along with additional DNS entries, 'force' browsers to open additional connections to a site
- PDF Dynamic Linearization
- A Performance Dashboard
- Symmetric and Asymmetric deployment options
- BIG-IP APM, ASM, and AAM layering
- iApps support
- Enterprise Manager Management

This Module is dependent on and can only be used in conjunction with LTM.

Application Security Manager (ASM)

ASM (based on technology gained through the 2004 acquisition of MagniFire Websystems) provides advanced web application aware 'firewall' (WAF) functionality. Unlike most modules it does not run within TMM but the HMS instead and therefore doesn't benefit directly from typical TMM performance and scale. It provides protection against a wide range of attacks and attack vectors including;

- Web scraping (the automatic (mass) extraction of data from a website or sites)
- SQL Injection (execution of SQL code, 'injected' via a website or service's user input methods (such as a form field), on the database backend used by that site's web servers)
- Layer seven (aka Application Layer) DoS and DDoS ((distributed) denial of service attacks aimed at application functions)
- Cross-site scripting (aka XSS) (malicious browser code injection and trusted site permission hijacking)
- JSON payload attacks
- FTP Application attacks
- SMTP Application attacks
- XML Application attacks

Other features include;

- Vulnerability assessment and mitigation
- Integration with vulnerability scanners from Cenzic Hailstorm, IBM Rational AppScan, QualysGuard Web Application Scanning and WhiteHat Sentinel
- Session awareness
- White and black listing
- Regulatory compliance reporting (PCI for example)
- An automatic policy-building engine
- Enterprise Manager management

Application Security Manager is available on a selection of BIG-IP application switches, as a Virtual Edition and as an LTM add-on module for physical and virtual editions and VIPRION chassis platforms.

Local Traffic Manager (LTM)

LTM is a TMOS system module that was named as such with the first release of TMOS, v9, in 2004. LTM Is the latest iteration of the original F5 Networks product, in the sense that it performs load balancing; it's clearly evolved a great deal from there and is now very different from the BIG-IP Controller products first released by the company.

So, what is LTM? In its purest form it's a load balancer; only a very sophisticated one with a significant amount of additional features designed to improve network, server and application performance, security, flexibility, control, visibility and management.

You could think of it as a layer 7 router, making routing decisions based on contextual application data as well as network conditions, business logic and rules, security policy, client host awareness and more. Features such as iCall, iControl, BIG-IQ and others extend this yet further into the operations, orchestration and SDN domains.

Local Traffic Manager is available on all BIG-IP application switches and as a Virtual Edition.

Global Traffic Manager (GTM)

Global Traffic Manager is a TMOS Module and is part of the core, long standing F5 product set. GTM primarily provides DNS based 'global' server load balancing (GSLB) for IPv4 and IPv6 (inter-Data Centre) rather than LTM's intended intra-Data Centre operation). In order to make this Module a more attractive proposition, its feature set has been significantly expanded since 2012 it now runs in TMM natively, rather than within the HMS. The considerable list of features and benefits include;

- Global server load balancing (using DNS to direct traffic between multiple DCs)
- Dynamic ratio load balancing (load balancing based on weights derived from Node metrics such as CPU and memory usage)
- Wide area persistence (DNS response persistence, a same client will get the same response and load balancing will be ignored unless/until a timeout is reached)
- Geographic load balancing (load balancing a client to its geographically closest DC)
- Advanced health monitoring
- QoS Awareness
- DNS Security Extensions (DNSSEC) support (including rate limiting and centralised key management)
- Up to 10 million DNS responses per second using the VIPRION platform
- DNS Caching
- DNS Server consolidation and offload
- DNS DDoS and Local DNS (LDNS) cache poisoning protection
- DNS server load balancing (similar to LTM server load balancing)
- Not BIND based and therefore not subject to BIND security vulnerabilities
- Protocol inspection and validation
- DNS record type ACLs
- IP Anycast support
- IPv6 support

GTM is available as a standalone appliance, a virtual edition and an LTM add-on module for physical and Virtual Editions and on VIPRION chassis platforms. DNS Services are also available as an LTM add-on Feature Set.

Enterprise Manager (EM)

I have to admit that large scale management and monitoring bore me rigid; I blame this on the incumbent vendors happy to milk the cash cow rather than innovate and please their customers. I've actually used Enterprise Manager (v2.x) and whilst I'm unlikely to describe it as exciting it's certainly an improvement over other so-called solutions I've seen and it is very focused. Enterprise Manager has numerous features and benefits;

- Aids with scaling up
- Improves device, application and service visibility and therefore troubleshooting capabilities and capacity planning and forecasting accuracy, as with other centralised management solutions
- Reduces cost and complexity
- Automates common tasks including device configuration backups, ASM policy deployments and reporting
- Custom Alerts and thresholds
- Manages and eases;
    - Device inventory tasks
    - Service contract monitoring
    - SSL TPS monitoring and certificate management
- Centralised configuration management including comprehensive search
- Allows for the use of configuration templates

- Granular (distributed) configuration management
- Uses a local or remote MySQL database allowing enterprise integration and high compatibility with various DB management and reporting tools
- Physical and virtual edition support for LTM, GTM, ASM, LC, WA, WOM (and therefore presumably AAM), APM and Edge Gateway

EM is available as a standalone appliance and a virtual edition. It supports and can manage all hardware appliances including VIPRION and Virtual Editions.

BIG-IQ Product

Planned as the eventual successor to Enterprise Manager, BIG-IQ is a management and orchestration platform with considerable scope. As with any centralized management system, the main goal is to reduce operational costs, reduce administrative overheads and improve scalability. Currently BIG-IQ has four main components each focused on specific functional areas; Cloud, Security, ADC and Device. The following modules are supported;

- LTM [ADC] [Cloud] [Device]
- ASM [Security] [Cloud] [Device]
- AFM [Security] [Cloud] [Device]

General features include;

- A comprehensive set of RESTful APIs
- So-called 'single pane of glass' management
- Centralized audit and control
- License management of BIG-IP Virtual Editions
- Role based access control (RBAC)

Here's a brief overview of each component;

Cloud

Orchestration of BIG-IP deployments in public and private clouds, with integration support for;

- Cisco APIC
- Amazon Web Services (AWS)
- OpenStack
- VMware environments

Additional features include;

- Automatic provisioning
- Dynamic application server 'bursting'
- Tenant awareness and service catalogue provision
- iApps management, provision and templating
- Health and performance monitoring

Security

Centralized

- Policy verification, staging, auditing and monitoring
- Multi-device policy push
- Rule monitoring, reporting and prioritization
- Configuration snapshots

ADC

Centralized management of LTM modules and functions including;

- Virtual Server and Pool state control
- Virtual Server configuration
- Multi-tenancy support
- Health and statistics monitoring
- Configuration templating

Device

Centralized management of physical and virtual BIG-IP appliances, including;

- TMOS Software upgrades
- Remote deployment of appliances hosted within VMware NSX, Cisco APIC, OpenStack or AWS
- Centralized license management for highly flexible provisioning
- Status and usage reporting
- Device discovery and monitoring
- Configuration backup and restore

BIG-IQ is available as a standalone appliance and a virtual edition. It supports and can manage all hardware appliances including VIPRION and Virtual Editions.

Carrier Grade NAT (CGNAT) Module

Introduced with v11.3 this Service Provider focused module provides highly optimised, available and scalable IPv4 and IPv6 Network Address Translation (NAT) and related features such as NAT44, NAT64, DNS64, DS-Lite, endpoint independent mapping, endpoint independent filtering and deterministic NAT.

A number of the Module's features rely on existing TMOS or LTM features such as HA, High-speed Logging (HSL), the full proxy architecture for translating or migrating between IPv4 and IPv6 objects and TCP Express.

CGNAT is available as an LTM add-on module for physical and virtual editions and VIPRION chassis platforms.

iApps Analytics (aka Application Visibility & Reporting - AVR)

Commonly referred to as simply Analytics or BIG-IP Analytics, this Module provides detailed historical and near-time HTTP and TCP/IP related statistics for iApps applications, Virtual Servers, Pool Members, URLs and even specific countries, allowing for in-depth traffic analysis.

The available metrics and counters include transactions per second, server latency, page load time, request and response throughput, sessions, response codes, user agents, HTTP methods, countries, and IP addresses.

Fine grained filters can be used to limit what is recorded, full transaction and data capture is possible and alerts (via SNMP trap, email or syslog) can be configured based on user defined thresholds. Remote logging of statistics data is also supported but unfortunately data cannot be collected via SNMP polling or iControl.

Analytics is available as an LTM add-on feature for physical and virtual editions and VIPRION chassis platforms and is included with the base LTM license. This wasn't always the case. Enterprise Manager can be used as a centralized Analytics reporting tool if required.

IP Intelligence Service

This subscription-based service is designed to be used in conjunction with ASM or LTM to block malicious traffic at the very edge of your network, thus increasing efficiency by avoiding processing overheads further within your infrastructure. The service provides a constantly updated database of IP addresses known to be used in relation to activities such as;

- Phishing sites and other fraudulent activity
- DoS, DDoS, SYN flood and other anomalous traffic attacks
- Botnet command and control servers and infected zombie machines
- Proxy and anonymization services
- Probes, host scans, domain scans and password brute force attacks

This database can then be referenced by iRules to allow for automated blocking, allowing for context aware policy decisions.

Link Controller Product (& Module)

LC Provides features to manage, aggregate and monitor multiple ISP internet connections (links) and controls the traffic flow across them, based on multiple dynamic factors and user specified criteria. Traffic optimization and prioritisation features are also available to improve application performance. TCPExpress, IPv6, iRules and SNAT are fully supported and there is an optional compression feature.

BIG-IP Link Controller is available as a standalone version and as a LTM add-on module for BIG-IP application switches.

MobileSafe Product & Service

This enterprise level product aims to protect and secure corporate mobile devices from various threats and ensure the company, its networks and its data are protected. The software is available for iOS and Android devices, with management achieved through a web portal run by the F5 Security Operations Center (SOC). Features include;

- Mitigates against various mobile device threats including; application tampering, unpatched operating systems, keyloggers, certificate forging and DNS spoofing
- Strong validation of SSL certificates
- Application-level encryption
- Malware detection
- Rooted and jail-broken device detection

Edge Gateway

Edge Gateway was available as a virtual edition and on a selection of BIG-IP application switches but not on VIPRION chassis platforms. It is a combination of the APM, WA and WOM modules, providing secure remote access (RAS) gateway features such as;

- ICSA Certified SSL VPN
- Clientless access
- End point validation and security and access policy enforcement
- Single Sign On (SSO) and credential caching
- Multi-factor authentication
- Symmetric acceleration (if the client is using the Edge Client software)
- Wide AAA protocol support
- Wide remote access protocol support (Citrix, RDP, ActiveSync etc.)
- IPv6 Support
- Enterprise Manager Management

Policy Enforcement Manager (PEM)

Available from TMOS v11.3, PEM provides mobile network subscriber and traffic reporting, management and control. The module provides a host of features and benefits, presumably based on the assets of the Traffix Systems acquisition;

- Comprehensive analytics including per session and per application statistics
- L7 Intelligent traffic steering (to appropriate caches, CDNs, proxies) and bandwidth control to reduce network congestion and increase performance
- Traffic classification (p2p, Voip, Web, streaming)
- Deep packet inspection
- Rate limiting, QoS, CoS and fair usage policy enforcement
- Charging system integration (PCRF, OCS)
- 3GPP standards based
- Subscriber awareness (IP address, IMSI, RADIUS data, Gx and/or mobile tower) and application context
- Function consolidation and further integration benefits when used with other modules (particularly CGNAT and AFM)

- Very high throughput and performance
- TCP Optimisations, reducing response times
- iRules and data and protocol manipulation
- Flexible scaling options and ScaleN
- Full standard HA feature support
- High speed logging (HSL)

Policy Enforcement Manager is available only as a standalone appliance on high-end physical appliance a virtual edition and VIPRION chassis platforms.

Secure Web Gateway (SWG) Cloud-based Service & Module

SWG Provides control, security and management of inbound and outbound user driven web traffic; it's effectively a secure internet proxy, or web access gateway as F5 like to call it. The module itself provides integration between Access Policy Manager and Cloud-based Websense security services and updates. Combined, these components offer;

- URL categorization and filtering
- User tracking
- Malware protection
- Endpoint integrity checking
- Policy-based blocking
- Real-time threat intelligence
- Detailed logging
- Splunk reporting

Silverline Cloud-based Service

The Silverline service (Software as a Service or SaaS) delivers two core internet related security functions; DDoS protection and web application firewalling. Rather than implement these yourself on-site, you can simply transparently route your inbound traffic through the F5 SOC and let them do the hard work for you. The services are as follows;

- **F5 Silverline DDoS Protection** - typical TMOS supported DDoS protection and features, along with the resources and bandwidth required to sustain a high volume attack.
- **F5 Silverline Web Application Firewall** - ASM features (see the earlier section), along with the processing resources and bandwidth required to mitigate attacks.

WebSafe Service & Module

The WebSafe service provides protection for the users and customers using your website properties, as well as the sites themselves. Traffic is transparently passed through the F5 SOC where it is analyzed and malicious traffic dropped before it reaches your site.

Additionally, the BIG-IP module component of this service, the Fraud Protection Service (FPS) provides additional features and protections at the local, Virtual Server level. This is fully integrated into the GUI from TMOS v11.6.

The protection and features provided by this combination include;

- Malware prevention
- Phishing and pharming attack mitigation
- Fraud detection and prevention
- Application-level encryption
- Transaction monitoring, analysis and integrity checking
- Device and behavior analysis
- Integration with MobileSafe
- Incident reporting
- Real-time alerts dashboard

ARX

Based on the acquisition of Acopia in 2007 and released under the F5 brand but continuing to use the original name, ARX is the data equivalent of a network load balancer, featuring file system virtualisation, load balancing and logical abstraction of the physical storage environment (referred to as the Global Namespace).

In the same way that BIG-IP platforms run TMOS, the ARX platform runs the Data Management Operating System (DMOS).

Features of ARX and DMOS include;

- Compatibility with the vast majority of Network Attached Storage (NAS) devices and file servers
- Capability for handling more than two billion files
- High performance and throughput
- No proprietary stub files on file storage assets
- Redundant hardware and network components and HA clustering
- 10Gb interface support
- CLI and GUI management
- SNMP, extensive logging and reporting, port mirroring and packet capture
- Data replication and automated tiering
- NFS (v2 and v3) and CIFS protocol support
- A patented split-path architecture separates the data and control paths in the system
- An open API

Benefits include;

- Physical storage changes are hidden from clients
- A single point of control (as with BIG-IP and TMOS)
- Reduced storage expenses with automated tiering policies and easy integration of new, cheaper storage (fewer costs, lower overhead, no disruption)
- Optimise existing storage by consolidating all storage into a single unified storage pool
- Easy, non-disruptive migration of data between devices, storage capacity and device moves, adds and changes.
- As with the ADC benefits detailed earlier, ARX abstracts the physical storage complexities as it works like a proxy for client connections
- Multi-vendor, multi-platform support

- Dynamic capacity balancing
- Reduced backups and backup time

 ARX Becomes end of sale on the 1st of November 2014.

End of Life Products

Products and modules that have gone end of Life (EoL) in the last couple of years include;

- ARX (file system load balancing)
- WebAccelerator (WAM)
- WAN Optimization Manager (WOM)
- Message Security Module (MSM)
- Protocol Security Manager (PSM)
- Firepass

iRules

iRules are available with LTM and other TMOS system modules including GTM and ASM. They are user created Tool Command Language (Tcl) programs or scripts that are assigned to Virtual Servers and run (or triggered) by one or more user specified Events related to that Virtual Server, such as a new TCP connection or HTTP GET request.

These Tcl scripts (a programmer might even call them 'event handlers') can contain any number of Commands that can be used to make load balancing decisions, modify packet content, direct traffic flow, collect statistics and do just about anything else you can think of between layers two through seven and beyond. This makes your network, traffic, routing and application flow programmable and contextual (at the point LTM handles it at least). This gives you a great deal of power and control.

Tcl itself is a relatively simple programming language to write, read and understand whilst still being very powerful and flexible. Variables, Functions, Operators, external files (iFiles), encryption, external UDP and TCP connections (Sideband Connections), Geolocation and security functions are all supported. To give you an idea of what an iRule looks like, here's an example that simply redirects an insecure HTTP request to HTTPS by returning a HTTP status code of 302 (a redirect) and the desired secure HTTPS URL;

```
when HTTP_REQUEST {
  HTTP::redirect https://[HTTP::host][HTTP::uri]
}
```

iRules are pre-compiled into byte code to provide fast performance, so don't think using them will impact your device (unless you use a really poorly written iRule!). iRules are challenging for most but stick with them and you'll soon learn to love them. They are great for handling unique customer conditions and customisations, controlling and routing traffic contextually, implementing business policy, using client specific decision making and much, much more. The possibilities are endless and the only limit is your imagination (although there is always room for improvement).

iApps

iApps is the name for a collection of features available from TMOS v11 onwards; a so-called 'framework' for deploying and managing application delivery services and their related BIG-IP configuration. This is done using custom templates and question-driven GUI based forms to automate complex tasks and/or processes. The templates (which control the possible configurations) are created using the tmsh scripting language. The related forms are created using a simple scripting language called Application Presentation Language (APL) and the overall iApp output (once a user completes the relevant forms) is the necessary configuration and objects. This 'package' can then be managed and administered (or even removed) as a whole to reduce administration overhead.

iApps can be used across a number of modules including APM, LTM and WAM.

As with any template derived automated configuration and process, particularly with complex configurations, iApps can help to reduce configuration time and errors and increase accuracy. iApps can also be used in tandem with other features such as User Roles and iRules to provide fine grained configuration control across administrative groups. Equally, iApps can be very complex.

iControl

iControl is an open SOAP (XML) web services and REST enabled API (and related SDK) that provides control of the configuration of an F5 BIG-IP as well as access to configuration object status and statistics. These interfaces are accessed using Web Services Description Language (WSDL) version 1.1 for SOAP and HTTP for REST.

The iControl API is only accessible using SSL/TLS via a device's dedicated management interface and uses HTTP basic authentication (via WWW-Authentication HTTP headers) using the same authentication method(s) configured for accessing the device's GUI or CLI via SSH.

Interestingly, the iControl SOAP API cannot be specifically disabled as it is a server-side module of the administrative web server (which serves the management GUI). Additionally as iControl is single threaded, performance, by today's standards, may be poor.

The benefits of iControl include;

- Standards based integration into existing extensible management, monitoring, workflow and application systems
- Automated provisioning and de-provisioning of servers and applications
- Automation and configuration management and efficiency
- Service Orientated Architecture (SOA) integration
- Software Defined Networking (SDN) integration

Some examples of products where iControl is used include; VMware vCenter integration, Microsoft System Center Virtual Machine Manager (SCVMM) with the F5 Management Pack, the F5 iRules Editor and F5 Enterprise Manager.

iHealth

iHealth is a free online tool available here: https://ihealth.f5.com/ that can be used to check the health, security and configuration of a device and ensure it is running efficiently.

The service revolves around Qkview files (uploaded by the user) which can be easily generated on any F5 BIG-IP device using the `qkview` command. This file contains the device configuration files, logs and other diagnostic command outputs.

The iHealth system parses and analyses the contents of the Qkview file and displays any information on identified configuration issues, known issues, common mistakes, software version bugs and best practice guidance, in a friendly, graphical format. Recommended remediation information is also provided along with links to relevant AskF5 articles.

The system benefits both F5 and the user; F5 get fewer support calls and users avoid the need for F5 support involvement in basic or commonly occurring issue scenarios. iHealth is updated on a regular basic to take account of new bugs and issues and TMOS versions.

iQuery

iQuery is an F5 Networks proprietary, TCP-based (port 4353) XML-like protocol that exchanges configuration, statistical, probe and metric information between BIG-IP platforms.

Communication is bi-directional, SSL secured (after initial device discovery when certificates are exchanged) and also gzip compressed. SSH is sometimes used as a fall-back when iQuery communication fails. iQuery Can be used through the management or TMM switch interfaces.

iQuery is used for a number of purposes when a device is under the management of Enterprise Manager but primarily for collecting statistics and configurations. It is also used for communication between the LTM and GTM modules.

Full Application Proxy

The first release of TMOS, v9 in 2005 introduced the Full Application Proxy; providing a significant improvement in functionality over the prior Packet Based Proxy architecture used in previous products. The Packet Based Proxy (covered in the next section) is still available and can still be the most desirable, high performance solution where only L2-L4 functions are required.

The Full Application Proxy architecture is just that; it functions as a proxy that fully and completely separates the client and server sides of a connection. There are in fact two connections; the client side connection is terminated on the proxy (the load balancer) and a new, separate connection is established to the server. The proxy acts in the role of server to the client and client to the real server. There are two related connection table entries too; one for client side, one for server side. Each can have independent parameters applied, such as idle timeouts, buffers, MTU, window size and so on. The following diagram demonstrates this full proxy functionality in respect to the TCP/IP connections;

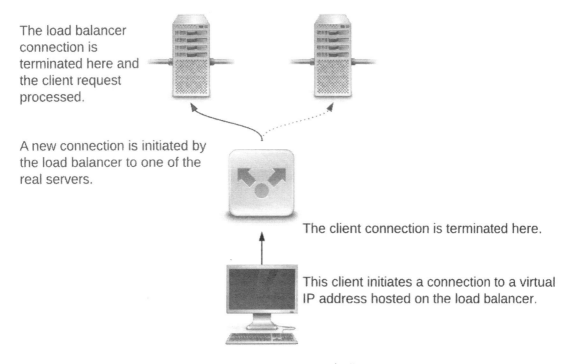

This allows for a huge number of features and functions to be dynamically applied to each connection separately, as well as the inspection, manipulation and modification of application layer data. This architecture provides the foundation for many of the advanced features described in this book (as well as many, many more that are not) such as; iRules (working above OSI Model layer four), advanced Persistence methods, SSL offload, TCP Optimisations and HTTP Compression, Caching and Pipelining. If you don't actually require any of these features or the benefits of two independent connections then using the Packet Based Proxy is probably preferable as it is simpler and will provide even higher performance.

Note in some documentation and other materials published by F5 the Full Application Proxy is sometimes referred to as the *Fast* Application Proxy.

Packet Based Proxy/FastL4

A Packet Based Proxy architecture is what was employed in the first generation of load balancers and generally only operates up to OSI Model layer four, the transport layer. Sometimes referred to as a Half Proxy, there is only a single connection which the load balancer modifies the TCP/IP parameters of, without the client or server being aware. The half proxy does not act as either a client or server from a TCP/IP perspective. The actual connection state and flow of packets is generally not controlled in any way. The following diagram demonstrates this half proxy functionality in respect to the TCP/IP connection;

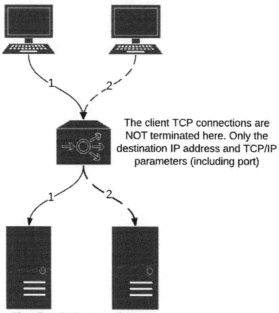

Unlike with the Full Application Proxy, the advanced features described in this book (as well as many, many more that are not) such as; iRules (working above OSI Model layer four), advanced Persistence methods, SSL offload, TCP Optimisations and HTTP Compression, Caching and Pipelining are not available with the Packet Based Proxy.

Even though a Packet Based Proxy operates up to layer four, the Full Application Proxy still provides some advantages over it even at this layer, due to its use of separate client and server side connections and the resulting ability to modify and control separate parameters for each.

 The lines between the half and full proxy can sometimes get rather blurry as one obviously evolved from the other resulting in features that can be common to both. In the most simplistic terms, the half proxy does not does not act as a TCP/IP client or server; it operates transparently with the single connection established between the real client and server. The full proxy acts as a TCP/IP server to the client and client to the real server; it terminates the first and initiates the second and thus there are two independent connections.

High Availability (HA)

TMOS Offers a wide range of software HA features when two or more BIG-IP physical or virtual appliances are deployed. HA is essential considering the BIG-IP's typically central position in the network and the applications and services provided through it. HA Also allows for traffic processing to be moved between devices when maintenance is required, for instance, when performing an upgrade. These features (along with many security focussed features don't forget) ensure continuity of service in as many failure scenarios as possible and include;

- HA Clusters (the focus of this section and the exam)
- Device Service Clustering (features for HA Clustering for up to 8 devices)
- Device Groups (a collection of devices providing HA)
- ConfigSync (configuration exchange within a Device Group)
- Traffic Groups (Virtual Addresses, NATs and related configuration objects that move between devices when failures occur)
- Floating Self IPs (interface or VLAN IP addresses that move between devices when failures occur)
- MAC Masquerade (Floating Self IP related MAC addresses that also move between devices to prevent the need for ARP relearning)
- Serial and Network Failover (device failure detection)
- Connection Mirroring (exchange of connection state information between devices)
- Fast Failover HA Groups (trunks and pool member failure detection)
- VLAN Fail-safe (VLAN traffic loss detection)
- System Fail-safe (services and switch board failure detection)

Trunking & LACP (redundant physical links and related failure detection). The exam only requires an understanding of two member HA Clusters and their two operating modes; Active/Active and Active/Standby, discussed in the following sections.

Active/Standby

With an Active/Standby two member HA cluster, one unit is active and processes all traffic and a second is standby and does not; the entire device configuration is typically synchronised between devices and connection and persistence state data can also be mirrored. In the event that a failure is detected on the active member, all traffic processing moves to the standby member, which becomes active.

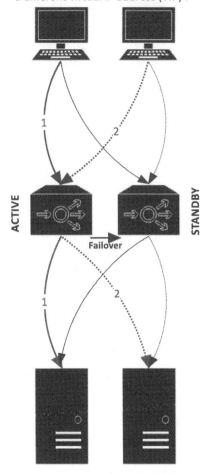

Two clients establish a TCP connection to a different virtual IP address (VIP).

Note that HA pair failover (or failback) is an all or nothing affair unless using active/active mode; *all* Virtual Addresses, Floating Self IPs, MAC Masquerade addresses, Address Translations, traffic and traffic processing moves between the two devices.

 Node and Pool Member Health Monitors, ICMP, ARP, Packet Filters and other security features and dynamic routing protocols always operate on all operational cluster members, regardless of state.

Active/Active

With an Active/Active two member HA cluster, specific traffic processing objects (Virtual Addresses, Floating Self IP Addresses, MAC Masquerade Addresses and Address Translations) are assigned to and process traffic (are active) on a particular cluster member until a failure occurs. Other objects are assigned to and process traffic on the other cluster member, again, until a failure occurs.

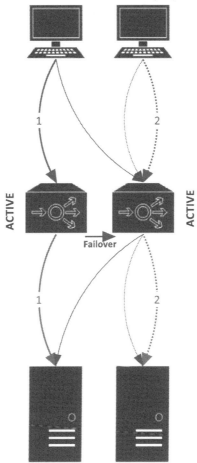

When a failure does occurs on a cluster member, only the traffic processing objects active on that member move to the remaining member. As with Active/Standby, the entire device configuration is typically synchronised between devices and connection and persistence state data can also be mirrored.

 Node and Pool Member Health Monitors, ICMP, ARP, Packet Filters and other security features and dynamic routing protocols always operate on all operational cluster members, regardless of state.

Device Service Clustering (DSC)

DSC Is the collection of features that allow for between two and eight Devices to be clustered in a Device Group to provide HA scaling; user-specified configuration object Traffic Groups are synchronised and can float between devices. DSC Allows for the Active/Standby and Active/Active HA clustering we've just covered. Connection state can also be mirrored (but only between two devices). Failback can also be controlled and preferred failover order specified.

DSC is configured and controlled through a number of objects and relationships as follows;

- Devices – individual devices participating in HA that each have a number of unique device attributes and objects
- Device Trusts – authenticated Devices and communications between them
- Device Groups – a defined group of Devices participating in HA
- ConfigSync – configuration synchronisation between member Devices in Device Groups - see the next section for more detail
- Traffic Groups – collections of local traffic configuration objects that failover between member Devices in Device Groups
- Failover & Fail-safe – features that actually cause a Traffic Group failover to occur
- Mirroring – stateful mirroring of connection and session information between member Devices in Device Groups

ConfigSync

ConfigSync is a feature which synchronises the configuration between two or more devices in a DSC Device Group, ensuring that in the event of a failover or the failback of a Traffic Group, the newly active unit for it has an identical configuration to that of the previously active unit and processes traffic in exactly the same way.

ConfigSync is performed manually unless the AutoSync feature is used.

You typically make changes on a single device and synchronise the new configuration to the Device Group (and therefore all its member Devices). You can also use it to reverse any configuration changes you've made to a Device by synchronising from the Device Group to the Device.

The complimentary ConfigSync Autodetect feature automatically checks the configuration of each unit, reports it to the other, determines if they are synchronised and reports the synchronisation status in the management GUI and CLI.

Traffic Groups

Traffic Groups (TGs) are the means by which layer three local traffic configuration objects; Floating Self IPs, SNAT, NAT Translation and Virtual Addresses are grouped and assigned to be processed by a Device in a Device Group. It's these objects that will move between Devices in the Device Group should a failover occur. Keep in mind that it's Virtual Addresses, not Virtual Servers that are assigned to TGs; multiple Virtual Servers can share a single Virtual Address and these couldn't be split across two TGs.

Whichever device is used to create the TG will become active initially. Until more are created, all relevant layer three local traffic configuration objects are placed in the default TG named: traffic-group-1. Layer three objects that do not move (or float) between Devices on failover are placed in the traffic-group-local-only TG.

You can see a list of what objects are in what TG using menu path: Network > Traffic Groups > 'Name' > Failover Objects. Note that any device with an active Traffic Group will show as Online (Active).

Floating Self IPs

A Floating Self IP is a virtual, shared IP address for a device interface or VLAN that is 'owned' and used by the Device with the active role for the Traffic Group the Floating Self IP is assigned to. Traffic to the Device would normally be routed to this shared address and traffic from the device has this shared address as its source IP address. Should a failover occur, the address 'floats' to the newly active Device to ensure traffic is directed to it.

The MAC Masquerade feature can also be used at the Traffic Group level to ensure the MAC address associated with the floating Self IP also floats and does not change when a failover occurs, which can avoid traffic loss.

MAC Masquerade

This feature is used to create a virtual, shared MAC address that is associated with a Traffic Group used by the active Device in a Device Group. When the Traffic Group floats to another unit so does the MAC address ensuring that neighbouring network devices such as firewalls and switches with MAC security features enabled are not required to accept Gratuitous ARPs (used to inform devices of the change in MAC address associated with the IP address that's normally required).

Force to Standby

The Force to Standby setting allows you to force any Traffic Group that's active on a Device to the standby state on that Device and have some other Device in the Device Group become the active Device. This is clearly very helpful when performing software upgrades, allowing you to move traffic processing off a device you'd like to upgrade and then back once it's done.

Note that forcing a Device into the standby state generates Gratuitous ARPs on the newly active Device, to the surrounding network informing devices of a MAC address change for the Floating Self IP(s) on relevant VLAN(s) unless the MAC Masquerade feature is used.

You can force one or more or all Traffic Groups on a Device to the standby state, at the same time.

Chapter Summary

- ❖ Access Policy Manager (APM) offers a unified, centralised access security solution for applications and networks, at typical TMM scale and performance; up to 1600 logins per second and 100,000 concurrent users.

- ❖ LTM is in its purest form a very sophisticated load balancer with a significant amount of additional features designed to improve network, server and application performance, security, flexibility, control, visibility and management.

- ❖ Global Traffic Manager is a TMOS Module and is part of the core, long standing F5 product set. GTM primarily provides DNS based 'global' server load balancing (GSLB) for IPv4 and IPv6 (inter-Data Centre) rather than LTM's intended intra-Data Centre operation.

- Edge Gateway is a combination of the APM, WA and WOM modules, providing secure remote access (RAS) gateway

- iRules are available with LTM and other TMOS system modules including GTM and ASM. They are user created Tool Command Language (Tcl) programs or scripts that are assigned to Virtual Servers and run (or triggered) by one or more user specified Events related to that Virtual Server, such as a new TCP connection or HTTP GET request.

- iHealth is a free online tool that can be used to check the health, security and configuration of a device and ensure it is running efficiently. It revolves around Qkview files (uploaded by the user) which can be easily generated on any F5 BIG-IP device using the qkview command or using the Web based GUI.

- iQuery is an F5 Networks proprietary, TCP-based (port 4353) XML-like protocol that exchanges configuration, statistical, probe and metric information between BIG-IP platforms.

- The Full Application Proxy architecture functions as a proxy that fully and completely separates the client and server sides of a connection. There are in fact two connections; the client side connection is terminated on the proxy (the load balancer) and a new, separate connection is established to the server.

Chapter Review

In order to test your knowledge and understanding of this chapter, please answer the following questions. You will find the answers and explanations of the questions at the end of this chapter.

1. The CEO wants you to set up a remote access solution for applications and networks and wants you to implement this on your F5 BIG-IP device. What BIG-IP module do you need to enable and configure in order to achieve this?

    a. EM - Enterprise Manager
    b. LTM - Local Traffic Manager
    c. GTM - Global Traffic Manager
    d. APM - Access Policy Manager

2. What BIG-IP module protects you from a wide range of attacks such as SMTP application attacks, SQL Injections and Web scraping?

    a. ASM - Application Security Manager
    b. WAM - WebAccelerator
    c. LTM - Local Traffic Manager
    d. APM - Access Policy Manager

3. What features does the BIG-IP module, Enterprise Manager (EM) have? Select all answers that apply.

    a. Centralized configuration management
    b. Load Balance incoming network traffic.
    c. Automates common tasks including device configuration backups
    d. Optimizes network traffic

4. What is the primary purpose of the BIG-IP module GTM?

    a. Provide load balancing for intra-Data Centre operation making decisions based on for example application data and network conditions.
    b. Provide central management for all BIG-IP devices located in your environment.
    c. Provide DNS based 'global' server load balancing (GSLB) for inter-Data Centre.
    d. Provide file system virtualization and load balancing of the physical storage environment.

5. What scripting language is iRules based on?

   a. Lua
   b. Perl
   c. PHP
   d. Tcl ✓

6. Which of the following is the correct description of an iRule?

   a. ✓ They are user created Tool Command Language scripts that can be used to make load balancing decisions, modify packet content and direct traffic flow.
   b. They are open SOAP (XML) web services and REST enabled API that provides control of the configuration of an F5 BIG-IP.
   c. They are used for deploying and managing application delivery services and their related BIG-IP configuration.
   d. They collect troubleshooting information that can be sent to F5 support.

7. In the F5 BIG-IP, which Proxy mode would you need to use to allow for full traffic inspection, compression, SSL termination?

   a. Packet Based Proxy
   b. ✓ Full Application Proxy

Chapter Review: Answers

You will find the answers to the chapter review questions below:

1. The correct answer is: D

   a. EM - Enterprise Manager
   b. LTM - Local Traffic Manager
   c. GTM - Global Traffic Manager
   d. **APM - Access Policy Manager**

- EM - Enterprise Manager is used to manage multiple F5 BIG-IP devices in your network.
- LTM - Local Traffic Manager is used to load balance traffic between your servers.
- GTM - Global Traffic Manager provides DNS based 'global' server load balancing (GSLB).
- APM - Access Policy Manager offers a unified, centralised access security solution for applications and networks.

2. The correct answer is: A

   a. **ASM - Application Security Manager**
   b. WAM - WebAccelerator
   c. LTM - Local Traffic Manager
   d. APM - Access Policy Manager

- ASM - Application Security Manager provides advanced web application aware 'firewall' (WAF) functionality such as web scraping, SQL Injection and SMTP Application attacks.
- WAM – WebAccelerator provides a host of features designed to optimise and increase HTTP-based website performance and responsiveness.
- LTM - Local Traffic Manager is used to load balance traffic between your servers.
- APM - Access Policy Manager offers a unified, centralised access security solution for applications and networks.

3. The correct answers are: A,C

   a. **Centralized configuration management**
   b. Load Balance incoming network traffic.
   c. **Automates common tasks including device configuration backups**
   d. Optimizes network traffic

EM - Enterprise Manager is used to manage multiple F5 BIG-IP devices in your network with features such as centralized configuration management and automation of common tasks.

4. The correct answer is: C

   a. Provide load balancing for intra-Data Centre operation making decisions based on for example application data and network conditions.
   b. Provide central management for all BIG-IP devices located in your environment.
   c. **Provide DNS based 'global' server load balancing (GSLB) for inter-Data Centre.**
   d. Provide file system virtualization and load balancing of the physical storage environment.

- GTM - Global Traffic Manager provides DNS based 'global' server load balancing (GSLB).
- File system virtualisation, load balancing and logical abstraction of the physical storage environment is something that the BIG-IP module ARX handles.
- Central Management is handled by the BIG-IP module Enterprise Manager (EM)
- LTM – Local Traffic Manager is responsible for load balancing intra-Data Centre operation and makes decisions based on for example application data and network conditions.

5. The correct answer is: D

   a. Lua
   b. Perl
   c. PHP
   d. **Tcl**

6. The correct answer is: A

   a. **They are user created Tool Command Language scripts that can be used to make load balancing decisions, modify packet content and direct traffic flow.**
   b. They are open SOAP (XML) web services and REST enabled API that provides control of the configuration of an F5 BIG-IP.
   c. They are used for deploying and managing application delivery services and their related BIG-IP configuration.
   d. They collect troubleshooting information that can be sent to F5 support.

- iControl is an open SOAP (XML) web services and REST enabled API (and related SDK) that provides control of the configuration of an F5 BIG-IP as well as access to configuration object status and statistics.
- iApps is the name for a collection of features available from TMOS v11 onwards; a so-called 'framework' for deploying and managing application delivery services and their related BIG-IP configuration.
- iHealth is a free online tool available here that can be used to check the health, security and configuration of a device and ensure it is running efficiently. This information can be sent to F5 support to help the troubleshooting of an on-going case.

7. The correct answer is: B

   a. Packet Based Proxy
   b. **Full Application Proxy**

The first release of TMOS, v9 in 2005 introduced the Full Application Proxy; providing a significant improvement in functionality over the prior Packet Based Proxy architecture used in previous products.

10. Load Balancing Essentials

So, now we've covered the OSI model, basic networking concepts and operation and the software products available it's finally time to move on to the heart of what application delivery is all about. It is not necessarily as simple and clear cut as you might think so please don't skip this section believing you know this subject inside-out already, you might be surprised.

What Is A Load Balancer?

In its most basic form a load balancer performs three interrelated functions; monitoring hosts (servers, caches, routers or anything else), acting as a proxy for those hosts and load balancing traffic across them.

Destination 'real' host availability and possibly metrics related to performance and load are constantly monitored by the load balancer (the monitoring function). The load balancer receives traffic (packets, connections or requests) that would otherwise be sent directly to a single host if it wasn't in place (the proxy function) and directs that traffic to one of any number of destination hosts (physical or virtual) that actually service that traffic (the load balancing function).

Monitoring information is used to influence load balancing decisions in real time. For instance, an unavailable server will not have any traffic sent to it; a server under high load can have less traffic sent to it and so on. Many different methods and algorithms can be configured and used to control the 'balance' of traffic across those hosts.

The following diagram illustrates these functions using the Full Application Proxy, in relation to a HTTP flow.

Load Balancer Primary Functions (Full Proxy)

Clients establish a TCP connection to a virtual IP address (VIP) hosted on the load balancer and send a HTTP GET request.

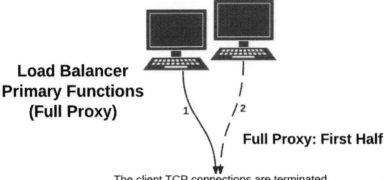

Full Proxy: First Half

The client TCP connections are terminated here by the load balancer.

Host Monitoring
The load balancer is constantly monitoring the status of each 'real' server host. The unavailable server (2) will not be used or considered in a load balancing decision.

Load Balancing
The load balancer makes a decision on which real server will receive each request. Round Robin is shown here.

A new TCP connection is established by the load balancer to each real server. The HTTP GET requests are sent.

Full Proxy: Second Half

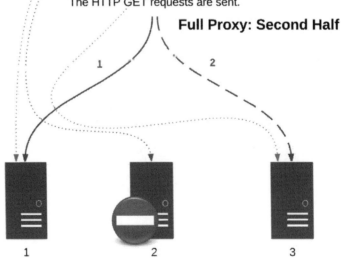

The load balancer TCP connections are terminated by the relevant real servers and each client GET request is processed and responded to.

Automatic Port & Address Translation

Just so you fully understand the TCP/IP implications, it is worth noting that when load balancing;

- NAT of the destination IP address occurs when the inbound traffic is sent to a real server host.
    - When using the Full Application Proxy architecture, as the load balancer is acting as a full proxy it's not actually NAT; the inbound connection is terminated and a new outbound one created with a different destination IP address. Of course it's far easier to think of it as NAT.
    - When using the Packet Based Proxy architecture, it is actually NAT.

- Translation of the destination TCP or UDP port occurs when the inbound traffic is sent to a real server host (if the Virtual Server and real server listening ports are different).
    - When using the Full Application Proxy architecture, as with NAT, port translation isn't really occurring but it's probably easier to think of it like that.
    - When using the Packet Based Proxy architecture, it is actually PAT.

- NAT of the source IP address occurs when the outbound traffic is sent back to the client (this is the reverse of the inbound NAT).
    - When using the Full Application Proxy architecture, as noted previously, as the load balancer is acting as a full proxy it's not actually NAT.
    - When using the Packet Based Proxy architecture, it is actually NAT.

- Translation of the source TCP or UDP port occurs when the outbound traffic is sent back to the client (if the Virtual Server and real server listening ports are different) (this is the reverse of the inbound port translation).
    - When using the Full Application Proxy architecture, as noted previously, port translation isn't really occurring but it's probably easier to think of it like that.
    - When using the Packet Based Proxy architecture, it is actually PAT.

- This all occurs transparently to the connecting client host.

- This 'NATting' does not need to be configured; it is automatic, even where the Virtual Address is IPv6 and the real servers use IPv4.

The following diagrams illustrate this automatic translation for inbound and outbound packets respectively, when using the Full Application Proxy.

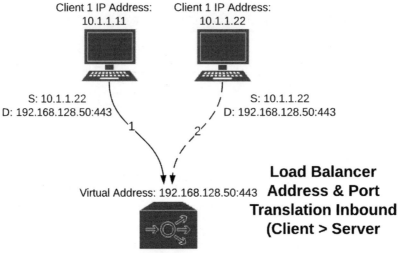
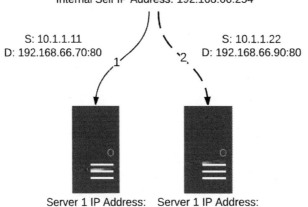

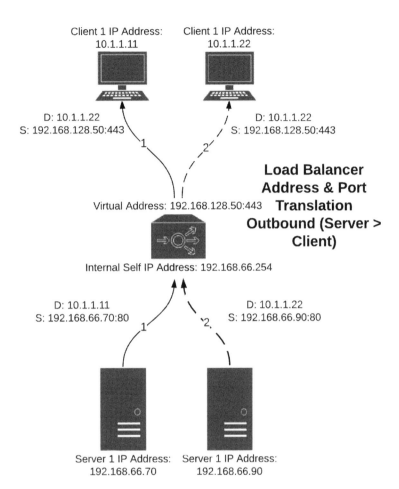

Load Balancing Methods

TMOS Supports a large number of load balancing methods (or algorithms) used to automatically distribute connections and traffic across real servers. The exam only covers two of the most popular and simple methods; Round Robin and Least Connections, which are described in detail next. As you'll find as you progress through the certification program, most of the more advanced methods are based on one of these two.

 Features such as Persistence can override the load balancing method and logic.

Round Robin

This is the simplest (and default) form of Load Balancing; each new connection is sent to the next Pool Member in the Pool in a strict circular (Round Robin) fashion. If there are two Pool Members and three clients connect one after the other, the first client connection will be sent to the first Pool Member, the second to the second and the third back to the first Pool Member.

This is a so-called static Load Balancing method; aside from Pool Member status, no real-time, near-time or historical information influences how load balancing occurs and the distribution of connections between Pool Members is strictly equal.

This method is suitable where the real servers have similar capabilities.

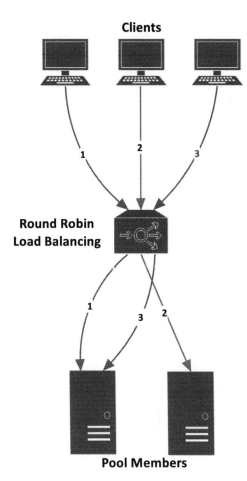

Least Connections

This method load balances new connections to whichever real server has the least number of active connections and is recommended by F5 in most cases.

This is a dynamic Load Balancing method; real-time information influences how load balancing occurs and the distribution of connections between Pool Members are unequal and changes over time.

This method is suitable where the real servers have similar capabilities.

As each connection can have differing overheads (one could related to a request for a HTML page, the other a 20Mb PDF document that needs to be generated and downloaded) this is not a reliable way of distributing bandwidth and processing load between servers.

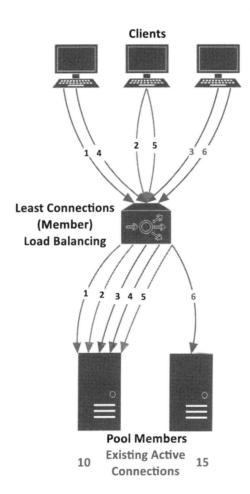

Persistence

In most cases Persistence, also known as stickiness, affinity or session persistence, is used to direct additional connections from a client to the same Virtual Server to the same real server as the existing (initial) connection. This ensures that any state information stored only on that server, related to the session the connections form a part of, is valid. If those connections were Load Balanced to different servers the lack of the session state context (and loss of server affinity) will most likely result in application errors.

Just to ensure clarity, let's define what a session is; an Application Session is the communication channel between two hosts, used to exchange information and complete Transactions of some kind. It can be comprised of one <u>or more</u> underlying TCP connections between the client and server (virtual or otherwise). A session is typically stateful, with various parameters and variables (including unique IDs and authentication information) assigned and valid only for the session in question. See the HTTP Pipelining section of the Application Delivery Platforms chapter for an example of a protocol that uses multiple TCP connections within a single session to increase performance.

With some message based protocols the opposite is true; rather than one session being capable of consisting of multiple connections, one connection may contain data for multiple sessions.

However, in other cases, such as when load balancing across caches, maintaining session state isn't required and persistence is instead used to ensure multiple requests (from multiple sources) for the same resource are sent to the same Pool Member.

The types of traffic or applications that Persistence is generally used with include; HTTP/S and related applications, SIP and other voice technologies, Remote Access and Diameter. In most cases any protocol or application that requires authentication which is performed by the real server and not shared between all real servers will require Persistence.

 Persistence only applies after the first load balancing decision is made.

The exam doesn't require you to have knowledge of any specific Persistence methods, but in order to aid your understanding of the concept in general; the simplest method available is discussed next.

Source Address (aka Simple)

This method persists connections based on the source IP address of a client and can also be configured with an IP netmask, which allows all connections from a particular IP subnet to be persisted together to the same real server.

The use of NAT, a proxy or other technologies which mask the true client source IP addresses and aggregate them behind one or very few addresses will make this Persistence method ineffective.

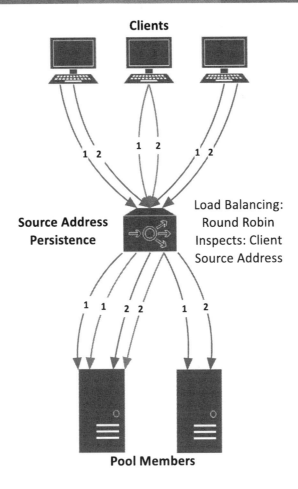

Cookie persistence

This method persists connections in a very different way to Simple persistence, overcoming most of its limitations. Rather than relying on TCP/IP data that is easily obscured by a proxy, or 'middle-box' as most RFCs refer to them; this method inserts a HTTP cookie and value to relevant server responses.

This cookie contains information that is used to direct all subsequent requests from the same client to the same real server/Pool Member. See The Application Layer in Detail chapter for more detail on Cookies. This persistence method is stateless (as is HTTP) and does not require any records to be maintained by the F5; all the relevant information is stored by the client. The following diagram illustrates how this method works;

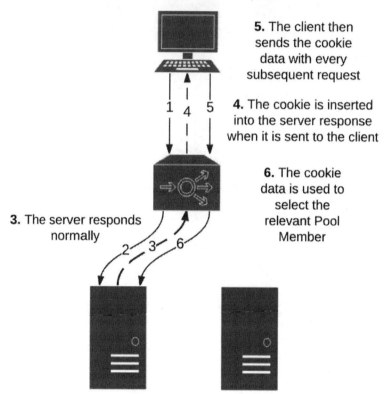

The use of NAT, a proxy or other technologies which mask the true client source IP addresses and aggregate them behind one or very few addresses **DOES NOT** make this Persistence method ineffective.

Despite its obvious benefits, this method does have some drawbacks, most notably with regard to security. The cookie data is obscured but does expose the Pool Member IP address, the Pool name and other details that are considered useful to a malicious party. There are however many ways to mitigate this risk, these are outside the scope of this book.

OneConnect

Also known as Connection Pooling, the OneConnect feature minimises server-side connections by re-using previously established connections for subsequent client requests. Rather than closing an idle connection to a real server (Pool Member) and reopening a new one for the next client request that gets load balanced to that server, the connection is maintained and re-used, within user configurable limits. This is demonstrated in the following diagram.

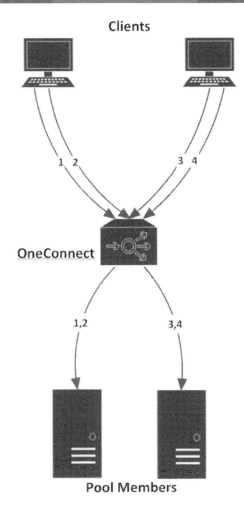

The Client & Server

In order to fully understand how network communications work, you need to be able to understand the difference between a client and a server. In most scenarios it is very easy to identify but there are occasions when you really need to think hard to tell which one is which. The client and server concept relates to layer three and more specifically IP.

Exam Tip Understanding the difference between a server and a client is fundamental for passing this exam. Since an F5 device sits between the client and the server things get slightly more complex, we'll cover this shortly.

What Is a Server?

In most cases a server is a large-scale computer which provides files or other services to clients and often has more processing power and other resources than a regular office computer. However, where TCP is concerned a server is simply a host that "serves" data or a service to clients. TCP isn't concerned with the size of a server; it might be a small NAS, a multimillion dollar mainframe, an office computer or an F5 device, it doesn't matter.

What does is that clients initiate the connection to a server, not the other way around.

What Is a Client?

With TCP a client is the host which connects to and receives data from the server. As with a TCP server, the physical attributes of a client are irrelevant. If a host initiates a connection it is the client.

F5 Device Acts As Both Server and Client

An F5 device can be both server and client and is often both. The server is the host that serves the data to the client and the client is the host that receives that data. Please view the following diagram.

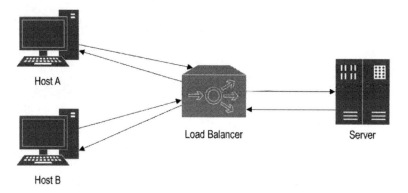

When you are communicating with a server through an F5 device (using the full proxy) there are actually two connections; one between the client host and the F5 and one between the F5 and the server host;

- The host initiates a connection to a virtual server IP address, which the F5 receives. In this case the host is the TCP client and the F5 is the TCP server.
- Next the F5 will initiate a new, related connection (on behalf of the host) with the server and passes the hosts data through to the server. Now the F5 is the TCP client and the server is the TCP server.

Exam Tip — In order to pass the exam it is very important to understand this concept. The F5 maintains two connections and acts as both a TCP client and server at the same time.

Chapter Summary

- In its most basic form a load balancer performs three interrelated functions; monitoring hosts (servers, caches, routers or anything else), acting as a proxy for those hosts and load balancing traffic across them.

- Round Robin is the simplest (and default) form of Load Balancing; each new connection is sent to the next Pool Member in the Pool in a strict circular (Round Robin) fashion.

- The load balancing method 'Least Connections' load balances new connections to whichever real server has the least number of active connections and is recommended by F5 in most cases.

- In most cases Persistence, also known as stickiness, affinity or session persistence, is used to direct additional connections from a client to the same Virtual Server to the same real server as the existing (initial) connection. This ensures that any state information stored only on that server, related to the session the connections form a part of, is valid

- An F5 device can be both server and client and is often both.

Chapter Review

In order to test your knowledge and understanding of this chapter, please answer the following questions. You will find the answers and explanations of the questions at the end of this chapter.

1. What load balancing method distributes connections between Pool Members in a strict circular fashion?

    a. Round Robin
    b. Least Connections

2. Is Least Connections a static or dynamic load balancing method?

    a. Static
    b. Dynamic

3. What feature ensures that the incoming connections are distributed to the same pool member as the initial connection?

    a. OneConnect
    b. Round Robin
    c. Persistence
    d. iQuery

Chapter Review: Answers

You will find the answers to the chapter review questions below:

1. The correct answer is: A

    a. **Round Robin**
    b. Least Connections

Round Robin is the simplest (and default) form of Load Balancing; each new connection is sent to the next Pool Member in the Pool in a strict circular (Round Robin) fashion

2. The correct answer is: B

    a. Static
    b. **Dynamic**

Least Connections is a dynamic Load Balancing method; real-time information influences how load balancing occurs and the distribution of connections between Pool Members are unequal and changes over time.

3. The correct answer is: C

    a. OneConnect
    b. Round Robin
    c. **Persistence**
    d. iQuery

Persistence, also known as stickiness, affinity or session persistence is used to direct additional connections from a client to the same Virtual Server to the same real server as the oxioting (initial) connection.

OneConnect minimizes server-side connections by re-using previously established connections for subsequent client requests. Rather than closing an idle connection to a real server (Pool Member) and reopening a new one for the next client request that gets load balanced to that server, the connection is maintained and re-used, within user configurable limits.

11. Security

Achieving high security has always been a significant challenge for any IT administrator. It seems that no matter how effective your network security is, hackers are always one step ahead. Nowadays it seems that every decision an IT administrator makes involves security of some sort.

There is always a balance to be maintained between security and convenience for the user (or administrator). Finding the right level of security can be a constant challenge. If security policy is too strict, users feel that it is an inconvenience rather than something worthwhile and beneficial for business.

In this chapter we will discuss the core concepts of security and take a look at some of the most common solutions that are used to provide security in organizations, without affecting availability.

Positive & Negative Security Models

In optimal environments, the security is impenetrable. In theory you can make any network environment safe from attacks; foreign or domestic, internal or external, but in reality this is very uncommon. First off, most hackers, governments or other 'actors' are far ahead when it comes to finding ways of exploiting systems and it seems they can always find a way to make a safe system unsafe. The main reason however, that most environments are not 100% secure is quite simply the cost.

Making a system impenetrable cost a lot of money and in many cases is not worth it. The security systems can cost more than the information is worth (or its loss would cost). With any system, host or network you need to evaluate many criteria including the potential risk of attack or compromise and the impact on the business, product or service. This can be measured in a number of ways including; financial loss, loss of trust, loss of reputation, downtime and legal or regulatory penalties. You need to balance your security based on the potential risks versus the investment needed to mitigate these risks.

IT decisions have become business decisions

With the growth in networking, the Internet and other technologies, IT departments started to adjust their security based upon this balance. Many business models started to change; security decisions were no longer purely IT decisions, they were also business decisions. Since most companies are almost completely dependent on IT to run the business, IT and IT security have become core business functions. Most IT products need to be business efficient but also as secure as possible and this combination is very difficult to achieve. In most cases security was the thing that had to step down. This leads to "good enough" security with high business efficiency. IT departments had to balance between total security and total functionality and this lead to the creation of two different security models that are often used today, the positive and negative security models.

Positive vs. Negative Security Models

Both these security models have the same base structure and both operate according to a set of simple rules. These rules can be Access Control Lists (ACLs), antivirus signatures or something else entirely. Even though these models have the same basic structure they are very different in the way they work. The positive security model starts with the approach of "block everything" and is then built upon by permitting specific, approved traffic, actions or other functions. Most operating systems and firewalls work in this manner as it feels safer. So an undefined positive security model should block everything from the start (what you allow is the positive).

A negative security model is the complete opposite of this. It begins with the approach "allow everything" and is then further constructed by blocking functions based on known previous attacks and unwanted content and behaviors (what you deny is the negative). Every rule that gets added to a negative security model will increase the security of the policy. So at the start, a negative security model will allow all traffic and as more restrictions are added the security increases. The traffic that passes through will be matched against a "bad" filter (a blacklist) and if there is a match it will be blocked and if not, it will be permitted.

To compare these models to a real world scenario, think of a private party, the party being for invited guests only. The people invited by the host are allowed in, anyone else is not. This would be the positive model.

If on the other hand you were in a public bar, everyone would be invited. As long as you were not causing any problems you could enter and leave at will. But if you caused problems (started a fight for instance) you would be thrown out and banned from entering the bar again. This would be the negative model.

The differences between these two security models have long been debated, with most security experts arguing that the positive security model is preferred because it begins from the most secure posture and gradually increases its functionality. However, most business experts claim that the negative security model is best because it starts off from the most functional posture and slowly increases its security.

Both groups have valid points but ultimately the positive and negative security models are just theoretical and in real life scenarios, a security policy falls somewhere in between. This creates a practical balance between the two. A negative security model that gets more secure will gradually become a positive security model and a positive security model that gets more functional will slowly become a negative security model.

Real-World Scenarios

In order to determine which security model is the most optimal for your environment there are a number of factors that need to be considered. The number of objects, the number of content types, how often the content changes and how the content works are all factors. These will form a variability scale. Note that the following examples relate to web content only. For instance if a site has 20-30 objects, it is much less variable than a site that has over 600-700 objects. A website with a few pictures and some texts is much less likely to change than, for example, a news site.

And if you have 600 objects that work with the same format they are less likely to change than 600 that are unique. A site that changes once every year is less variable than a site that changes every day. The last measurement of variability is based on the complexity of the site.

The aim of the variability scale is to achieve the maximum security for your needs with the least effort. This way you will use the most functional model while having the best possible security. There is therefore no security model that is better than the other; it all really depends on the content.

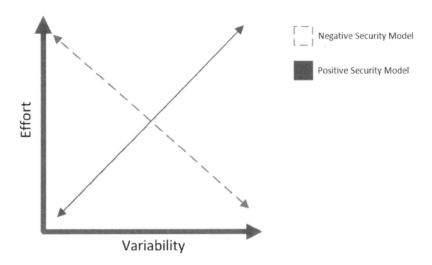

A positive security model will still likely be the more common model because you know what type of content you offer. You know that you need to allow HTTP or HTTPS to your webserver or SMTP to your email server. These content types will never change on their servers so that is why a positive security model is used.

But if you have an R&D department which introduces new services on new ports on a daily basis, all of those requests will be denied from the start and they will have to make a request for changes to the firewall every day. In such an environment it is easier to have a negative security model so the department does not have to request changes all the time. Attacks that are known to the network will continue to be blocked. But still, a negative model could allow unknown malicious traffic which is unattractive to most.

A great example of a useful negative security model is anti-virus or anti-spam. Either will only prevent activity or block content based on signature or content matches (a list of known attacks, behaviors or keywords) they have been configured to use. Anything that does not match the signatures is permitted.

Conclusion

As we've explored, the positive security model is the most common security model and the appropriate model for most network devices operating at layer four and/or above. The negative security model is most efficient for anti-virus, anti-spam and environments that change a lot.

The security model you choose depends on what environment you have and what content you are securing. There really is no right or wrong way and since IT decisions have become business decisions you might have to adjust according to the business' best interest.

Authentication and Authorization

When working as an IT technician it is necessary to understand the difference between authentication and authorization. *Authentication* verifies the identity and validity of a user. This is the most fundamental part of user-based network access and is used often in our daily lives. When, for instance, you try to retrieve a package at the post office, you need to produce some sort of identification to prove you are the intended recipient. In networking though that identification could be a username and password, an SSL certificate, something else entirely or a combination of these.

Without authentication, an administrator could never control user (or machine) access to networks and related resources. *Authorization* is closely related to authentication and they are easily confused.

When logging into a system and entering your username and password, this is authentication, not authorization. When the system has authenticated you (verified your identity) it then checks its internal database to see what resources you are permitted to access, this is authorization.

Authentication Processes

There are many different ways to confirm a user's identity and it all depends on what level of security your business (or its customers) requires. There are three different methods of identifying a user and you can use one or more of these;

- **Something you know** – This usually takes the form of a username and password but can also be a PIN code or something similar
- **Something you have** – This can be either a smartcard or a physical token that generates a random number which you send to the server. A smart card is like a credit card which you insert into a device that is attached to your computer.
- **Something you are** – Some environments require that you provide a physical attribute (a biometric). This is achieved by scanning a unique body part like a finger print or the retina of the eye.

In many scenarios, password authentication is sufficient and this has been the case for many years. However, more and more companies are starting to use smart cards and security tokens in addition to passwords to verify a user's identity. This is more likely when users are trying to gain access to internal resources from outside the office. Combining two or more authentication forms (or factors) is often called *multifactor authentication or two-factor authentication*. Combining password authentication and security tokens is currently the most common combination.

Centralized Authentication

To provide simplified account management and greater control over user identities, *centralized authentication* is used. With centralized authentication, you rely on a single (but likely redundant) system to authenticate users. When the user enters their credentials at the system they are trying to access, that system relays the request to the centralized authentication system, which then confirms the user's identity (or not if it isn't valid). You can configure many resources, for instance a file share or the intranet to authenticate against this centralized system. This saves both time and administration because you do not need to maintain multiple user account databases.

If a group of users need access to a new resource, all you have to do is configure the resource to use the centralized authentication system rather than its own and add the correct user rights.

Authentication also enables you to deploy *single sign-on* which is advantageous. We will cover single sign-on in greater detail in the SAML section.

There are several different types of centralized authentication technologies and protocols available which we'll explore briefly in the following sections.

RADIUS

RADIUS is commonly used and stands for *Remote Authentication Dial In User Server*. It uses UDP port 1812 and is a standard that defines a client/server application protocol running at layer 7 of the OSI model, the application layer. The RADIUS server provides authentication and authorization for the different resources and systems that receive the originating request. The resource in the following example is the server. The server prompts the user for credentials and then forwards what is supplied on to the RADIUS server using the message Access-Request. The RADIUS server checks the credentials supplied against its database and if they are correct and the user has permissions to access the resource, it sends back an Access-Accept message to the originating server. The whole process is illustrated next;

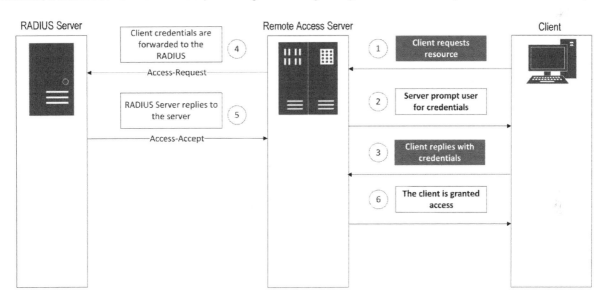

TACACS+

TACACS+ is also a centralized authentication technology and stands for, *Terminal Access Controller Access-Control System*. There is however a big difference as to how TACACS handles its authentication process. It separates authentication and authorization into individual processes and uses TCP (port 49) instead of UDP. Cisco originally developed TACACS+ as an open standard in the beginning of 1993.

Authentication, Authorization & Accounting (AAA)

To efficiently control user access to computer resources, a framework called Authentication, Authorization and Accounting (AAA) is often used. This framework combines many different related processes that are very important in securing and recording access to the IT-environment. These processes include controlling access to resources, auditing the usage of these resources, enforcing IT policies and providing the right access to the right user.

As we already discussed, authentication validates the user's identity; this is the first function of the AAA framework. You can validate a user's identity through various means as explored in the previous section.

The next function of the AAA framework is authorization. When a user has been validated there is a need to ensure that the user has access to the resource(s) required. If a user is trying to access a file share or a server, this will be validated by a database in the directory service which can confirm that user is authorized; this is covered in the previous section.

Last but not least we have accounting, which we've not discussed so far. Accounting is used to measure the user's access in some way. This could include how often a user accesses a certain resource or the amount of data a user has sent or received during a particular session. You can use this information to analyze trends and resource utilization. This can help control authorization and limit access if people do not use this resource often enough or plan upgrade activities based on when and how often a user or group of users accesses a resource. Accounting information can also be used for user and customer billing in relation to, for instance, a mobile phone data plan.

The AAA framework is often implemented by a server that controls all of these processes. RADIUS and TACACS+ are two examples of protocols and related server software that support AAA.

Security Assertion Markup Language (SAML) Authentication

Single Sign-On (SSO) is exactly what the name implies. SSO enables you to log on to multiple systems or sites but only being prompted for your user credentials once. This is something end-users love as it minimizes (almost entirely eliminates) delays caused by authentication that most users consider an interruption and inconvenience. In this day and age we need to remember so many different passwords and codes, as well as carry around security tokens and making it easier for the users is much appreciated.

SAML is a standard developed for this purpose and especially for web browser single sign-on. Previous implementations of web browser SSO involved cookies but this was only available on a single domain. The reason for this was that cookies were not transferred between domains and sites so if you obtained a cookie at www.abc.com it could not get transferred to www.xyz.com.

SAML provides a solution beyond the intranet and is based on an XML framework. It exchanges user authentication, entitlement and attribute information.

You can find out more about how SAML works in Appendix A but note this is not required for the exam.

Exam Tip — It is very important that you remember what SAML is used for.

Virtual Private Networks (VPNs)

Being able to access your business and office resources (files, websites, applications and administrative tools) yet work from any location is something that has been possible for many years thanks to VPNs. Yet there is a constant drive to improve this, to further enhance security and functionality without affecting easy access.

In the early days of remote access, you had to use a dial up modem and analogue phone line and call in to your office which would be using a dedicated serial line which was both slow and expensive. Today this problem no longer exists thanks to the wide availability of high speed domestic broadband (and cheap high bandwidth circuits in general). There have been quite a few VPN technologies over the years and they keep getting better and better in terms of functionality and security.

Some of the early VPNs required certain software to be installed and configured. The most recent and most popular VPN of choice for remote user access is SSL VPN. This technology makes it possible to access the corporate network simply by visiting a website and provide valid credentials. Once you have been authenticated, the web browser will launch an application or JAVA applet that automatically connects you to the corporate network.

Being able to connect branch offices to a company's headquarters or head office and globally connect everyone has also been very difficult and expensive in the past. This also required dedicated or leased lines and as mentioned before, this was very expensive. Now there are IPsec tunnels that connect the different branch offices; they both secure the connections and lower the costs because the Internet is used rather than a dedicated private network.

Even though IPsec tunnels have made it easier to connect branch offices you still need a suitably high capacity Internet connection in order for them function properly.

IPsec – IP Security

VPNs were initially based on the standard IPsec Protocol suite, which was developed to create a site-to-site tunnel between branch offices (or any two remote sites) and secure its communication. By using this technology, a lot of companies were able to save money on expensive dedicated lines and use cheap and high bandwidth Internet connections instead.

IPsec establishes a tunnel between two locations and secures the data by digitally signing and encrypting it prior to transmission. IPsec provides several different types of security including:

- **Spoofing Prevention** – You cannot trick the recipient by claiming to be someone else; the identity of each end point is verified
- **Modification Prevention** – You cannot capture a packet, modify its payload and send it on without it being detected
- **Protection** – You cannot read the contents of the packet payload/data because it is encrypted
- **Reuse Prevention** – You cannot reuse any encrypted packets or discover any passwords or keys.

This provides end-to-end protection, which means that the information is secured (as just detailed) until it reaches its destination (there's no guarantee after that). IPsec is an extension to the IP protocol; any traffic that takes the form of IP datagrams can be encrypted and it doesn't matter what type of information is carried within. The OSI layers above the network layer are not aware that the traffic has been encrypted or part of a VPN in the first place; it is truly remarkable.

In the early days of VPNs, IPsec was the only option available for secure remote access. Originally IPsec was only intended for securing communications between locations using site-to-site tunneling and it therefore had its limitations when it was used in securing user remote access. To solve this problem, another remote access method was introduced, *SSL VPN*. SSL VPN operates using the Secure Sockets Layer protocol (which also secures HTTPS) and has become the most common VPN solution that is in use today for user access. This will be discussed later in this chapter.

When Should You Use IPsec?

Since IPsec VPNs were originally designed for site-to-site access it is still the best method. It is the perfect solution when you need to have a constant connection between two locations. This could be between the headquarters and the branch office or a connection between two highly secured internal servers.

There are still organizations that implement remote access using IPsec but they are decreasing in number and instead organizations are relying on the much more convenient solution, SSL VPN.

SSL VPN

SSL stands for *Secure Sockets Layer* and its purpose is to secure transmissions between servers and clients. SSL is a protocol that has been implemented into many different applications and adds a good layer of security. For instance HTTP uses SSL as part of the HTTPS protocol.

SSL encrypts the data generated by applications; it was originally developed by Netscape Communications and was intended to protect data transmitted between a server and client using HTTP.

In January 1999 Transport Layer Security (TLS) was introduced as an upgrade of the highest SSL version (v3). The difference between TLS and SSL was not dramatic but significant enough that it was given a new name. The latest TLS version at the moment is TLS version 1.2. Despite this, even use of TLS is still widely referred to as SSL, a VPN over TLS still referred to as an SSL VPN.

An SSL VPN protects the data in the following ways:

- **Spoofing Prevention** – Server and clients provide their credentials in order to confirm the identity of both systems.
- **Modification Prevention** – Every packet is signed with a hash function called HMAC which ensures that there has not been any modification to the packet.
- **Protection** – The data is encrypted by the public key which makes sure that only the recipient is able to decrypt and receive the information.
- **Reuse Prevention** – You cannot reuse any encrypted packets or discover any passwords or keys.

SSL is supported by all web browsers used today which enables an organization's employees to gain remote access from anywhere they have an Internet connection, without installing additional software that the IT department has to manage. SSL VPNs are even implemented in some recent versions of operating systems. For instance, in Windows 7 and 8 you can specify Secure Sockets Tunneling Protocol (SSTP) when configuring a new VPN connection. SSTP sends traffic through an SSL tunnel.

In most cases when you use an SSL VPN with your web browser, you will visit a URL using HTTPS and get prompted for your credentials. After entering the credentials an Active X or Java based application will launch and after a couple of seconds you will be remotely connected to your organization's environment. When you use a SSL connection directly in the operating system you can save your credentials in the settings and launch the VPN very easily. Since SSL is included in all of the different browsers and major operating systems, users will have an easier time connecting. HTTPS operates on TCP port 443 by default so it is probably already permitted through relevant firewalls.

Chapter Summary

- Authentication verifies the identity of the user so that it can determine if the user is valid or not. This is the most fundamental part of network security and it is used in our daily lives.

- Authorization is the process of determining what resources the user has the right to access after logging in. Authentication and authorization are very easily confused.

- Accounting is used to measure the user's access. This could include how often a user accesses a certain resource or the amount of data a user has sent or received during a session. This information is used to analyze trends and resource utilizations.

- Authentication, Authorization and Accounting are also known as the three-letter acronym AAA.

- There are three different forms of identifying a user and they are: something you know, something you have and something you are.

- Centralized authentication is used to simplify management of users and groups and it also enables SSO (Single-Sign-On). RADIUS and TACACS+ are two examples of centralized authentication.

- SAML enables you to have SSO (Single-Sign-On) on multiple external sites through the use of an Identity provider. SAML stands for Security Assertion Markup Language.

Chapter Review

In order to test your knowledge and understanding of this chapter, please answer the following questions. You will find the answers and explanations of the questions at the end of this chapter.

1. Which of the following correctly explains authentication?
    a. Authentication determines what access a user should have.
    b. Authentication is responsible for making sure a user has the right access.
    c. Authentication verifies the identity of the user so that it can be determined if you are a valid or invalid user.
    d. Authentication is a security system that handles all incoming request.

2. What is multifactor authentication?
    a. When a client request goes through multiple authentication servers.
    b. It is multiple ways of identifying the user.
    c. It is used when you want to access multiple resources using the same credentials.
    d. You use it when multiple users have different operating systems and they are trying to access the same resources.

3. What is SAML (Security Assertion Markup Language)?
   a. SAML is used to enable Single-Sign-On to multiple systems/sites through the web browser.
   b. SAML is an authentication protocol created especially for multifactor authentication.
   c. SAML is used to enable Single-Sign-On to multiple systems/sites directly on the computer.
   d. SAML is the system that authorizes users after they have been authenticated.

4. True or false: Authorization verifies a user's identity based on the credentials the user has provided.
   a. True
   b. False

5. Your company recently expanded and you have opened up a new branch office on a different site. As a network technician you are now responsible for providing access to the servers located at the headquarters for the branch office users.

   In the following scenario, what remote access technique is preferred?

   a. Site-to-site IP Sec VPN
   b. SSL VPN
   c. Hire a dedicated leased line between the two offices
   d. Site-to-site SSL VPN

6. As an IT-technician for a large organization you have to make changes to the network environment every day because the R&D department is constantly implementing new features that you have to allow through the organization's firewall.

   Which security model is best suited for your needs?

   a. Positive security model
   b. Negative security model

Chapter Review: Answers

You will find the answers to the chapter review questions below:

1. The correct answer is: C
    a. Authentication determines what access a user should have.
    b. Authentication is responsible for making sure a user has the right access.
    c. **Authentication verifies the identity of the user so that it can be determined if you are a valid or invalid user.**
    d. Authentication is a security system that handles all incoming request.

Authentication is the process when the user is prompted for credentials. The authentication system does not care what resources you have access to, it only wants to know that you are who you claim to be.

2. The correct answer is: B
    a. When a client request goes through multiple authentication servers.
    b. **It is multiple ways of identifying the user.**
    c. It is used when you want to access multiple resources using the same credentials.
    d. You use it when multiple users have different operating systems and they are trying to access the same resources.

Multifactor authentication is used when you have combined multiple ways of authenticating a user. There are currently three ways which are: Something you know (password), something you have (physical token) and something you are (finger print).

3. The correct answer is: A
    a. **SAML is used to enable Single-Sign-On to multiple systems/sites through the web browser.**
    b. SAML is an authentication protocol created especially for multifactor authentication.
    c. SAML is used to enable Single-Sign-On to multiple systems/sites directly on the computer.
    d. SAML is the system that authorizes users after they have been authenticated.

SAML is a Single-Sign-On technology used for web browsers. Previously web browsers used cookies for this but this was only possible on the intranet. This was not efficient because they could not be transferred between domains. So SAML was invented instead.

4. The correct answer is: B
    a. True
    b. **False**

Authorization is the process after a user *has been* identified. After the user has been identified it looks through its database to determine what resources a user should be able to obtain.

5. The correct answer is: A

    a. **Site-to-site IP Sec VPN**
    b. SSL VPN
    c. Hire a dedicated leased line between the headquarters and the branch office.
    d. Site-to-site SSL VPN

Since you are required to provide access between two remote sites the best option is to setup a Site-to-site IP sec VPN tunnel between the headquarters and the branch office. You could also hire a dedicated leased line between the HQ and the branch office but this would not be the preferred solution.

SSL VPN are not used for Site-to-site VPN, they are only used when you need to provide separate users with access to resources located in the office.

6. The correct answer is: B

    a. Positive security model
    b. **Negative security model**

Since the environment is constantly changing the best suited security model is the negative security model. Policy rules are created that will keep out all known attacks which will keep the network secure while allowing all new traffic through.

12. Public Key Infrastructure (PKI)

How do we know that the file we are sending to our colleague has not been tampered with and arrives safely? How do we know that no one is actually sniffing the network and downloading sensitive data?

What is Public Key Infrastructure?

Public Key Infrastructure (PKI) was invented in order to increase security. PKI is pretty complex and can be hard for people to grasp initially; it involves *encryption, digital signing* and *certificates*. These are used in technologies like SSL and VPNs which we have covered in previous chapters.

The Basics of Encryption

Encryption is used to protect data against unauthorized people. This ensures that only the intended recipient can read the file or application data that is being sent. In order to understand how encryption works, the terms used in relation to it needs to be explained.

When you encrypt data you need two inputs; **an algorithm** and **a key**. The algorithm describes how the data should be transformed into unreadable cipher text and how we can convert it back to its original format. Cipher text is the result of encryption performed on plaintext using an algorithm. The key is a piece of unique information (like a password, certificate or shared secret) that is used as an input to the algorithm to be able to create a unique value that can only be obtained by using the correct algorithm and the key.

To present an example, when configuring a site-to-site tunnel you have the possibility to use pre-shared-keys (a shared secret that both routers/firewalls know because it has been configured on both devices) and this works just like a password. In order to establish the tunnel both tunnels need to have the same pre-shared-key to be able to encrypt and decrypt the data that travels over the tunnel. In this sense the pre-shared-key is the **key** and the encryption used in the tunnel, is the **algorithm**.

To summarize,

- Unencrypted data is known as **plain text**
- The **algorithm** describes how you encrypt the data
- The **key** is used to encrypt and decrypt the data
- Encrypted data is known as **cipher text**

When you encrypt a file you can either use *symmetric encryption* or *asymmetric encryption, the difference being the number of keys used*. This all depends on the level of security you need.

Symmetric Encryption

When you use symmetric encryption you use the same key for both encryption and decryption. The good thing about symmetric encryption is that in theory it is very fast, but the encryption algorithms are not as complex (and thus less secure) as those used with asymmetric encryption. Therefore they are ideal for environments that require speed.

Below you will find an example of how symmetric encryption works:

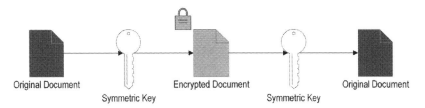

 When using symmetric encryption, we use the same key for both encrypting and decrypting the data.

The system that encrypts the file generates a random symmetric key which is defined by the algorithms (and some user input). The algorithm determines the size of key together with the application using it. Once the key is created, it is used to encrypt the data. The encrypted file is then made available to the recipient. The key must also be made available to the recipient through some secure method (not the one used to exchange the data). Once the user receives both the encrypted key and file they can then decrypt the file and access the data.

 A pre-shared key (PSK) can also be used as a key in symmetric encryptions. This is a secret that both systems know that will enable both parties to both encrypt and decrypt the file.

The important thing is that the encryption key is transferred (or shared) using a secure channel between users or end hosts. The encrypted data can be exchanged over an insecure network or through an insecure method as only those with the key can decrypt it. The greatest security risk is if the key is intercepted by a malicious user, who can then unencrypt the file or communications (if they can access them).

Symmetric Algorithms

The greatest benefit of symmetric algorithms is the amount of data it can encrypt in a short period of time. Some common symmetric algorithms are;

- ❖ **Data Encryption Standard (DES)** – Uses a generated symmetric key that consists of 56-bits. This standard was selected by the National Bureau of Standards as an official Federal Information Processing Standard (FIPS) for the United States in 1976 but has now been withdrawn. DES is considered to be insecure for many applications because the symmetric key is too small (56-bit).

- ❖ **3DES** – An algorithm that is the very similar to DES except it is applied three times to the data payload. The payload is encrypted with key A, decrypted with key B and then re-encrypted with key C. This method is called Encrypt-Decrypt-Encrypt cycle (EDE) and is explained below:

    a. Encrypt using first key and plaintext (non-encrypted file) that produces the first ciphertext.
    b. Decrypt using the first ciphertext and second key that produces a second unreadable ciphertext.
    c. Encrypt using the second ciphertext and third key to produce the final ciphertext.

    It can also be encrypted with only two keys. In this case only keys A and B are used. It is very important that you use three separate keys, if two of the keys are the same it will severely degrade security. 3DES is three times stronger than DES but also three times slower.

- ❖ **Advanced Encryption Standard (AES)** – An algorithm intended to be the successor to 3DES which uses, 128-bit, 192-bit and 256-bit keys instead of a 56-bit one. It uses the Rijndael algorithm which makes it possible to encrypt data in just one pass instead of 3DES which uses three. Despite being more secure, AES Is faster than 3DES.

Exam Tip   You do not need to remember the different types of algorithms available and their key lengths. But it is important to understand how PKI works.

Asymmetric Encryption

Asymmetric encryption uses two keys instead of one; these keys are known as *public* and *private keys*. This increases security significantly, but at the cost of speed. The keys are separate but mathematically related. The reason why this technology is more secure is because the private key is only possessed by the host that generated the key pair (the private and public key). The private key never leaves the original system. The public key on the other hand is distributed to other systems and does not have to be protected. This way, the sender uses the public key to encrypt files that is destined for the system that holds the private key (only the system holding the private key can decrypt the data).

As mentioned before, asymmetric encryption uses two keys. One key is used for encrypting the data and the other is used for decryption. The algorithms used in asymmetric encryption are more complex which causes the encryption and decryption process to take much longer. Things change over time and vendor focus and new technology can change the picture but in theory symmetric algorithms can be 100 to 10000 times faster than asymmetric ones.

Asymmetric Encryption is explained in the illustration below:

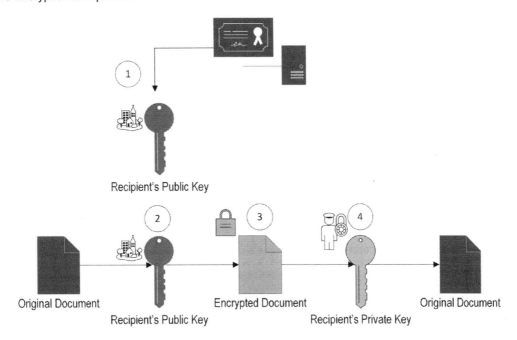

1. The sender retrieves the recipient's public key. This can be sent from either the recipient itself or it can be obtained from a server. This key really can be public; there's no need to protect it.
2. The document is then encrypted using the asymmetric algorithm and the recipient's public key. This transforms the original plain-text into unreadable cipher-text.
3. The encrypted cipher-text is sent to the recipient and since asymmetric algorithm is used there is no need to send the encryption key too. The recipient will use its own private key to decrypt the text.
4. The recipient decrypts the document using the private key which transforms the encrypted text into the original document (the plain-text).

 Documents are used as an example of encryption. You can apply encryption to pretty much any data type including documents, emails and technologies like FTPS, HTTPS and SSH.

Since asymmetric is in theory is so much slower than symmetric encryption it is very uncommon to use asymmetric encryption for the data payload. Most of the time a combination of both asymmetric and symmetric encryption is used. You create a symmetric key which you use to encrypt the document and then use the recipient's public key to encrypt the symmetric key. Both the encrypted file and the encrypted symmetric key are sent to the recipient.

Since the recipient has the private key, it will be able to decrypt the symmetric key. The symmetric key will then be used to decrypt the encrypted document. Using this method we can use, in theory, the faster symmetric algorithm on the data and still have high security because we use asymmetric encryption on the symmetric key. The illustration below explains this concept:

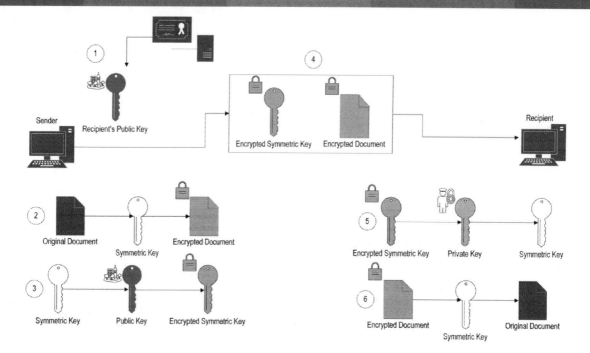

1. The sender obtains the recipients public key.
2. The sender generates a symmetric key and uses this key to encrypt the document.
3. The symmetric key is encrypted using the public key obtained earlier. This is done to secure the symmetric key during transfer.
4. The encrypted document and the encrypted symmetric key are transferred to the recipient.
5. The recipient uses its private key to decrypt the encrypted symmetric key.
6. Finally the encrypted document is decrypted using the symmetric key which transforms it to the original document.

Asymmetric Algorithms

Below you will find the most common asymmetric algorithms used:

- **Diffie-Hellman (DH) Key Agreement**: This algorithm does not rely on public and private keys for encryption. Instead it uses a mathematical function that helps generate a shared secret between two parties. Understanding how this algorithm works is beyond the scope of the exam and thus this book.

- **Rivest Shamir Adleman (RSA)**: An algorithm based on a series of modular multiplications that can be used for both encrypting and signing. You can control how secure this encryption is by using different key lengths. For instance you can use a 128 bit key or you can use a 256 bit key. Remember, longer keys (normally) result in a slower encryption and signing process but higher security.

- **Digital Signature Algorithm (DSA)**: This algorithm uses a series of calculations based on a selected prime number and it is only used for digital signing. The maximum key size used to be 1024 bits but longer key sizes are now supported. Digital Signing will be covered in greater detail later in this chapter.

Asymmetric Signing

This technology is used when there is a need to protect data from modification and confirm the identity of the sender. To do this the asymmetric encryption process is reversed. Instead of using the public key to encrypt the file, the private key is used instead. Since the sender is the only one with the private key, we can ensure that the file is coming from the sender. If the private key is jeopardized or stolen, the whole PKI structure fails. That is why it is very important to keep private keys safe.

The asymmetric signing process is illustrated below:

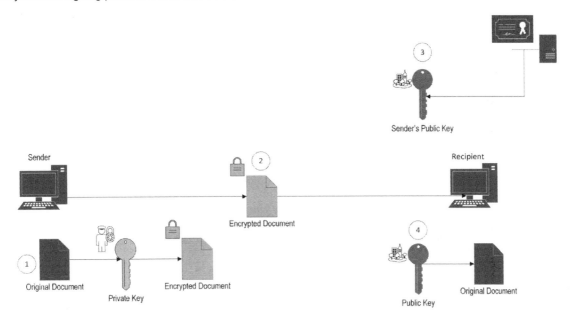

1. The sender will encrypt the document using its own private key. The private key is only available to the sender so this ensures that the document comes from the sender.
2. The encrypted document is sent to the recipient.
3. In order for the recipient to decrypt the document, it needs to download the sender's public key.
4. Finally the recipient will decrypt the document using the sender's public key thus, confirming that the sender is who he claims to be.

Since anyone can get a hold of the public key, anyone will be able to decrypt the file. But that is not the purpose for Asymmetric Signing. The purpose is to confirm the identity of the sender and make sure it's correct.

 Remember that with Asymmetric Signing you do not encrypt using the public key, you use the private key in order to ensure that the file/document is coming from the original sender since it's the only one containing the private key.

The Hash Process

A hash algorithm takes a plaintext document and produces a mathematical result. This mathematical output is referred to as a hash value, message digest or digest. If a single character is changed in the plaintext document, the mathematical result will not be the same. We use this to determine that the original file has not been modified in transit.

Hash Algorithms

These are the most common hashing algorithms used today:

- **Message Digest 5 (MD5)** – This algorithm is used in many security applications. It is used to produce a 128 bit hash value of messages of any size. It was designed by Ron Rivest in 1991.

- **Secure Hash Algorithm (SHA-1)** – This is an algorithm designed by United States National Security Agency and was first published 1995 and produces 160bit hash value. It is widely used in many security applications and protocols. It is considered to be slower than MD5 but it is harder to find two data inputs that result in the same hash value. It has been upgraded several times and SHA-3 is currently the latest version that was released in 2012. SHA-3 is superior to SHA-1 and offers greater security.

Digital Signing

The main purpose of encryption is to *prevent data from being modified, ensuring the source of the data and keeping the data secret.* This is also known as:

Integrity: If someone was able to capture the information, even if they could not understand the data they could still change the bits and alter the data. That is why there is a need to recognize what is happening and refuse the information.

Authentication: You do not want to send critical and classified information to the wrong host; therefore it is essential that the recipient is who he claims to be.

Confidentiality: Keep the data secure so that no man in the middle can obtain the information. If someone was able to capture the data, it would appear to be meaningless to the thief.

Even though encryption can provide protection for the data and prevent it from being altered; only digital signing has the ability to ensure the source of the data. Digital signing also provides protection against data modification. In order to digital sign a document or application we need to use a digital signature.

In short, a Digital Signature is the same as asymmetric signing. In other words, the use of a private key to digital sign a file, application or even a hash value.

Summary:

1. The digital signing process uses a hash algorithm to determine if the data has been modified.
2. The digital signing process applies a *digital signature (the private key)* to the message digest that identifies who actually signed the data. Since the signer is the only one with the private key it means that you can be certain the data comes from them.

One real-life example of digital signing is digitally signed drivers. This will ensure that the device drivers you install on your computer come from the manufacturer and not from an unknown publisher. Hashing is usually also used together with the digital signature to ensure that the device driver has not been modified. Digitally signing device drivers are entirely up to the manufacturer. If your operating system detects an unsigned driver, it will most likely warn you about it as it is considered a security risk.

Combining Asymmetric Signing & Hash Algorithms

When working with digital signing, you can combine both asymmetric signing and hash algorithms. The hash algorithms make sure that the data has not been modified and the asymmetric signing provides proof that the hash value was created by the sender. Below is an illustration of this:

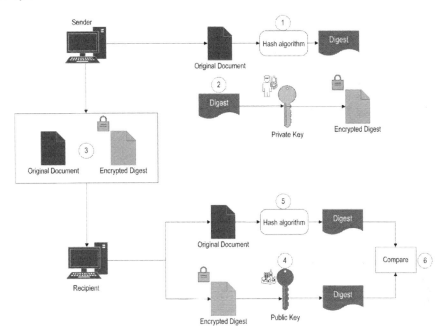

1. The sender takes the original document and runs it through a hash algorithm. This creates a message digest.
2. Then the sender encrypts this message digest with its own private key.
3. Then both the orignal document and the encrypted digest are sent to the recipient.
4. The recipient will download (or already have) the sender's public key and decipher the message digest.
5. The recipient will also run the original document through the same hash algorithm that the sender did, this will create another message digest.
6. In order to verify that the document has not been modified during transit, the recipient will compare both digests to see if they are both the same.

With digital signing no encryption is used on the original document. The original document can be modified but this will be proven when the message digest is compared.

Certificates, Certificate Chains and Certificate Authorities

Now that we have talked about all the different types of encryption technologies, hashing algorithms and so forth let's consider some real life scenarios. Many of you have probably visited your bank online or bought something from Amazon or eBay. When you are accessing high security sites which involve payment or some sort of confidentiality requirement, you will most likely encounter a website protected by HTTPS.

HTTPS provides confidentiality, integrity and authentication. It achieves this by using a SSL/TLS *certificate*. A certificate is a file that contains information such as e-mail address, owner's name, certificate usage, duration of validity and a lot of others. It also contains the certificate ID of the entity that signed this information and the public certificate. The public certificate is the same as the public key. The certificate itself is signed by a hashing algorithm to ensure that it has not been modified.

This certificate is created by a *root certificate authority* (CA), which can be compared to the entity that issues your passport. A Certificate Authority is a very important part of PKI and it has several functions. Below you will find some examples:

- **Verify the identity of the requestor**: Before the CA will issue a certificate; it must ensure the identity of the requestor.
- **Issue certificates to the requestor**: When the administrator has validated the identity of the requestor; the next step is to issue the certificate. This could be a user, a computer, network device or service certificate. It is important to choose the right purpose for the certificate. Depending on what you choose, the certificate will have a different set of options. A HTTPS certificate is very different from a IPsec certificate
- **Manage certificate revocation**: The CA also keeps track of certificates that have been revoked. They could be revoked for several reasons which will be discussed in next section of this chapter. The CA publicly publishes something that is called a *certificate revocation list*.

Certificates can represent users, computers, network devices or services and every one of them has a public key and a private key (public and private certificate). Since we are using two keys, this means that we are using asymmetric encryption.

Since the CA is managed by administrators, the administrator needs to verify the identity of the requestor before granting a certificate. There are several different ways of identifying the requestor and it all depends on what type of IT-security policy your company uses. Some examples of identifying the requestor are driver's license, proof of address, company or logon information. Some companies even involve a face-to-face meeting. When the identity has been confirmed the administrator can issue a certificate to the requestor and signs it with the CA's own private key. This is done to protect the certificate from any changes. If you were to change anything in the certificate it would fail the digital signature check and be marked as invalid.

Below is an example of the www.google.se certificate information that I get when accessing Google Sweden.

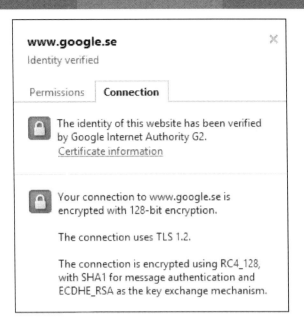
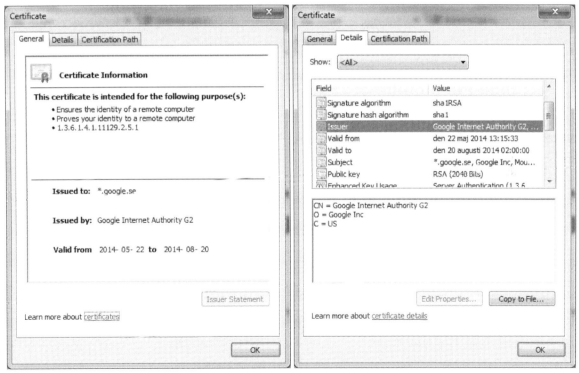

Certificate Revocation Lists (CRLs)

Sometimes the CA must revoke a certificate before the validity period expires. The CA stores and publishes this information in a *certificate revocation list* or CRL.

The Different Revocations

Certificates can be revoked for a number of reasons;

- **Key Compromise**: The private key of the certificate has been compromised. This can happen if the private key related to the certificate has been stolen or the hardware that contains the private key has been stolen.
- **CA compromise**: The CA private key has been compromised. The same happens with this key, either the hardware has been stolen or the private key itself has been stolen.
- **Certification Hold**: Indicates that the certificate has been temporarily revoked. This can occur when an employee in an organization takes a leave of absence for some reason (maternity leave for instance).
- **Affiliation Changed**: This is used when the subject (typically a user) of the certificate has changed. This may be when a user has left the organization. This is indicated in the DN attribute of the certificate. In other words, the user has been fired or quit their job and therefore the certificate has to be terminated.
- **Cessation of Operation**: The certificate's subject has been decommissioned. This can happen because the server which holds the certificate has been replaced by another one with a different name.
- **Superseded**: The certificate has been replaced with a new certificate. This can occur when some of the options in the certificate have been changed.
- **Remove From CRL**: A certificate has been unrevoked and taken off the CRL.

Chapter Summary

- Encryption is used to make data unreadable against unauthorized people. This ensures that only the intended recipient gets access to the file or application data that is sent. There are both symmetric encryptions and asymmetric encryptions.

- Some symmetric encryption algorithms are DES, 3DES and Advanced Encryption Standard (AES).

- Diffie-Hellman key Agreement, Rivest Shamir Adleman (RSA) or Digital Signature Algorithm are examples of asymmetric algorithms.

- Asymmetric signing is used to protect data from modification and confirm the identity of the sender

- A Certificate Authority is a very important part of PKI and it is responsible for verifying the identity of a certificate requestor, issue certificates to the requestor and manage certificate revocations. The certificate revocations are stored in the CRL (Certificate Revocation List)

Chapter Review

In order to test your knowledge and understanding of this chapter, please answer the following questions. You will find the answers and explanations of the questions at the end of this chapter.

1. What is the advantage of symmetric encryption compared to asymmetric encryption?
    a. Symmetric encryption is faster than asymmetric encryption.
    b. Symmetric encryption is safer than asymmetric encryption.
    c. Symmetric encryption is easier to setup than asymmetric encryption.
    d. Symmetric encryption requires less hardware than asymmetric encryption.

2. Which of the following are symmetric algorithms?
    a. DES
    b. AES
    c. Diffie-Hellman Key Agreement
    d. MD5

3. Which of the following are asymmetric algorithms?
    a. 3DES
    b. Diffie-Hellman Key Agreement
    c. DSA
    d. SHA1

4. True or false: A Certificate Authority issues certificates to the requestor
    a. True
    b. False

Chapter Review: Answers

You will find the answers to the chapter review questions below:

1. The correct answer is: A
    a. **Symmetric encryption is faster than asymmetric encryption.**
    b. Symmetric encryption is safer than asymmetric encryption.
    c. Symmetric encryption is easier to setup than asymmetric encryption.
    d. Symmetric encryption requires less hardware than asymmetric encryption.

The main advantage of symmetric encryptions is the speed of it. Symmetric algorithms are in theory at least 100 times faster than asymmetric encryption in software-based encryptions and 10,000 times faster in hardware-based encryptions. But they are less secure because they only use one key for both encryption and decryption.

2. The correct answer is: A and B
    a. **DES**
    b. **AES**
    c. Diffie-Hellman Key Agreement
    d. MD5

3. The correct answer is: B and C
    a. 3DES
    b. **Diffie-Hellman Key Agreement**
    c. **DSA**
    d. SHA1

4. The correct answer is: A
    a. **True**
    h. False

13. Application Delivery Platforms

In this chapter we'll cover the basics around F5's application delivery hardware, its virtualised software-only equivalent, the differences between the two and the drawbacks and benefits of each. Additionally we'll explore some more advanced protocol specific features for TCP and HTTP now that you understand more about these protocols and their relation to basic load balancing and application delivery.

BIG-IP Hardware

BIG-IP Application switch hardware comes in a wide range of fixed and modular models. Both the physical hardware and the Virtual Edition are considered a form of application delivery platform; in other words, they run TMOS. I'll summarise the differences between the hardware and virtualised software forms shortly but it's worth exploring the benefits and drawbacks of dedicated hardware and related design considerations here first.

Hardware provides superior performance and throughput using Field-Programmable Gate Array (FPGA) circuitry, specialised high performance network interfaces and optimised data paths. Further benefits are gained from the inclusion of additional dedicated hardware for SSL processing (all models) and compression processing (higher end models only) which provide much higher performance than commodity processors. Due to this higher performance the number of TMOS modules you can install on an appliance is also typically quite high, which lends itself well to functional consolidation.

Clearly more suited to high workloads, hardware appliances are therefore typically placed in a logically central position in the network to maximise their benefits and ensure the maximum amount of traffic is easily processed through them. The built-in always on management (AOM) subsystem is a useful inclusion and vendor support is also simplified as both the hardware and software are supported and designed by the same vendor.

Of course, for all these benefits there are some downsides, the primary ones being cost and a lack of flexibility. The hardware (and related support) is expensive, however, make good use of their high performance and capacity and the cost is low compared to their true value. This is a primary design consideration, the higher the throughput (within suitable limits) the greater the return on your investment.

Moving to the second and related drawback, with the exception of VIPRION, hardware appliances in general simply don't scale. If you need to do more than your current device has capacity for you have to (rip and) replace it with a larger device. Equally, future (estimated) capacity requirements must be incorporated in the original purchase, which may mean the hardware is not used to anything like its full capacity for a significant time.

You don't need to know this for the exam but, if you're interested, all physical BIG-IP platforms (with the exception of VIPRION systems detailed in the next section) have a minimum specification of;

- LCD Panel & Physical Controls
- Intel dual core CPU
- Dual power supply capable (AC and DC)
- Four Gigabit Ethernet interfaces
- Front mounted LCD panel
- Dedicated management network interface
- Serial console interface
- Failover/HA serial interface
- One Rack Unit (RU) height
- Front to back airflow
- Software HTTP compression
- Hardware SSL encryption via 'Cryogen' card
- 4Gb RAM
- 500Gb HDD
- Up to 5,000 1k SSL transactions per second (TPS) [reduce by 80% for 2k keys]
- Up to 1Gbps Layer four and layer seven throughput
- Up to 1Gbps Bulk encryption
- Up to 100,000 Layer seven requests per second
- Up to 60,000 Layer four connections per second

Specifications increase up to the following for the higher end models (excluding the VIPRION platforms discussed shortly);

- Intel 12 core CPUs
- 40GbE Fibre interfaces
- Three RU
- Hardware compression (up to 40Gbps)
- FPGA Acceleration
- 128Gb RAM
- Dual 10,000RPM 1Tb HHDs with RAID (SSDs are an option)
- Up to 240,000 2k SSL transactions per second (TPS)
- Up to 84Gbps layer four throughput
- Up to 40Gbps layer seven throughput
- Up to 40Gbps Bulk encryption
- Up to 4,000,000 Layer seven requests per second

Up to 1,500,000 Layer four connections per secondThe only hot swappable components are the power supplies (assuming two are installed), SFP network interfaces and fan tray (in some models only). Hard disks are not hot swappable even on models that support RAID. FIPS Compliant and Turbo SSL versions of some models are also available.

VIPRION

VIPRION is F5 Networks' high density hardware consolidation platform; the Cisco Catalyst 6500 of the BIG-IP range if you will. The three VIPRION models are modular chassis with capacity for up to eight hot-swappable blade modules, all featuring hardware compression. The larger 16 rack unit (RU) high 4800 can accommodate dual hex core CPU full-width blades, the smaller 4RU 2400 holds single quad core CPU half-width blades.

The features and benefits of these chassis are similar to those of other modular, expandable network devices;

- Hot-swappable blades, multiple power supplies and field replaceable components increase uptime and provide a high level of redundancy
- Consolidation of multiple devices in a high density form factor reduces and/or fixes hardware, environmental, operational and management costs
- High interface density and capacity
- Non-disruptive capacity scaling
- High maximum capacity
- Fewer points of administration and monitoring
- Easy expansion capabilities (aka vertical scaling or scale up)

You don't need to know this for the exam but, if you're interested, the technical highlights of the VIPRION platforms include;

- Load is dynamically shared across all available blades
- All physical interfaces on all blades are fully meshed using high-speed bridge Field Programmable Gate Arrays (FPGAs)
- The entire system is managed through a single interface
- Everything from firmware, software and configuration settings is automatically duplicated from the primary blade to every other blade
- The SuperVIP feature allows a VIP to span multiple blades
- vCMP – A hypervisor allowing for multiple ADC guest instances
- CMP - multicore and multiple processors (not VIPRION specific)
- Device Service Clustering (DSC) support provides horizontal clustering with any mix of physical, modular or virtual devices (not VIPRION specific)
- Scale^N support
- NEBS Certification
- 96Gb RAM
- 40Gb Ethernet interfaces
- Up to 30,000 2k SSL transactions per second (TPS)
- Up to 80Gbps layer four throughput per second, per blade
- Up to 40Gbps layer seven throughput per second, per blade
- Up to 20Gbps bulk encryption per blade
- Up to 2,500,000 Layer seven requests per second, per blade
- Up to 1,400,000 Layer four connections per second, per blade
- Up to 20Gb hardware compression per blade

BIG-IP Virtual Edition (VE)

LTM Is one of many modules supported by BIG-IP Virtual Edition, the others are; Access Policy Manager, Application Security Manager, Edge Gateway, Global Traffic Manager, WebAccelerator and WAN Optimization Manager.

LTM was the first TMOS module to be supported by VE with the introduction of TMOS v10.1. There is a maximum throughput restriction of 1Gbps throughput but regardless, for smaller deployments, VE is a very cost effective option. Note v11.3 vastly improved the Virtual Edition, v11.4 adds a 5Gbps throughput option and v11.5 a 10Gbps option.

The Lab edition is a <u>very</u> cheap (**now only $95 or so**), very bandwidth limited (10Mb) version highly suited to test and development environments and includes LTM, GTM, APM (10 user) AFM, ASM, AVR, PSM, WAM and WOM.

Mixed platforms (hardware/VE) are not supported for some HA features but this has improved greatly in v11.4.

There are FIPS options for VE but these require an external, dedicated network HSM appliance of some kind.

I'll summarise the differences between the hardware and virtualised software forms shortly but it's worth exploring the benefits and drawbacks of the virtual edition and related design considerations here first. Keep in mind VE performance is highly dependent on the host hardware and hypervisor software used.

Virtual Edition is available at lower cost to hardware and a wide variety of throughput levels, which provides licensing flexibility and the ability to use a pay as you grow model. You also benefit from the various advantages of using virtualisation in general. Of course, you lose the performance gains of hardware acceleration (particularly for SSL) but you don't have to initially over-specify hardware to accommodate future growth.

Potentially poor SSL performance is slowly being eliminated with recent advances and contemporary features now available with commodity Intel processors. It's argued that network performance is a bottleneck introduced by most hypervisors and that's probably true at present but I don't see this being an issue for too much longer as the vendors focus on it and even now this is only an issue of your traffic profile includes a large number of short lived connections.

The hypervisors supported are;

- Citrix XenServer (v5.6 sp2 and 6.0)
- Microsoft Hyper-V (Lab license only, Windows 2008 R2) (Fully supported in v11.3)
- VMWare vCloud Director (v1.5)
- VMWare ESX/ESXi/vSphere (v4.0 to v5.1 inclusive)
- KVM (From v11.3)

BIG-IP Features not available in the Virtual Edition include;

- CMP (until v11.3)
- Spanning Tree Protocols (vSwitches don't run STP; interestingly it's also not supported on the 2000s, 2200s, 4000s or 4200v hardware platforms)
- Link Aggregation Control Protocol (LACP) – but Trunking is still available
- The hard-wired failover functionality and interface
- Federal Information Processing Standards (FIPS) 140-2 compliance (specific hardware is required)
- Interface mirroring
- The Serial console interface
- Always On Management (AOM)
- Use of more than 4Gb of memory (until v11.3)
- Throughput of more than 1Gb (until v11.4)
- There are downgrade restrictions depending on your hypervisor.
- The Link Controller (LC) module
- Advanced SSL functions
- Advanced TCP profile settings

Virtual Edition vs. Hardware

With the increasing use of virtualisation and cloud computing as well as the ever decreasing cost and increasing power of commodity servers and their processors, the argument for using customised hardware such as BIG-IP application switches grows ever weaker I believe. Unlike some other vendors who continue to impose unnecessary restrictions on their virtual products in order to protect their hardware sales, F5 have shown they have no such issues.

The benefits and drawbacks of each form of application delivery platform are as follows;

Type	Benefit	Drawback
BIG-IP Hardware	Customised, task specific hardware	Fixed number of network interfaces
	SSL Hardware offload and higher maximum throughput	Expensive, does not scale up without replacement (bar VIPRION). Future capacity requirements must be incorporated now.
	Compression hardware offload	
	Layer 4 packet offload, hardware acceleration	
	Full module support	
	FIPS support	
	Serial, hard-wired failover	
	Holistic support – simplicity	
	LACP support	
	CMP	
	Spanning Tree Protocols	
	High performance even with a high number of short lived connections	
	High maximum throughput (less of a benefit with later TMOS VE versions)	
	May match the production implementation	Very expensive for testing and development environments
	Multiple subsystems	Higher complexity, greater knowledge required
Virtual Edition on Generic Server Hardware	Unlimited number of network interfaces	Hardware is not task specific
	Cheaper Scales well Flexible	No SSL Hardware offload, greater CPU resource use and lower maximum throughput
		No Compression hardware offload, greater CPU resource use
		No layer 4 Packet offload or hardware acceleration, greater CPU resource use
		Lower maximum throughput (less of an issue with later TMOS versions)
	Can run on commodity server hardware	Hardware is not supported by the software vendor
	Low costs suitable for testing and development environments	May not match the production environment
	Good hypervisor support	Possible poor performance with a high number of short lived connections

TCP Optimisation

TCP/IP v4 is ancient, seriously, the original TCP protocol specification: RFC793 was published in 1981, over 30 years ago. Of course, the only way TCP has remained relevant and useful over those years and to this day, is through constant evolution through additions and modifications to the protocol. It's hard to count how many there have been but it's in excess of 100 and a fair number of these are focussed on optimising performance and increasing throughput.

 TCP v6 really only solves only one problem with v4, by increasing the size of the address pool significantly.

In addition the highly tuned TMOS TCP/IP stacks dynamically tune each connection on either side of the proxy to achieve the best possible performance. You could have a LAN connected server on one side and a client connecting over a slow WAN on the other and an F5 will dynamically manage and maintain separate TCP parameters and options for each to get the highest possible performance and throughput. Whilst mostly applicable to the Full Application Proxy described earlier (and another example of its benefits) some TCP optimisations are still available with the Packet Based Proxy.

 Even though using the Packet Based Proxy means you can't take advantage of most of these optimisations, the hardware acceleration and resulting performance that's possible instead *can* make up for this.

If you're interested, these are some of the open standard TCP optimisations TMOS supports;

- Nagle's Algorithm (RFC896)
- Delayed Acknowledgements (RFC1122)
- Extensions for High Performance; TimeStamps and Windows Scaling (RFC1323)
- Selective Acknowledgements (RFC2018)
- Slow Start with Congestion Avoidance, (RFC2581)
- Limited and Fast Retransmits, (RFC3042 and RFC2582)
- D-SACK (RFC 2883)
- Extended Congestion Notification ECN, (RFC3168)
- Adaptive Initial Congestion Windows, (RFC3390)
- Slow Start, (RFC3390)
- Appropriate Byte Counting (RFC 3465)
- Selective Negative Acknowledgements, SNACK (RFC4077)

HTTP Pipelining

A HTTP/1.1 performance improvement technique in which multiple client HTTP requests are sent on a single TCP connection, <u>without waiting for the corresponding server responses</u>. This can provide a significant performance benefit particularly over high latency connections where waiting for a response before sending the next request can cause considerable delay.

As part of HTTP/1.1, conforming servers are required to either support Pipelining, or at least not fail when a client attempts to use it. The server must respond to each request in order. Pipelining relies on HTTP Persistent Connections, more commonly known as HTTP Keepalives, described in chapter one. The two are often confused, to ensure you are not, take a look at the following two diagrams which should make things very clear. You can also calculate the time saving gained by Pipelining over a high latency connection; if the one way latency is 0.2s the three requests and responses take 1.2s, with Pipelining it only takes 0.4s.

HTTP Persistent Connections/Keepalives

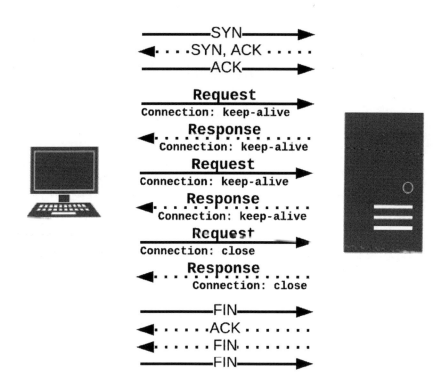

HTTP Pipelining

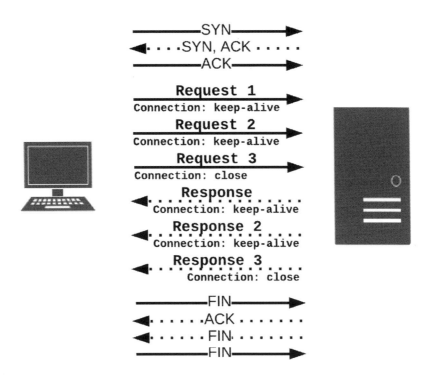

Pipelining is supported by Firefox and its variants (still the case as of v35) but disabled by default. It is not supported by any version of Internet Explorer. It is supported by Google Chrome but disabled and cannot be enabled in standard builds. Despite its potential benefits, issues with server and proxy support and head of line blocking explain the lack of browser support or default disabled state.

HTTP Caching

HTTP caching is an application level protocol performance optimisation and also another form of server offload. Caching can be performed by a client, a proxy server, a dedicated cache, or in the F5 case, the load balancer. Often caching is performed in multiple ways by multiple devices at once, the benefits are somewhat cumulative. In all cases, caching typically reduces the number of end to end client server requests which reduces bandwidth usage and client page load times.

- With client browser software, response content is stored in a local cache which is consulted when new requests for content are made. If the request is for content that is in the cache (that has already been requested and received) the cache content is used and displayed. This negates the need to request it from a remote server. This is typically known as client-side caching.

- Proxy servers (forward proxies) also cache content in a similar way, typically on behalf of multiple clients within a large network, reducing the load on external Internet connections.

- Dedicated caches are typically used to provide content on behalf of servers, thus reducing the load on them in respect of commonly requested objects. These caches may be placed close to the servers (the offload benefit still applies) or, more likely, closer to clients (providing additional bandwidth savings). This is typically known as edge and/or transparent caching.

- In the case of F5, server offload is the primary focus and benefit and operation is similar to that of a dedicated cache located close to origin web servers (OWSs). This is typically known as server-side caching.

The following diagrams demonstrate the operation of caching in respect of server-side caching on a F5;

Object is not in the Cache

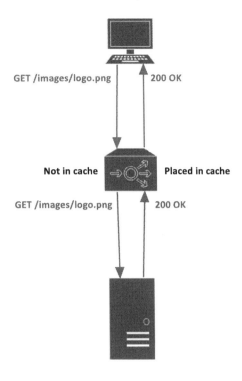

Object Is In The Cache

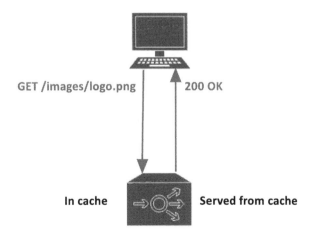

HTTP Compression

HTTP Compression, part of the HTTP/1.1 standard, allows for the compression of text-based responses (and requests although this is rarely seen) using the gzip or deflate algorithms. This compression can greatly reduce the size of the content by up to 80% and improves performance dramatically, as far less data is sent to the client and bandwidth used. Offloading this compression from the real servers to the load balancer obviously also removes the processing overhead on those servers.

HTTP Compression is supported by all modern web browsers.

The following diagram provides a visual representation of HTTP compression offload

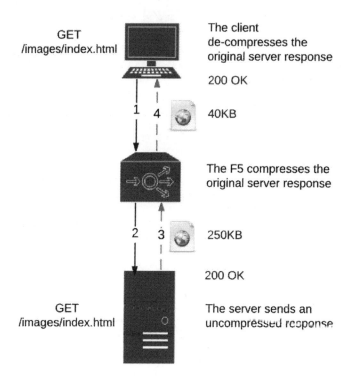

Further Reading

The O'Reilly published book: High Performance Browser Networking, authored by Ilya Grigorik, is available online for free and provides significantly more detail on the TCP and HTTP performance related subjects covered in this section. If you are interested in learning more, you can view the book here:
http://chimera.labs.oreilly.com/books/1230000000545/index.html.

Chapter Summary

- BIG-IP Application switch hardware comes in a wide range of fixed and modular models. Both the physical hardware and the Virtual Edition are considered a form of application delivery platform; in other words, they run TMOS.

- Hardware provides superior performance and throughput using Field-Programmable Gate Array (FPGA) circuitry, specialized high performance network interfaces and optimized data paths. Further benefits are dedicated hardware for SSL processing (all models) and compression processing (higher end models only) which provide much higher performance than commodity processors.

- HTTP caching is an application level protocol performance optimization and also another form of server offload. Caching can be performed by a client, a proxy server, a dedicated cache, or in the F5 case, the load balancer.

- HTTP Compression, part of the HTTP/1.1 standard, allows for the compression of text-based responses (and requests although this is rarely seen) using the gzip or deflate algorithms. This compression can greatly reduce the size of the content by up to 80% and improves performance dramatically, as far less data is sent to the client.

Chapter Review

In order to test your knowledge and understanding of this chapter, please answer the following questions. You will find the answers and explanations of the questions at the end of this chapter.

1. What F5 platform offers modular chassis with up to eight hot-swappable blade modules?
   a. Virtual Edition
   b. All physical editions
   c. VIPRION
   d. All F5 platforms

2. What feature is not available on the Virtual Edition platform?
   a. SSL Hardware Acceleration
   b. Unlimited number of network interfaces
   c. OneConnect
   d. iRules

3. What feature enables you to send multiple client HTTP requests on a single TCP connection?
   a. TCP Optimisation
   b. HTTP Pipelining
   c. HTTP Caching
   d. HTTP Compression

Chapter Review: Answers

You will find the answers to the chapter review questions below:

1. The correct answer is: C

    a. Virtual Edition
    b. All physical editions
    c. **VIPRION**
    d. All F5 platforms

VIPRION is F5 Networks' high density hardware consolidation platform; the Cisco Catalyst 6500 of the BIG-IP range if you will. The three VIPRION models are modular chassis with capacity for up to eight hot-swappable blade modules, all featuring hardware compression.

2. The correct answer is: A

    a. **SSL Hardware Acceleration**
    b. Unlimited number of network interfaces
    c. OneConnect
    d. iRules

With the Virtual Edition you lose the performance gains of hardware acceleration particularly for SSL.

3. The correct answer is: B

    a. TCP Optimisation
    b. **HTTP Pipelining**
    c. HTTP Caching
    d. HTTP Compression

- HTTP Pipelining offers a performance improvement technique in which multiple client HTTP requests are sent on a single TCP connection, <u>without waiting for the corresponding server responses</u>
- HTTP caching is an application level protocol performance optimisation and also another form of server offload. Caching can be performed by a client, a proxy server, a dedicated cache, or in the F5 case, the load balancer.
- HTTP Compression, part of the HTTP/1.1 standard, allows for the compression of text-based responses (and requests although this is rarely seen) using the gzip or deflate algorithms.

Appendix A - How Does SAML Work?

There are three entities that are defined and used by SAML; the client, the Service Provider (the company that provides the service) and the Identity Provider. The Service Provider is usually a cloud based application but it could be any application (website) that has SAML support.

There are two methods to authenticate a user using SAML and both methods are described below.

Service Provider Initiated

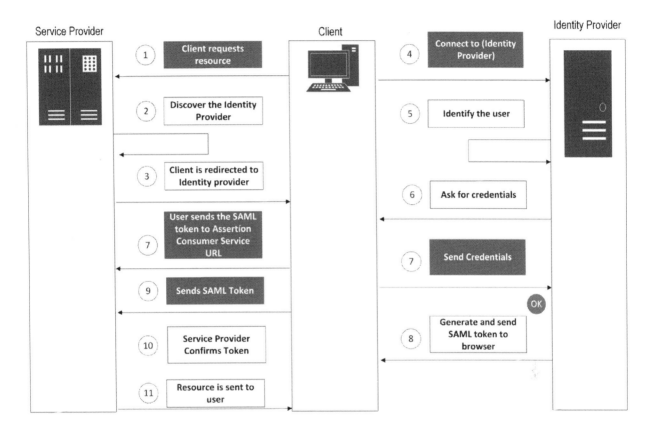

1. Client requests the resource from the server via a web browser. The URL will most of the time include the company name in order to discover what Identity Provider the user should get redirected to. For example https://f5.example.com/myresource. If there are no company name in the URL the user might be asked for its username in order for the service provider to discover the Identity Provider.

2. The server performs a security check on behalf of the target resource and discovers the Identity Provider.

3. The client is redirected to the Identity Provider. The URL could look something like this. https://f5.example.com/SAML2/SSO/Redirect?SAMLRequest-request

4. Now the client sends an AuthnRequest to the Identity Provider. The web browser issues a GET request to the Identity Provider where the value of the SAMLRequest parameter is taken from the URL query string

5. The Identity Provider processes the AuthnRequest and performs a security check on the user.

 The Identity Provider has multiple ways to identify the user and it all depends on how you have configured it. The Identity Provider could be connected with your Centralized Authentication system and automatically grant you permissions or the Identity Provider would ask you for your credentials.

6. The Identity Provider asks for credentials

7. The client responds with credentials and the Identity Provider confirms the user's identity.

8. If the Identity Provider was able to authorize the user it will create a token that is send back to the user. This token will be sent back to the service provider in order to verify its identity. It will also be used for other sites supporting SAML so the process of identifying the user will not occur every time a user tries to access a resource.

9. The SAML token is forwarded to the server

10. The server confirms that the SAML token is valid.

11. And finally, the resource is sent to the client.

Identity Provider Initiated

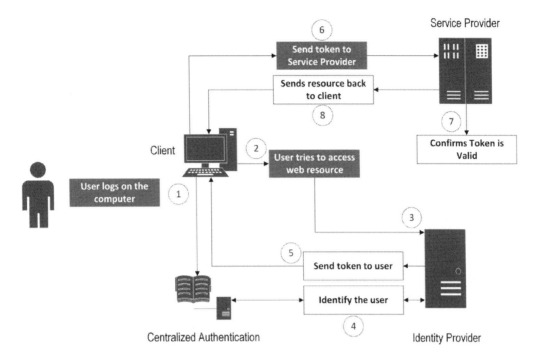

1. The user logs on to the client computer and authenticates to the Centralized Authentication system

2. Now the user tries to access the web resource.

3. Instead of sending the user to the Service Provider directly, the user is sent to the Identity Provider that is connected to the Centralized Authentication system.

4. Since the user has already provided its credentials when it logged on, the Identity Provider can verify the user's identity by asking the Centralized Authentication system.

5. The Identity Provider creates a token that is sent back to the client.

6. The client forwards this token to the Service Provider (the web resource)

7. The Service Provider confirms that the token is valid and grants the user access to the resource.

8. The resource is sent back to the client.

Appendix B – A History of Load Balancing

Here you'll find a visual representation of the company and, to a lesser extent, product history of the load balancing/application delivery field. You'll note there are some interesting clusters;

- There's a huge amount of companies being founded or going public between 1995 – 2000
- Cisco and Citrix are clearly the 'beasts' in this field, perhaps due to their 'early start'
- F5 Seems to have been well motivated by the crashes of the early 2000's to release major features
- There is much acquisition activity in the mid to late 2000's
- Lots of product withdrawals in the late 2000's

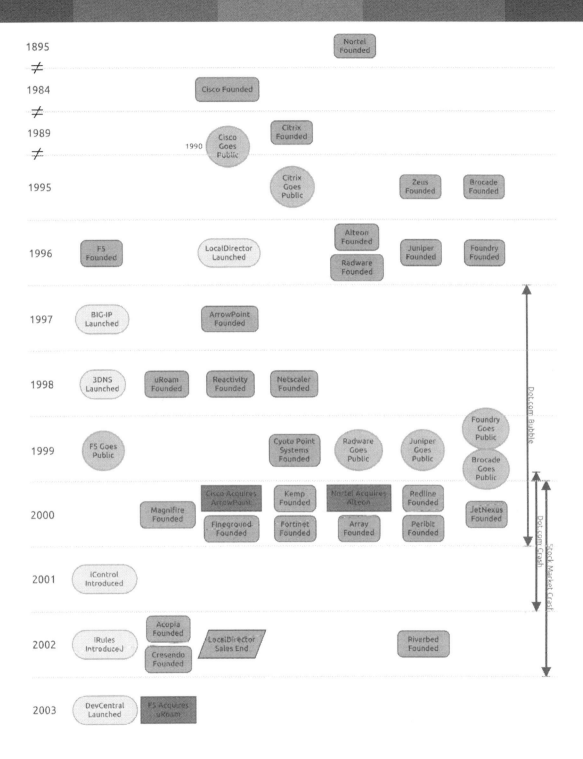

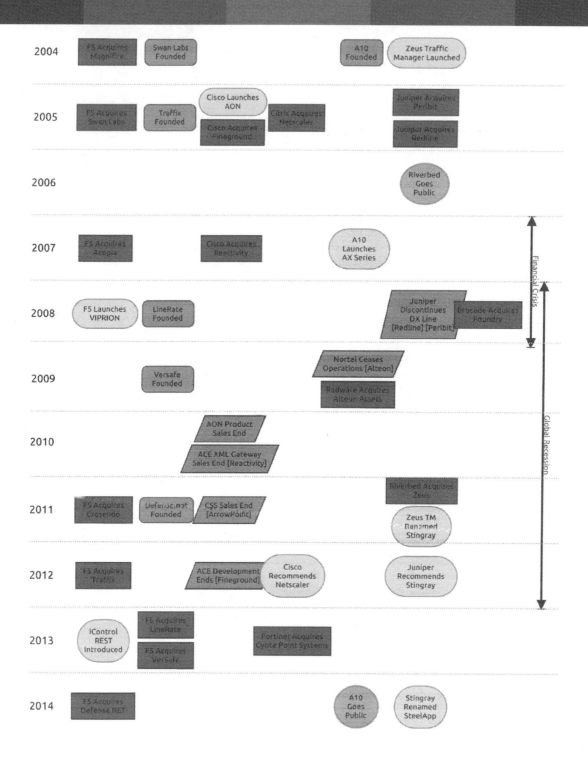

Made in the USA
Middletown, DE
21 September 2017